COACHING
Fastpitch Softball
SUCCESSFULLY

Kathy J. Veroni
Western Illinois University

Human Kinetics

Library of Congress Cataloging-in-Publication Data

Veroni, Kathy.
    Coaching fastpitch softball successfully / Kathy Veroni.
        p.   cm.
    Includes index.
    ISBN 0-88011-546-7
    1. Softball--Coaching.   I. Title.
    GV881.4.C6V47   1998
    796.357'2--dc21   97-47016
                                   CIP

ISBN: 0-88011-546-7

Interior photographs by **Laurie Black:** pp. 5, 9, 11, 17, 25, 33, 38, 47, 54, 55, 59, 69, 70, 71 (top), 72-73, 76, 77, 78, 79, 80, 85, 90, 91, 93, 94, 95, 102, 103, 104, 105, 106, 117, 118, 119, 120, 121, 122, 123, 124, 125, 126, 128, 129, 131 (top), 131 (bottom right), 132, 134, 135, 137, 163, 182, 188, 189, 190, 192, 194, 195, 218, 220, 232; **Larry Dean:** pp. 2, 7, 14, 19, 23, 26, 67, 68, 71 (bottom), 101, 110, 127, 131 (bottom left), 155, 161, 183, 191, 196, 205, 207, 209, 211, 222, 226, 228, 229, 231; **D. Hulett:** p. 66; **Tom Roberts:** pp. 116, 200, 214.

Acquisitions Editor: Jim Kestner; **Developmental Editor:** Julie A. Marx; **Assistant Editor:** Laura Ward Majersky; **Copyeditor:** Tony Callihan; **Proofreader:** Erin Cler; **Indexer:** Craig Brown; **Graphic Designer:** Nancy Rasmus; **Graphic Artist:** Tara Welsch; **Photo Editor:** Boyd LaFoon; **Cover Designer:** Jack Davis; **Cover Photographer:** Western Illinois University/Larry Dean; **Illustrator:** Tom Roberts; **Printer:** United Graphics

Copies of this book are available at special discounts for bulk purchase for sales promotions, premiums, fund-raising, or educational use. Special editions or book excerpts can also be created to specifications. For details, contact the Special Sales Manager at Human Kinetics.

Printed in the United States of America   10 9 8 7 6 5 4 3 2 1

Human Kinetics
Web site: http://www.humankinetics.com/

United States: Human Kinetics
P.O. Box 5076
Champaign, IL 61825-5076
1-800-747-4457
e-mail: humank@hkusa.com

Canada: Human Kinetics, Box 24040
Windsor, ON N8Y 4Y9
1-800-465-7301 (in Canada only)
e-mail: humank@hkcanada.com

Europe: Human Kinetics, P.O. Box IW14
Leeds LS16 6TR, United Kingdom
(44) 1132 781708
e-mail: humank@hkeurope.com

Australia: Human Kinetics
57A Price Avenue
Lower Mitcham, South Australia 5062
(088) 277 1555
e-mail: humank@hkaustralia.com

New Zealand: Human Kinetics
P.O. Box 105-231, Auckland 1
(09) 523 3462
e-mail: humank@hknewz.com

This book is dedicated to the women in my life. To my grandmother, Anna Cascio, who taught me courage and strength. To my mother, Josephine Veroni, who taught me to have a dream and to live it. To my sister, Julie Pro, who always cheered for me and stood by me as my friend and confidante. To my best friend, Kathy Orban, who always loved and believed in me. As we lived and worked together it was her ear and shoulder I leaned on, her compassion and love that saw me through many challenges and adventures. To my friend and colleague, Kelly Hill, who said "You can do it." To Marion Blackinton, who taught me to be fair. To my three favorite nieces: Aliza Pro, who taught me about being independent and confident; and Kelly and Kayla Veroni, who always sparkle when they smile. To Abby Browne, for her thoughtfulness. To my aunts, Marge, Marie, and Dorothy, who have always been there for me and who taught me kindness. To my extended sisters, Jan Veroni, Sherry Browne, Chris Dinesen, Pat Taflinger, and Missy Orban, who enjoy sisterhood, and to Pauline Orban, keeper of the lighthouse.

This book is dedicated to the men in my life. To my father, Jim Veroni, who wanted the best for me and who told me "Go for it." To my brothers, Jim and Joe Veroni, who taught me sensitivity and the importance of a strong work ethic. To my nephew, Mike Pro, who taught me to have fun in anything I do. To my nephew, Dan Pro, for his creativity and honesty. To Russell Browne, for his friendship, and to Dave, Matt, and Brian Taflinger, who love life.

CONTENTS

FOREWORD

What a great time to be associated with the great game of fastpitch softball. As we approach the year 2000, the faces of the game will continue to change, but the game itself will always be built around fundamental skills.

From the USA's Gold Medal performance in Columbus, Georgia, to the NCAA College World Series in Oklahoma City, Oklahoma, the proper execution of fundamental skills is synonymous with winning.

As I have had the privilege of traveling around the country to speak at various clinics, I cannot help feeling the excitement and thirst for knowledge about the game of fastpitch softball. As I have shared my knowledge about the game, many have been so kind to share their ideas and verbiage in teaching the fundamentals of our great game. As a result, players are getting better and better each year.

One aspect of the game that will never change is the thrill of victory and the agony of defeat. As coaches, we must do our part in becoming competent teachers of the game, but let us not forget the bigger game of life. We must learn to cherish our relationships with one another and pride ourselves on our ability to make an impact in the maturation and development of young people. It is time to enjoy each moment because you never know when that moment will be taken away from you.

Kathy Veroni has made an impact in the game of softball and in the lives of many young athletes. I know you will enjoy her vast knowledge of the game. *Coaching Fastpitch Softball Successfully* will give you the insight to make a positive impact on your quest to be the best!

Mike Candrea
University of Arizona

ACKNOWLEDGMENTS

I would like to thank Mindy Dessert for her help in writing *Coaching Fastpitch Softball Successfully* and helping put our system of coaching and training into this book. Mindy has been a player and is now a coach for Western Illinois University, and her friendship, talent, great wit, humor, and perseverance are gifts I will always treasure. I would also like to thank Mindy's parents, Ron and Pat Dessert, for supporting Mindy and me in our careers at Western. I also wish to acknowledge and thank the tremendous women athletes I have had the privilege to teach and coach throughout my seven years with the Macomb Magic and my 26 years with Western Illinois University.

I would also like to express appreciation to Julie Marx and Jim Kestner at Human Kinetics for their professionalism, creativity, and support of this book.

I am so happy that this book is now in the hands of teaching coaches. It was a labor of love, but unfortunately my best teacher will not be able to read it—my mother passed away October 21, 1997. Josephine Lillian Veroni was my hero, my teacher, and my best friend. She was a softball player in the 1940s as well as an equestrian, bowler, and super sports fan. For 26 years she watched as I coached teams from Western Illinois University to the Macomb Magic. She saw many tremendous athletes play the game she loved.

The 1943 Roper Manufacturing softball team, with Coach Veroni's mother, Josephine Veroni (front row, far left), and aunt, Dorothy Cascio (back row, second from right).

As coaches, we are all dream weavers, and we have the ability to make young girls sparkle as they realize their dreams. My mom bought me my first glove. She let me play sports whenever I wanted. She watched me throughout my life with the Rockford Comets and later with the Pekin Lettes. She came to Connecticut to see the Falcons win a world professional fastpitch title and saw every WIU and Macomb Magic team. The players named her "Mama Magic."

She made me laugh and we rarely argued. If we got into a disagreement she would soon change the subject. She taught me how to cross the street when I was very little, how to go to school by myself, and she taught me to be grateful for all we have in our lives . . . and to remember not to take anything for granted, not a person or even one moment in time.

She loved to read and recently really shared that gift with her twin granddaughters. My brother Jim recalled that when he took the girls over to visit, he would sit and watch the love she showed Kayla and Kelly, sitting on either side of her as she would read to them the book she had bought them. As teachers we are kindred spirits with our mothers. The important lessons my mother taught me, I, in turn, try to teach my young athletes. As teachers and coaches we must pass on a legacy from one generation to the next, and from one season to the next. Just as we want our mothers to be proud of us, so too, do our players want us to be proud of them. Reward them with your praise.

During halftime of a basketball game that was televised for our school I was asked to speak with the announcers about the upcoming softball season. My mom got the same channel so I called her and told her I would be on TV and that I would tug on my ear, which meant "Hi, I am thinking about you." By the time I got home after the game she had already called and left me a message on my answering machine. She told me I had done a very nice job and that she was proud of me. She said, "I saw that little ear tug you gave me." Well, mom, I write this book in your honor and memory, as a thank you for all you gave me and taught me. You gave me the gift of life and the support I needed. I hope that I have passed that on to other young women who want what you and I wanted—to have fun and to play the game to the best of their ability.

Thanks, Mom, for all of the wonderful memories. Until we meet again.

INTRODUCTION

The idea of writing a book was overwhelming. I had not yet decided whether to begin when I was called to the bedside of Mary Ellen "Mickey" McKee, a dear friend and tremendous fan of softball. Mickey asked me to pick up a notebook and as I sat down with it I realized it was a book she was writing about her brother. She instructed me to get a piece of paper and pencil, and then proceeded to dictate the conclusion of the book. I wrote furiously, read it back, wrote some more, and on and on. We worked together for a couple of hours, sharing stories and thoughts. Before I left I picked some lilacs, brought them in, and left them in a vase by the bed. The next morning, I told Lu Harris, a wonderful friend, colleague, and coach, about my afternoon with Mickey and it was right then that Lu and I decided to write this book. We had just begun our labors when the associate athletic director, Kathy Orban, came into our office and told us Mickey had just passed away. We sat for awhile in disbelief, then cried and went to Mickey's home—her spirit and the lilacs were still there. On that day, we planted a lilac bush next to our softball field, and on that day the book and the bush took root.

Coaching Fastpitch Softball Successfully covers the fundamental skills, strategies, and drills of the game, and it also discusses the all-important behind-the-scenes areas of every softball program. Part I focuses on the elements that make up a solid coaching foundation: coaching philosophy, communication, motivation, and program development. With this foundation in place, coaches can then concentrate on the many other details that go into successful coaching. For example, it is difficult to have a successful season without considering all of the people and details involved in coaching a softball team. Part II covers planning and organizing, from preseason administrative details like arranging for medical care, uniforms, and equipment; to hiring assistants and student managers; to developing conditioning programs and practice plans for your team.

Parts III and IV, which focus on offensive and defensive skills, respectively, comprise the heart of this book. These sections cover the basic offensive and defensive techniques all fastpitch players will need to know. They describe drills that will hone your players' offensive and defensive skills, and they contain discussions on how to successfully use various softball strategies with your club.

One of your main goals as a coach is to help your athletes perform their best both physically and mentally in game situations. With this in mind, part V includes information about scouting your opponents, pregame practice and motivation, creating the lineup, and specific game strategies. Finally, no softball program is complete without player and coach feedback. Part VI explains how and when a coach should evaluate, and also what and who a coach should evaluate and be evaluated by throughout the season.

I wanted to write a book that would help coaches build a softball program with the emphasis on the athlete. I have read and seen many books and videos about fastpitch softball that offer the reader techniques in developing skills, but none that look beyond the technical. Over the years my student athletes have taught me about sport, life, and living beyond the foul lines, and these are other lessons I want to share in this book and emphasize for fellow coaches. The ideas in this book are ones I have used and developed throughout my career. They have proven successful for me and my student athletes, who have gained knowledge and awareness in how to play this great game of fastpitch softball.

Part I

COACHING FOUNDATION

Chapter 1

DEVELOPING A SOFTBALL COACHING PHILOSOPHY

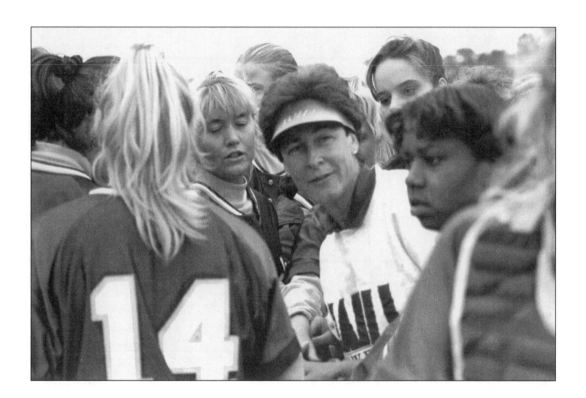

A coaching philosophy is your belief in the way your program should be run. It is very important to have a solid, consistent philosophy. As a coach, you touch people's lives, beginning with your players and extending to their families, along with administrators, the media, and others. By being consistent, you ensure that your players understand what is expected of them.

Consistency also sends the message to the athletes that you are going to be fair in all decisions because you will base each decision on the principles and values that you have created and followed. When you are consistent, the athletes as well as the media and administrators can expect certain behaviors from you. This knowledge will enhance the athletes' performances both on the practice field and during games.

DEFINING YOUR PHILOSOPHY

My philosophy is the sum of my coaching beliefs. I believe a lot of things have to combine for a team to win a conference championship or a national championship. Some are obvious factors: hard work, dedication, teamwork, discipline, and skill in the fundamentals of the game. Other factors for success are more subtle: the emergence of leaders, development of the team's "chemistry" and confidence, and the surprise of young players growing into roles with enthusiasm and ability. And some components are intangible but no less real, such as spirit, tradition, and the will to win. My philosophy is to attempt to bring these aspects together every season consistently with my belief that the most important part of coaching is to give athletes the opportunity to participate and to be the best they can be.

I have always stressed performance rather than winning. Through our team objectives, we ask the athletes to do only the best they can. If circumstances combine for a victory, we can celebrate; however, sometimes events that occur in the game are beyond the athletes' control. Performance then becomes the ingredient to team success. I believe in athletes first, winning second.

During my years of coaching, I have had my coaching philosophy tested on different occasions. I try to stress that winning is not everything and that if you do the best you can, then you can be congratulated on a job well done. It is this belief that has been tested the most. Athletes come off the field after playing great softball but losing, and hang their heads. I always want them to be proud of their performance, and though I do not expect them to cheer or smile, I do expect them to respect the game. After performing at their optimal level, they should be able to applaud their efforts, congratulate their opponents, and respect the competition. They should feel the loss, but I also ask that they acknowledge the efforts in the game—their efforts, as well as those of the coaches, umpires, fans, and opponents. In acknowledging the efforts, they should be able to hold their heads up and not curse the game's outcome.

In developing my philosophy I realize that with my position comes the power to influence those I teach—with that power I hope to elicit a positive change. My father told me to "go for it" when I was debating whether to change softball teams. I had the option of staying home to play or moving away to play for a great traveling team. Those three little words sent me on a journey of many positive influences. My mother taught me not to be afraid and to try new things. She taught me strength and courage and determination. My sister taught me to dream dreams and to trust in the future, that roots are strong and you can be anything you want. My brothers taught me kindness and sensitivity, that nothing is impossible. My assistant coaches taught me to laugh and give my all.

THE BASICS OF A COACHING PHILOSOPHY

Your coaching philosophy should not be developed overnight. You should gather different views of coaching the way you would visit a buffet—choosing and trying different methods and observing what works for others, as well as remembering certain techniques that worked (or didn't work) for you both as an athlete and a coach. Once you have gathered what you feel is right for you, then try it out. You will no doubt have to throw out some beliefs, but others will become the backbone of your coaching style and success. When putting your philosophy together, remember to look for tools that will cover what is important in a team, that is, how to lead a team to success and how to make the most of the game for everybody. Finally, do not think that you should have all the answers from personal experiences. Reading literature and attending coaching seminars will be very rewarding.

Be Yourself

Many jobs may call on you to be an actor or an actress. Sometimes you will find yourself playing a role that fits a situation but that you cannot support in your heart. I find these situations in coaching to be rare. The coach who follows her heart and does what she believes is right will come out ahead. Athletes are smart and they spend a lot of their time trying to figure you out.

They will test you, push you, pull you, and see what they get from you in return. If you try to respond in a way that is truly not you, they will see through your façade. They want you to be genuine, just as you want them to be genuine.

Many first-time coaches want to do a great job, and thus, they put on a serious face when they hit the field. They see coaching as strictly business. Sometimes they hesitate to let down their guard and laugh with the athletes. But it's important to show your full personality when coaching. The athletes want to see that you are real so they can relate to, trust, and confide in you. It is best to be yourself and to be relaxed. Pretending to believe in something you do not or acting like someone else is being dishonest. The first thing to tear down any relationship is dishonesty. You must be honest with your athletes and your staff if you wish honesty in return. So when in doubt, be yourself and listen to your heart. You will not always be right, but at least you can say, "I did what I believed was the right thing to do." People have a hard time arguing against that case.

Go Ahead and Yell

I once had an assistant coach who told me after a few practices that she did not like to yell, and moreover, she felt uncomfortable yelling. Without letting me talk, she went right into how she was going to work on it and get better at it. I smiled at her and knew she thought that being able to yell was part of the job requirement. As she sat behind her desk and began working and looking discouraged, I told her not to yell. She looked confused, and I said, "Just be yourself. If you want to correct a situation or confront an athlete, do it the way you feel comfortable. They will see through anything else." My assistant seemed much more at ease knowing that she could teach the way she felt comfortable and that it would still be a correct method. She has since developed more of her own style. When she is tested she even yells a little, and everyone knows she means it.

You must develop and follow your own coaching style. It is good to have mentors but not to imitate them. If you look at famous coaches you will see that each one is different. Some are quiet and use their body language, while others are more vocal. They motivate in different ways as well as teach with different tools, yet all have found success. Their diversity shows that there is no one way to coach. You must find what will work for you from within yourself. By all means, learn some coaching techniques from others, but build them into *your* style; otherwise, your athletes may sense that the style you are using is not your own.

Be Eager to Learn

I once attended a workshop in another state at my own expense. When the speaker began, I found my mind wandering. Sitting in that comfortable seat with the lights dimmed made it difficult to concentrate. At that moment I realized the importance of being "eager to learn." It is very difficult to truly listen and pay attention. I realized the challenge facing my athletes when they have to listen. I decided to give my full attention to the speaker and to hear every single word she said. By the end of the lecture I was fatigued and my mind was tired, but I knew I had experienced what it actually feels like to learn.

Touch People's Lives

As I look back at the players I have coached, I am rewarded by their success in coaching and life. Many of my players have gone on to coach winning teams and are sharing their love of the sport. I know these women are making a positive imprint on the young lives they touch because I know the kind of athletes they were when they played for me.

Coaches need to use the influence they have on their athletes to help them make good life decisions. If your athletes can walk away from your program feeling they have learned important life tools that will help them in the future, then you have done your job. The teacher of these life tools is you, the coach. I try to influence the athletes to increase all positives in their lives. I start by providing them information on better eating habits and health choices for their bodies. We talk about how what we put into our bodies will affect the way we feel, perform, and grow. Often I require them to listen to guest speakers on campus. These lectures have been about drug use, depression, eating disorders, abusive relationships, time manage-

ment, and study skills. Sometimes they growl about going but always seem to learn something positive from the discussion.

On the field, I stress leadership and responsibility. These two characteristics are critical not only in sports but also throughout life. If I demand these things from my athletes, I hope that they not only take these values with them out onto the field, but also into life situations.

I am realistic and realize that I will not be everyone's favorite person. I know some athletes will leave and not put me on their Christmas card list. But I hope that there will be some on whom I have made a great impression, or who feel they can call me for advice. With this in mind, I only hope that they all leave learning some valuable lesson or with some newly found strength to face future challenges.

Have Fun

Martha Ewing and Vern Seefeldt of the Youth Sports Institute of Michigan State University conducted a study with the cooperation of school systems in 11 cities. Questionnaires were filled out by more than 10,000 young people, aged 10 to 18, and the results were released in 1990. The study underlined a number of truths about children and sports:

1. Fun is pivotal; if it is not "fun," young people won't play a sport.
2. Skill development is a crucial aspect of fun and is more important than winning, even among the best athletes.
3. The most rewarding challenges of sports are those that lead to self-knowledge.
4. Intrinsic rewards are more important in creating lifetime athletes than are extrinsic rewards. Intrinsic rewards include the self-knowledge that develops out of self-competition, and extrinsic rewards include victory or attention from others.

As a coach, it will benefit you to become a communicator and to recognize the needs of your team and balance those needs with yours. Remember the "truths" and plan activities with them in mind. Seek out clinics and workshops that teach interpersonal skills that will help you work with parents and get the most out of your players.

I try to keep the fun in all practices, and I think you should do the same. Encourage laughter and smiles. When the coach laughs and smiles, the team relaxes and executes with less stress. Laughter is a great reliever of pressure. Give your players a reason to smile at practice, during warm-up, and in games.

Sports are recreation. They should be enjoyable. When you stop having fun, you should stop playing. Do not forget, though, that you can have fun whether you win or lose a ball game. If you play hard and smart and yet you lose, you may not be satisfied with the ending, but somewhere within the game you experienced enjoyment. If you play hard and smart, you will have more fun than if you do not.

Give Them What They Want in Practice

On certain days in practice we divide our squad into two even teams and play a game of seven innings. In an envelope I put seven pieces of paper with a prize written on each: get a candy treat, watch the losers do 10 jumping jacks, get a piece of gum, watch the losers do 10 sit-ups, you're exempt from equipment duty today, and you're exempt from field maintenance today.

Each inning has an objective, such as to move the runner, to hit well, to score the most runs, or to make the fewest errors. At the end of each inning, the team that has accomplished the objective gets to select a prize from the envelope and each team member receives the prize. This game is a lot of fun because rewards are given each inning and smiles and cheering resound!

ESTABLISHING OBJECTIVES

Your objectives come after you establish your philosophy. There will be objectives for you, your staff, the athletes, and the team. These objectives will surface from what you believe is important in the game and will be in your mind at every softball hour: during practice, pregame, game, and the off-season. The athletes will have the majority of objectives because they play the game. Many of those objectives are set to help the athletes reach their optimal performance. Team objectives help you decide if you have really won or lost the game beyond the scoreboard. If the team accomplishes the majority of its missions, you will often feel victorious even when the scoreboard reads defeat. I

believe it is the coach's goal to help the athletes reach theirs.

Player Objectives

Player objectives are difficult to write about because, although I have objectives for them, I want them to develop their own. With this in mind, I offer the following list of possible objectives.

- Treat players, officials, and coaches with courtesy and respect.
- Represent your team and school with pride and respect.
- Always cheer for and support your teammates.
- Arrive everywhere early.
- Run if you must be late.
- Always be honest.
- Work hard and give your all.

I want the athletes to be the best they can be as athletes, as students, and as people. They should use our program and coaching staff to add to their talents and strengths, and to minimize their weaknesses. I want them to be team players in life, to be worthy employees as they are worthy athletes now, and to find happiness in all they have accomplished and in what they strive to conquer tomorrow.

Team Objectives

These objectives will develop from what the team wants from the season. Most importantly, the players are to work as a team and support each other. Softball is like an assembly line—if everyone is doing her job at the highest level then the end product is quality. I think a team wants the end product of all its efforts to be quality team play. Its players will set their sights on a goal in hopes that, with each team member giving her best, the goal will be reached. Some common team objectives follow.

- Be completely focused as a team at practice and games.
- Support and respect each other.
- Represent the team first and yourself second.
- Play one pitch at a time.
- Give a winning effort.

I'll discuss some of these objectives in more detail throughout the rest of the chapter.

Play Hard

A coach should never have to speak these two words: "Play hard." As coaches we need to instill in our athletes the concept of playing hard, but then it should be something every athlete does without being told. That is what sports are all about. If a player is out on the field and does not play hard or give it her all, someone else eager for the moment will give what it takes to be "out there" and will pass her by.

What does it take to be out there? What is playing hard? Giving 100 percent of what you've got. That is what I tell my players I want from them. I ask that not only from my starting nine but from the whole team. You never know when a smart pinch runner is going to score the winning run or a pinch hitter is going to swing in your runners. Everyone has got to be prepared to give 100 percent when opportunity knocks.

Play Smart

Playing smart wins ball games. I know I say it all the time to the athletes: "Be smart." I want them to think ahead, not only to want the ball, but to know where to go with it when they get it. We have won crucial games because we have out-smarted our opponents. It is as simple as your hitters not swinging at bad pitches but drawing a walk, or faking a throw with an aggressive runner on second and just holding onto the ball. It is about judgment and thinking ahead.

To play smart you and your players have to communicate with each other and make sure you see the same things. I try to give input and ask for input from them. If you communicate, think ahead, and trust your instincts, then you are playing smart and will come out ahead.

Practice as You Play

We know that "perfect practice makes perfect." In practice we must do things as we wish to see them done in the game. Fundamentals must be taught and executed correctly in practice. Intensity must be planned for in practice. Hustle and determination must be incorporated into practice drills.

Utilize pressure drills during practice. When you apply pressure drills you must have a consequence if an error is made. For example, in a game situation with the negative outcome being a run scored, in practice the negative outcome would result in having to do 10 jumping jacks.

If players take practice too easy the game will become hard. Practice must be intense and fun at the same time. They have to give 100 percent in practice so that when game time arrives, the game pressure becomes routine. The athletes will go onto the field with confidence. Your shortstop will know she can field the short hop because she did 50 of them at practice the day before. Your outfielders will get good jumps on the ball because they spent time with you going over technique. Your team will play as they practice because the practice comes first! The practice is the foundation for the game, and your players can only go as high as their foundations will hold them.

A Winning Effort

We read the saying on T-shirts and it is quoted many times by athletes and coaches: "Winning is everything." I know that it should not be, but still I have discussed winning with my assistant and we do in fact talk about the wins and the losses and match them up in our hearts. Winning the game gives us something that losing could never give us. In one such discussion my assistant and I ended up talking about our most recent win. The whole team had been elated. The athletes got on the bus and played a tape and sang along at the tops of their lungs. We were all laughing as they began dancing up and down the aisle. I even began dancing with them. This feeling that winning gave us, which caused us to want to dance and sing, we never had gotten from losing and playing well, nor do I think we ever will.

What a Finish!

Our team was playing in a tournament in Decatur, Illinois. Because of rain delays, games were limited to one hour or were to end in the fifth inning on all the games in pool play. We were on a winning streak with three wins behind us when we were scheduled to play our longtime rivals, Illinois State. We started off with a one-run lead, but after a few hits and an error we were behind 3-1. We were the visiting team and we were now in the top of the fifth inning, so this was our last chance to score.

We started the inning with a groundout by our freshman pitcher. Next, one of our senior outfielders came up and got on with a walk. Up came another senior outfielder who slashed a base hit. Then a sophomore popped out for the second out of the inning. Our junior third baseman was next, and she batted for another base hit up the middle to score the runner on second base. Our senior catcher came up and drew a walk to load the bases. The score was now 3-2 and our senior shortstop was deep in her battle against the pitcher with two strikes and two outs. She then perfectly executed on an outside pitch and lined a shot to right field, scoring two runs to put us ahead 4-3. Our defense held them and we ran away with the win.

That game was full of leadership and good execution. Our veterans went to the plate and executed. They showed maturity and their winning efforts sent the whole team singing on the way home.

Coach's Objectives

The objectives of the coach are similar to those of the athlete and can include the following:

- Keep getting better as a coach.
- Know your strengths as a coach.
- Believe in your abilities.
- Stay committed to your plan.
- Keep a balance in your life.
- Be yourself.

You want to be able to give it your all, enhance your strengths, and minimize your weaknesses. I do this by furthering my knowledge of the game so that I can always give my team new techniques and drills. Another way is by listening and observing other coaches and teams. I read up on the sport and stay active on committees so that I can represent my team's issues, such as rules, strategies, and techniques. I try to be a constant student of the game. I want to be able to give quality time to my athletes, and to do this, I ensure that if I do not have the answer to what they need or want I will find it. With all this in mind, I still believe my number one objective is to love what I do, and this is the easiest objective to reach.

SUMMARY

This chapter examined some key points in building a coaching philosophy, that is, your belief in the way your program should be run.

- Be consistent so your players understand what is expected of them.
- Stress performance rather than winning.
- Gather different aspects of coaching as you would visit a buffet; choose and try different methods and observe what works for others.
- Be yourself, be eager to learn, and be relaxed.
- Remember, children and young adults playing sports want to have fun.
- Love what you do.

Chapter 2

COMMUNICATING YOUR APPROACH

We can teach and learn only if we are effective communicators. Successful coaches must be able to exchange information with players, assistant coaches, umpires, players' parents, and the media. As coaches, we play such a major role in the development of young athletes that it is crucial that we effectively communicate with our players.

Communication is the essence of the team structure. The better we communicate, the stronger the fabric of our organization. It is our responsibility as coaches to help the athletes understand how to play the game and how to relate sport to life.

COMMUNICATION OFF THE FIELD

One of the most important aspects of coaching is to have good communication with the athletes off the field. This is the area in which we get to know more about each other. We can reach an understanding about each other off the field and away from the stress that sometimes surrounds games and practices. Through off-the-field communication, I can show the players my concern for them and the respect I have for them.

In addition to your athletes, there are a number of other people you'll have to communicate with on a regular basis, including assistants, parents, members of the school faculty and administration, and other students. Communicating effectively with all of these different groups will help you spread the word about your softball philosophy and program.

Communicating With Players

I try to teach the athletes that it is very important for us to have good communication. It is hard for the coaching staff to know where people are, how they are feeling, what is going on in their classes, and how their families are doing if we are not communicating. One of my expectations is that the athletes say "Hello" to the coaches when arriving at practice. This greeting opens up the door for further conversation, which will give a sense of how things are going for both parties that day.

Athletes and coaches will see each other many hours of the week in practice and games. At those times, coaches teach skill development and teamwork, along with other facets of sports participation. But the chance to really allow the athlete to know the coach and the other way around occurs during planned one-on-one conversations. I meet each student athlete once a week for a 15-minute conversation. This gives me a chance to praise and encourage her performance on the field and to find out how college life is treating her.

Four times a year, I have a one-hour meeting with each player. These meetings take place partway through the fall season, at the end of the fall season, at the beginning of the spring season, and at the conclusion of the spring season. At these times, we discuss the athlete's goals and expectations and my evaluation of her practice and performance.

Communication off the field is the most important sharing that will go on between coach and athlete. Within these conversations, the athlete will find her comfort zone with the coach and will discover that the coach values her as a person, not just as an athlete. I value the time I spend with my athletes off the field, both in and out of season. This is the time when we get to know each other better. These one-on-one conversations are when we both forget our roles of coach and player and become people.

It's Never too Late

I once had an athlete call me and leave the message that she had finally gotten her degree. She had left school five years earlier and the only thing keeping her from graduating was an Illinois constitution test for the out-of-state student. Jenn Jackson had told me several times she was going to come up and take it, but things never seemed to work out. She had earned a job as a St. Louis police officer without the official degree and had been doing well. It was not until she came up for our fall tournament that a friend talked her into taking the test. She did and she passed! She would receive her diploma and a considerable raise in salary. She was excited and really proud. It felt good that she wanted to share the accomplishment with me even after being gone for five years. I called her back and congratulated her on a job well done! She told me that she knew I would want to know and that I had always been there for her, encouraging her along the way.

I work with an "open-door" policy, which means that I am always in and available to talk to anyone who drops by. Communication is a two-way conversation. It involves both parties getting the opportunity to talk and share thoughts, concerns, and ideas. I try to define what communication is for the athletes so that they know I want their input and that when I am speaking I want them to listen. Your athletes want to be able to talk with you and know that you will listen, just as you want that from them.

Communicating With Assistants

I always try to incorporate my assistants in every aspect of the game. I give them their time to teach as well as try to teach them all that I have learned. I have had a great variety of assistants who have taught me different aspects of the game. Most of my assistants have been

former players of mine who shared my love for the game and my philosophy of developing athletes to be the best they can be. I want my assistant coaches to have a vested interest in the program and to know that their ideas matter. I give them responsibilities and allow them to develop programs and plans for the team.

Some assistants have a strong specialty, such as pitching, which allows them to work in their area of expertise. If they begin in an area in which they have had success, it helps develop their confidence. We make sure that no one feels totally responsible for any one area of the program. I oversee all aspects and will request progress reports of any "assignments." I work hand in hand with my assistant coaches in planning the schedule, the budget, the workouts, and all other aspects of the program.

From the first day, I give feedback to my assistants about their strengths and weaknesses. I always have more positive than negative feedback, and the constructive criticism helps them to learn more about the game.

The communication between you and your assistant is a give-and-take. You will not always agree, and this is healthy and will always be a learning experience. If you agree on everything, then neither of you will benefit. Keep the communication lines open and find value in your assistant's opinions, skills, and insights. Remember, it is your program and you want good

people representing you. Trust your judgment and confront all problems head-on so they will not grow. Loyalty is critical in this relationship; build it with honesty and communication.

Communicating With Parents

Try to work with parents and make them a part of the team rather than viewing them as critics to be avoided. It is important that the parents are able to approach you and talk with you about their daughters. They should be able to discuss their child with you, and they want you to take the time to answer all their questions. In most cases they want to know that their child is doing well and that she is in good hands. Take the time to approach the parents also. It is a nice feeling when the coach initiates the conversation and lets the parents know that their child is a fine young athlete.

The majority of the parents have always been great fans, volunteers, and supporters of their daughters. I know that parents want their children to be playing and enjoying their time on the team. It is easy to see their disappointment when their daughter is not in the starting nine or not performing well. I do not avoid the issue, and if the parents ever want to talk with me about the "whys," I am more than willing to do so, yet I cannot recall a situation where this has happened. I don't know if this means they always understood my choices or just did not want to hear the answers. It's nice to see parents and families of all the athletes come and support the team. If you take a good look at the family when you are recruiting and realize the athlete is a product of that family, you should be happy with your athletes and parents. I know I have been.

Recycled Grandparents

I had a woman on the team about six years ago who had the most wonderful parents and grandparents. Lisa's family came to all the games they could and were always willing to lend a helping hand. One year we were flying to California from the Quad Cities on an early morning flight. The Cities were an hour and a half away from Macomb, so we were looking to stay somewhere close the night before. Four of our athletes were from the Quad Cities, so their parents offered to put us up for the night. I had the opportunity to stay with Lisa Hernandez's grandparents in a small upstairs apartment of their home. It was a great visit and I really enjoyed them. It is hard to watch your athletes go—you not only miss them but their families also.

It was not too long ago that I received a phone call from an athlete who wanted to transfer from another Division I school to Western Illinois University. I was delighted to hear Jen wanted to come here because she was a fine athlete and a cousin of Lisa Hernandez's. I knew she had great genetics for softball, and the icing on the cake was that her two biggest fans were two of my favorites—Mary and George, her grandparents. I felt like Jen had found a new home with us at Western and at our first tournament in the fall Mary and George looked very pleased to see Jen playing with the Westerwinds. She brought with her a fine athletic package full of great tools and a great group of people to support her and the Westerwinds.

In the beginning of each year we have a picnic where all the athletes and their families come together and meet one another. Every year there are new athletes and families, and I feel it is important for these new people to get the chance to meet the other athletes and families before the first competition. This allows them to ask questions, get to know each other, and learn what the program is about. This bonding time offers so much to the players as well as to the parents. It is a mixer in the truest sense because they are the ingredients of the up-and-coming team. It is nice to have the opportunity to recognize how well we will blend. I recommend this type of gathering for high school players, too.

Communicating With School Faculty

Regardless of the ages or abilities of your athletes, you want them to receive a great education. A university provides a great opportunity for your student athletes to receive a degree and play in the sport they love. At Western Illinois University we try to create a working relationship with the professors who teach our athletes. From day one, we ask our athletes to introduce themselves to their professors as student athletes. We write a letter that tells the professor the days the athletes will miss because of competitions and asks for the athlete to be excused. The athlete is to arrange with each professor how to make up the work. We realize not all professors are going to be fans of athletics, and we try to work the best we can with them so that everyone understands the role of the student athlete. This same approach can be followed in high school, with the students (or coach) informing the teachers of their schedule and the times they might be away in competition.

As coaches we want our athletes to be able to compete; therefore, their academics come first and eligibility standards must be met. If the athlete is not a good student, it may cost her the opportunity to play. I believe coaches are teachers first and should share academic monitoring with other faculty members. We request feedback from professors and work directly with student athletes, and we try to ensure that our athletes are attending classes, getting the help they need, and staying on schedule. Staying abreast of each athlete's classroom performance shows your interest in the student first.

Communicating With Administrators

I often meet with the athletic director or other administrators at Western regarding particular athletes or issues related to my program. Common courtesies prevail here. My assistant and I try to stop in and visit briefly every so often. If there is something I need for my team or an important issue has come up, I send a letter and then ask for a meeting at their earliest convenience. In this way they are prepared when we sit down to our discussion.

It is important to be organized when meeting with an administrator. Be sure to bring the necessary paperwork with you to the meeting and realize their time is valuable. Communication is an integral part of success when dealing with administrators. The athletic director is a key staff member and needs to be informed of every major issue concerning your team.

Communicating With the Community

Coaches at the high school and college level need to communicate with the community. For one month each summer and two months each spring, usually in June, January, and February, one of our team's goals is to be the center of attention in our community. People are very active and busy these days and numerous activities compete for their time and attention year round. But for a short time we work with individual community members to keep the spotlight on our team. We want to gain their support of our team and of the sport itself, because this helps build a better program for Western and for the young athletes. We work with the community in the following ways:

- Our athletes and coaches do clinics for young athletes.
- Our athletes and coaches periodically do a local radio show one day a week with ticket giveaways.
- Our athletes deliver our posters, media guides, and schedule cards to area businesses.
- We have designed a program called "Community Corporate Teammates."

A more in-depth discussion of community projects can be found in chapter 4.

Communicating With the Media

Give the members of the news media your time and patience. This might be easier said than done, but it is critical if your athletes are to get the exposure they deserve. I want the media to talk to the players to better understand what it takes to be a strong Division I female athlete. I do not keep the media waiting. Immediately following our game, if there is anyone present from the media, I tell them I will be right with them. I then gather my thoughts and meet for the interview. At this time the players are packing their equipment prior to our team meeting.

If we have a unique story, I try to notify the media supporters first. They enjoy getting a "scoop." I encourage the reporters to call me at home as well, and if they would like to call us on the road I let them know where we are staying.

COMMUNICATION ON THE FIELD

The athletes learn the game on the field, during practices and games, through the communication we have with them. What we say and how we communicate with each athlete can determine the outcome of the game and the success of the program. If the athlete understands that we are on her side and want to help her be the best she can be, then the communication line is open.

Communicating With Players

My main objective with my athletes is to let them know that I respect them and the efforts they make, and that I am concerned about the forces that impact their ability to play to their potential. When the coach is on the field she is visible to all who watch the game or watch the practice, so I try not to overreact or embarrass the athletes—as they play their positions with poise and technique, so do I. The image that you project on the field is viewed by many others and it is vital to conduct yourself at the highest level of professionalism.

Never Humiliate

I have made it a point in my career to never yell at a player during a game. I will not raise my voice to them when there are other people and fans around. I may do that during a practice but never when the athlete could be embarrassed in front of nonplayers. I work with my assistants to make sure they follow this philosophy. If a player is having a difficult time hitting or fielding, I will pull her aside between innings and talk quietly. Most of our game communication is praise, leaving criticisms for practice.

Always remember that the athletes are young adults who need to be treated with respect and dignity. If you treat them otherwise, they will eventually lose trust in you and respect for you. This makes them less likely to perform at their best under your coaching. Keep the communication lines clean and clear and do not damage those lines with humiliation, but rather strengthen them with words that instruct.

Linking

I have noticed an interesting phenomenon that I call "linking." It occurs when a player asks a routine question directly of the coach. This may not sound special, but have you ever corrected or criticized a player and then a few minutes later they ask a basic question? I believe the player is trying to reconnect with you on a one-on-one basis and that she is showing you that she is there and looking for an answer. She wants to have you acknowledge her again in a positive light, and so she asks you a question, usually a simple one, so that you can respond in a nonthreatening manner. I call this "linking" because the player wants to reestablish her relationship with you.

Instruct, Don't Dictate

Go out every day of practice with a lesson in mind. Follow that lesson plan by telling the team what that day's objectives are and then, at the end of each practice day, reviewing what was accomplished. This method will help you feel prepared to teach what you want to teach that day. Coaches should give direction to their athletes to help them reach the optimal outcome of each day's lesson. You do not want to order a

certain behavior from your athletes. Students, in general, learn from instruction when they have input and can work together with the person in authority. Usually, giving a command or ordering a desired behavior does not reinforce that behavior or teach it to the student.

We must be sure we have taught a skill before we can criticize the athlete for her failure to execute a skill or to carry out a play. I try to always remember that I am a teacher first and foremost and that it is my responsibility to instruct the student in how to play the game at the highest level. When I feel agitated because my players are not trying or paying attention, I try to remind them and myself that we are learning to be the best we can be.

Game Communication

In softball we have communication lines going on all over the field at all different times of the game. On defense, the pitcher gets signals from the catcher who might be getting signals from the coach on what pitch to throw to the batter. The shortstop and second baseman get signals from the catcher and give them to the outfielders. When on offense, the batter and the base runner receive signals from their coach on what play to execute. This communication goes on for every pitch of the game. This type of communication could be given with signals or code words. The game relies on the use of communication so that all participants are informed and receive the right message.

As we come off the field to get ready to bat, we have a quick huddle to praise the defense and discuss the upcoming ways to score. This is a time to unite each player with hands in the middle of the huddle and a chant: "Hit, hit, hit."

At the conclusion of each game we meet as a team in the outfield to briefly discuss the game. We sit in a circle in assigned spots. In this way I know where each player is and can look at her to address her. I use this time to acknowledge the well hits (or well-hit balls), the good execution of plays, the RBIs, and the defensive plays that stand out. If we made mental errors, we talk about them at this time as well. The focus of this meeting is on praise and instruction.

Communication Failures

There will be communication failures on both ends of the athlete-coach relationship. These failures can be as simple as changing where practice is and forgetting to tell someone on the list, or taking someone out of a starting position without communicating why. I try to avoid these scenarios as well as I can. But finding the athletes when events have been rescheduled can become a difficult task and sometimes we just miss someone. I try to never let the second scenario happen, yet I fear in some delicate instances I might.

The Game Ball Goes to . . .

We were playing in Tampa, Florida, over spring break. One of the games was against Michigan State University. The game was very intense and both teams were playing great ball. It seemed that for every great play we made they made one. The hits were scattered and the score tied. It was our turn up to bat when our shortstop, Natalie Salerno, hit a home run to put us in the lead. Our senior pitcher, Becki Warner, held the Spartans and we won the game. It was a great win for us and set the pace for a great tournament. As my assistant, Mindy, and I were closing up the

game we asked for the game ball to give to Natalie. We had the team in a circle and talked about the great win and tossed Nat the ball. Everyone seemed to be enjoying the moment, but one of our starting captains, Robyn Stark, looked down. This upset both Mindy and me. What would she have to frown about after such a team triumph? Later that evening we figured out that Robyn had hit a home run the day before in a game that we lost. It was also a great hit, yet we did not celebrate it because we were focused more on the loss and how to fix our mistakes for the next day.

In this scenario the communication lines went bad on both ends. Robyn should have told us why she was upset, and we should have spoken of the great hit after the game and given her the ball that went over. We apologized and everybody signed a ball for Robyn and her home run. It is important that the athletes know their efforts are not overlooked. We try our best to communicate this to them, but sometimes we fail.

Communicating With Assistants

My assistant coach and I make it a point not to disagree in front of the team. We present a united front to the players, and if we have disagreements we use a more private opportunity to discuss them. I do make game decisions based on her input. I feel two heads are better than one, so I try to confer with her often during the game. As a general rule, I coach third base and determine the particular plays. I will discuss any pinch-hit or pinch-run possibilities throughout the game. I have given the responsibility of calling the pitches during the game to my assistant. I feel that we know what it takes from our squad to be successful because we have talked about our opponent's strengths and weaknesses prior to the contest. During the game, I do not hesitate to call time-out or take my assistant aside to discuss changes in our game plan.

We plan out every practice together and do a follow-up evaluation after practice. We take notes from the evaluation and work in our suggestions for future practices. We share the same office so our discussions are free flowing, but we do plan our day in blocks of time with the first task of the day being to plan that day's practice.

Each Monday we evaluate the previous week's games and practices and determine the emphasis for the upcoming week. We ask the athletes to notify us in advance if they are going to be late or unable to attend a practice. In this way we are better able to plan around those occurrences.

Communicating With Umpires

Let the catcher set the rapport with the plate umpire in determining balls and strikes. Quiet conversations between the two will establish a strike zone the battery can work with. I may ask the catcher if a particular pitch was a strike, and I want an honest opinion back. In that way I do not have to get into a strike zone discussion with the umpire.

Don't Call Me *Honey*

In a regional Amateur Softball Association game where my summer team, the Macomb Magic, was vying for a chance to win the title and go on to nationals, I had to draw the line in order to keep my starting pitcher, Margie Wright, on the mound. The game was highly charged and neither Margie nor our catcher felt the umpire was as sharp as he should have been with balls and strikes. They showed their displeasure to him with facial expressions and quiet comments. I had known the umpire for quite awhile and could tell he was becoming agitated as well. In the sixth inning, as I was walking to the coach's box, he said to me, "Listen, *honey*, you better do something about your pitcher." As soon as he said the word *honey*, I knew I was going to win an argument with an umpire. I stopped, spun around, and said, "You can call me Kathy, or you can call me Coach, but you can never call me honey. I am not your honey, never was, and never will be." The crowd within earshot roared, and the umpire blushed. He spent the rest of the game apologizing to me. The best part was, my pitcher stayed in the game, quite a bit more relaxed, and we went on to win the regional title.

It is important for the coach to be able to ask the umpire a question about a play and to then have a brief discussion, if necessary, with her. Oftentimes, however, the umpire is too sensitive to hear the question or the debate is too highly charged. My approach is to make my point quickly, and leave it at that. If it is a situation, for example, where the umpire says my player missed a tag, on my way out to the umpire, I will first quickly ask the player if she did indeed apply the tag. If the player says yes, I will continue my trip out to the umpire. I believe in this manner the umpire has heard it from the player and then from me. There is little to talk about after that, but the umpire knows we know a call was missed. The umpire is just trying to do the best job possible and it does not serve a purpose to embarrass her or argue with her.

SUMMARY

Communicating your approach allows you to put your philosophy into action. This chapter studied how the coach communicates with athletes, assistant coaches, parents, umpires, administrators, the community, and the media.

- Let athletes know you are always available to talk.
- Instill in the athletes the importance of good communication.
- As a coach, realize that communication is a two-way conversation.
- Never humiliate a player.
- Make it a point to instruct and not to dictate.
- Give your assistant coaches responsibilities and allow them to develop programs and plans for the future.
- Let the umpires do their job.
- Keep your relationships with parents professional.
- Keep the faculty and administrators informed; they are crucial to team success.
- Win or lose, be available to the media. Promote your players!

Chapter 3

MOTIVATING PLAYERS

Motivation means helping players improve to a higher level of performance. I do this by calling upon skills and strategies that assist each athlete in reaching for, meeting, and stretching beyond her expectations as an athlete. My job as the coach is to find the mechanisms that challenge my athletes to work harder to be the best. These tools, or motivational devices, must keep the job at hand fun and interesting or no growth will occur. I try to motivate the athletes so that they can reach the goals they set.

I often use our competitive schedule as motivation. An athlete is going to work harder when she knows her opponent might be a little bit better. Haven't we often heard that the team will play up or down to the competition? I also try to do things for my players that make them feel special and unique. In this chapter you will find some of those techniques that can help motivate and keep motivating your players.

WHAT MOTIVATES YOUR ATHLETES?

In so many ways softball is an individual sport. When the athlete is the batter, there is little a teammate can do to enhance her performance. She must work long and hard on her individual skills and often delay gratification throughout many months of training.

This is intrinsic motivation and must come from within the player. Some intrinsic motives are success, recognition, self-worth, and peer acceptance. A high level of motivation results in athletes who are committed and driven toward success.

There are essential elements needed to get the most out of your players. While some athletes already possess these qualities, the coach tries to instill and further develop them in all her athletes as a motivational technique.

1. Players need the ability to work for delayed rather than instant gratification. Greatness is achieved through constant repetition of softball tasks. The great athlete separates herself from the good athlete when she shows a willingness to practice hard now for a payoff later.

2. Players must have the ability to take feedback as help, not criticism. To achieve her maximum, the athlete needs to receive coaching and instruction—this is the coachable player. The athlete must recognize that progress, not perfection, is the goal. She must accept instruction openly rather than defensively.

3. Players must have a vision of where they want to be and could be. Success and greatness come with a vision of being so. The athlete must have a sense of purpose, a vision to guide her efforts. This vision is the fuel which drives the delayed gratification. It is imperative that the athlete's motivation is not external, but internal.

4. Players must have the ability to look for solutions, not problems. These are the athletes who love a challenge, who see opportunity in difficulty, and persist with hard work and alternatives rather than quit.

It is vital that an athlete learns from the coach that success is ensured when she perceives a loss or mistake as information to prepare her for the next event. When she learns to *learn* from her mistakes, she will not beat herself up over a failure. This is what we have all experienced as constructive criticism.

Verbal Reinforcement

Reinforcement means to strengthen with new assistance. When using verbal reinforcement to strengthen a player's focus or confidence, you are saying something in a positive light about her or her performance. There are several different ways to go about this. In this chapter I will share with you what has been most successful with the athletes I have worked with.

One of the most common ways I reinforce my athletes is through verbalizing their strengths. I will often, when addressing the whole team, choose one of my athletes and name her as a great leader, hitter, defensive player, and so on. I do this so that she gets the recognition she has worked hard for and also so that her teammates see that hard work is acknowledged.

Approaching an athlete at practice and reinforcing her efforts with one-on-one communication is important for me. One-on-one communication has a place in every game as well. I find that those athletes who give the extra day in and day out need to be applauded by the whole team. Athletes like hitting home runs in the game, where everyone can appreciate their talent. The same principle applies here. If Natalie has hustled all practice, point out in front of everyone that you see and appreciate her efforts and that you feel the team should recognize them as well and follow her example.

Verbal reinforcements are not always expressions like "good job." They can be skill related also—for example, telling a hitter "great hands" because she kept her hands stationary on a bad pitch. Overall, I feel I verbalize more about the skills that are being polished during practice time. I find this appropriate because I want the athlete to know why I said "good job." So I go straight to the skill and say, "Lisa, great balance." That way I am saying "great job" about the skill she performed. Through this technique you find that everyone does something well.

When you need to correct an athlete or give constructive criticism, I feel the best way is to sandwich the criticism between two positive reinforcements. For example, you might say, "Missy, great balance (positive reinforcement). You need to keep your bat still (constructive criticism), but your hands are coming through the zone nicely (positive reinforcement)." This helps the athlete better absorb constructive criticism because she is also hearing things she is doing correctly.

You want to make sure that you are not always picking the same athletes to praise in front of the team. Everyone has a strength. It could be that they are quick or strong, or have good balance, a good eye, or even keen insight into drills. Make sure to point out that not only does your starting lineup have great skill but so do those players on the bench. I often remind the team that the starting lineup is so good because of the competition their teammates who do not start offer them in practices.

Team Praise

There are crucial times when you want to make sure you verbalize the team's strengths both as a whole and individually. It might be before a big game, after a tough loss, or if the season seems to be a roller coaster of ups and downs. These times represent crucial moments when the group needs to be reminded of its talent and effort. I sometimes take the time to pull out each individual's strengths for display. When I have touched upon everyone, I combine all those attributes and talk about the team as a whole. This technique helps the team members respect each other for their own individual strengths and illustrates how they all make up the team they are a part of. Hopefully, with this in mind, they find a comfort zone on the field and can begin performing at an optimal level. Verbal reinforcement is the quick and easy high that an athlete or a team needs. As coaches, we are the providers. You will also see other athletes picking up on it and using it daily to support their teammates. This helps but should not take the place of the coach's verbal reinforcement.

Individual Attention

Individual attention is a special way to motivate players. The motivational power an athlete receives when she feels like the coach is paying attention to her in practice is great. I believe the coach and the athlete need to have a 10-second contact within the first 10 minutes of practice. The trick to this is requiring the athletes to say "Hello" when arriving at practice. This provokes a response from you and even possibly a small exchange of a smile, pat on the shoulder, or short conversation about their day. Saying "Hello" is the doorway to communication, comfort, and caring. For example, one of your athletes walks up and says "Hi." She is looking a little down, so you say "Hi" back and ask if everything is all right. She may respond that she had a bad day or she may not disclose anything, yet you have shown your interest in why she is

upset. If the same athlete does not pass by and say "Hi," but just instantly becomes a part of the mix, you lose the opportunity to communicate and show you care.

During practice you should give individual attention to the majority of your athletes. You may not be able to reach them all in one day; though that would be optimal, it is not always feasible. I try to make sure our staff provides some type of verbal reinforcement to everyone. The easiest way to reach everyone is when they are working in small groups. If your staff can work at different stations, they are likely to have the opportunity to teach and provide insight to the athletes on a more individual level. As the athletes move through the practice stations, they should be reached by at least one of you and receive some individual attention about the task at hand.

NONVERBAL REINFORCEMENT

There are absolutely hundreds of nonverbal reinforcers. In coaching we are always looking for ways to send a message and make it stick. Verbal reinforcement is good, but I feel it is a quick fix. Nonverbal reinforcement can be both a quick fix and a lasting message.

Physical cues or our body language can send a message and be a nonverbal reinforcer. These might include clapping, patting a back, a high five, or a nod of approval. These types of non-verbal reinforcement are very good but are something of a quick fix also. They convey your approval or congratulations, but within moments the athlete and you are doing something different and the transaction is over.

Token reinforcement—that is, the use of a token such as a sticker to reward a player for an accomplishment—has been a fun motivator for our athletes. We have stickers for singles, doubles, triples, home runs, stolen bases, RBIs, Ks, great defense, great offense, and great hustle. After every game, our staff votes on an offensive and defensive player of the game, sometimes picking more than one in both categories. These athletes receive a sticker picked out for their specific accomplishment. The other stickers are allotted to the athletes who earn them during each game. After an athlete receives the sticker, she places it on a sign that hangs on her locker with her name on it. This allows other athletes to see each player's talents and contributions.

Everyone seems to need a few daily words of inspiration; the quote-of-the-day book has taken America by storm. There are books for sisters, mothers, different religious affiliations, and so on. I think what this tells us is that we all search for some type of motivation on a daily basis. After reading a quote, we ponder it for a moment and go on.

Taking the quote-of-the-day approach with my athletes is like fishing for their attention. The quote I offer is the bait and their thoughts are the fish. I take a quote I feel is relevant to what we need to accomplish that day and hand out copies to the athletes to all read silently. For a moment we are pulled to one common thought and what it means to us. I like to start practice this way. It is a true exercise of focusing. I sometimes read the quotes but many of the players like to have them written down. I type them up and sometimes add a few graphics and then hand them out. Several of the athletes put them in their handbooks; this is an excellent place, since they can return to the quotes and refocus.

Trading Cards and Posters

I once saw a great poster of Michael Jordan with the caption DESIRE under it. I thought that my athletes should have a poster of themselves with an inspirational message as well. I let them choose their saying, and I then located the action picture of them that best depicted their abilities and designed a poster for them. I took the 8 1/2-by-11-inch sheet to a color copier and made an 11-by-14-inch poster. I then laminated it and gave it to them. Some were used by the athletes as Christmas presents and many hung them on their residence hall wall.

I also designed trading cards for them. Again, the color copier did a super job! On the front I put each athlete's name and position along with our school's name and an action photo. Information about their career and statistics appeared on the back. When they saw their cards they beamed!

MAKE SOFTBALL FUN

To ensure that the athletes enjoy their time with their sport and as a way to motivate them, I try to add humor to situations that might be stressful or tense. I have stooped so low as to put bugs in athletes' gloves and fake dog poop by the dugout or even in the dugout. One time I gave my new assistant a piece of fire hot gum on her first trip with the team. She laughed and took it very well. It seemed to break up her nerves a little. Such jokes get the teammates and coaches to let down their guard and laugh at themselves or those around them. The shock effect is a great one! I believe this also helps the athletes relate to me better and thus enhances my communication with them.

PRACTICE AS A MOTIVATOR

When your athletes are practicing in the gym at 6:00 A.M. on a cold January morning you sometimes need to remind them that they are fortunate to be there. You can talk about the ones who are not fortunate enough to play on a softball

One Hot Trip to Texas!

While in Dallas, Texas, on spring break in 1991, I took the team to a barbecue rib restaurant and we all sat at a huge table. This restaurant was just what we needed. It pulled us all together with the huge table and crazy balloon hats they gave us to wear. One of the athletes had ordered a dish that had whole jalapeño peppers as a garnish, and I noticed her putting them aside and commenting on how nobody could eat a jalapeño. I bet each athlete a dollar I would eat a whole pepper. They all laughed and started digging in their pockets for change. Once there was a pile of change on the table, they all began chanting "Go, Go, Go!"

I picked up the jalapeño and sent it down the hatch. They could not believe I did it. They laughed and seemed to be waiting for smoke to come out of my ears. I held my composure, kept my mouth shut, and just smiled. They could not believe that I had survived the green fire bomb without a sound or drink of water. We all laughed and their faces were great to watch. After they left the restaurant to go shopping, I took my assistant to a yogurt shop and put the fire out in my throat. I never knew the effect this episode really had until my new assistant, who at the time was one of those athletes who chanted around the table and stared in disbelief, asked me this year, "How hot was that jalapeño you ate in Texas?" I just smiled.

team—those athletes who got cut or just were not seen. As competitors we work harder when facing a challenge. Athletes need to hear about their opponents who are practicing every day to beat them. I sometimes wear the sweatshirts of the teams we cannot wait to play in the upcoming season. It is a subtle reminder that those opponents are out there practicing and preparing for us, just as we must do today for them. As competitors we motivate ourselves for the very purpose of competition.

Many times I bring in a video of the country's high profile athletes in competition. We watch these games as a team and critique them. This helps my team see that there is always room for improvement. It also helps them relate to those athletes, since they find themselves facing some of the same stumbling blocks in the game.

In practices you want to hit all the important details, but you also want the athletes to come to practice with their own personal agendas. I believe each athlete has an idea of what she wants to work on, who she wants to outhit, who she wants to strike out, or how many ground balls she wants to make a play on without making an error. Let these things be part of practice. Create competitions. Congratulate your freshman pitcher in front of the team when she gets your best hitter to fly out. Hit your shortstop ground ball after ground ball and let the team applaud her as she makes the plays. There should be clapping and cheering during practice. It is at those instances that the athletes recognize why they love the game and its intensity.

GOAL SETTING

Every practice, every day, every week, the athlete needs something to inspire her. I believe a goal is a pep talk an athlete gives herself.

To get somewhere you must first know where it is you want to go. Some of the teams I have coached have gone to a national tournament and some have not. But it was not always based on talent or lack of talent. I believe those who go believe they can and never question the possibility they won't. The team sets the goal to win it all, and though they might come up short, they do go a lot further than they would have if they had never strived to be champions.

Performance Goals

Athletes should stay away from outcome goals and focus on performance goals, which they can control. Some things in the sport of softball are out of the athletes' hands. For example, a pitcher might want to throw a shutout. This is an outcome goal and one over which she has little control. She might be pitching great, getting batters out, having good ball movement and location, but the team may make some errors and allow a run to score. The pitcher had no control over the players on her team and how well they were fielding that day. If her goal was based on the outcome—the shutout—she will not have achieved her goal, even though her performance was outstanding.

However, performance goals are specifically within the athlete's control. Examples of performance goals might be to hit the ball hard, to stop swinging at bad pitches, or to stop 10 grounders in practice without an error. These are all goals that the athlete can meet without depending on the performance of others.

Goals should be set up like a pyramid. The *now* goals make up the base of the pyramid. These goals are abundant and create a strong base for the others to rest on. Athletes need to constantly strive for something during each moment of practice or competition.

A *now* goal is one that an athlete wants to accomplish at this present moment. In softball a player might say she wants to follow every ball into her glove for the entire practice. These are goals that the athlete makes in the present and attempts to accomplish in the present.

Short-term goals occupy the center of the pyramid. They are the most important portion, the building blocks. They work off the base or now goals and ask for a real commitment from the athlete. They are goals the athlete expects to meet in practice or within a two-week period. If they are accomplished, the heart of the pyramid is strong.

Much of the athlete's goal setting needs to involve short-term goals since these are the building blocks of the success pyramid. Short-term goals must be realistic and attainable, and they can be verbal or written. Every two weeks I have my athletes fill out a "goal card," which they carry with them at all times. On this card they list four short-term goals for the 14-day period: a personal goal, a family goal, a school goal, and a softball goal. I put a motivational quote on the bottom of the card every two weeks.

Long-term goals make up the peak of the pyramid. This is the highest point of goal setting. If the athlete reaches the peak successfully and she has followed the steps correctly, then she is probably playing up to her "peak" performance. Once the athlete has met her long-term goal, she can see and feel all the great reasons why goal setting is important. Having been to the top once, she will create another pyramid and set out to conquer it.

Team Goals

Team goals are developed and discussed by the team. They could be spoken or written words, such as "Let's have the best defense in the conference." During this discussion our athletes create a list of all the team goals for the season. This list is made into a large poster with the opponents for the season across the top and the goals down the side. This chart is then posted after every game with a star next to the goals the team met.

Changing Goals

If a goal set in the beginning of the year becomes unattainable at some point in the season, a new attainable goal needs to be made. If, for example, one of your athlete's goals was to have a fielding percentage of .970 and there is now no possible way to raise it that high, she needs to change her goal. You can first help her evaluate why she did not meet her original goal. After she has reflected over the first goal, let her put it away and create a goal that can be met in the remainder of the season. This allows her to still have something to shoot for and also to learn from her failure to fulfill the first goal. She might realize that she did not reach her first goal because it was too unrealistic for the position she plays or even possibly that she did not follow the steps needed for the end result desired. When goals are made in the beginning or in the middle of a season they first need to be attainable to be effective.

Misdirected Goals

These are the goals that are either unattainable or too obvious. It would be silly to set a goal like going undefeated in a season. Although everyone hopes for it to happen, it's not a goal that can be controlled. Different things will happen throughout the season that will cause teams to win and lose games. Though being undefeated in a season is attainable, it is a misdirected goal because it is controlled by too many other forces. Another example of an unattainable goal is for your weakest hitter to say she wants to hit .380 for the season. You know she struggles to keep a .250 average. This goal is too lofty and will most likely only collapse this athlete's goal pyramid. It would be better for you and the athlete to find an attainable goal.

An example of an obvious goal is to say, "I want to do the best I can." Of course most athletes usually want to do the best they can. To make this a goal is an easy way out. They need to strive for something to increase their level of play. "I did the best I could" is often an excuse for not rising to the occasion.

DISCIPLINE

Discipline has a dual meaning. Coaches both teach and perform types of discipline during their careers. They teach time management, healthy eating, and behavior control, for example, which affect the athletes' everyday lives whether in practice, at school, or on personal time. Coaches perform discipline in cases where an athlete has broken a rule. The two mingle with each other and help strengthen each other.

When prompting an athlete to perform at the level I feel she can, I have to use several motivating tools to get the end result. One tool I use, as needed, is discipline. Discipline works best when you use discipline to get discipline.

Every sport has its rules and every team has its own laws or code. This is where the first type

Fix the Problem With Sweat

I once had a pitcher who could not get her drop ball to drop like it should. In practice it was unmatched by the other pitchers, but in the game she seemed to lose faith in it. We felt it was psychological, that she did not believe in her pitches, or herself for that matter. She was more inclined to argue it was something else. After listening to every excuse and tolerating bad performances, I decided she needed to throw the drop ball so many times that throwing it in the game would be easy. I sent her over to a brick wall with a strike zone painted on it and gave her a bucket of balls. Her practice that day consisted of throwing drop balls to a designated area on the wall. After she threw a ball, it would bounce off the wall and she would have to pick it up and then throw another. In the end she had thrown hundreds of drop balls. She was sweaty, tired, and disciplined. We both got what we wanted out of the experience. She got a drop ball and I got an athlete who realized the game is easy. In the game you get to throw to a catcher and batters; you don't have to pick up every ball. She valued the experience and did not fear throwing her drop ball in the game again.

of discipline begins. Discipline in one's behavior is the first discipline I address. The athletes are informed of a formal code of ethics put out by the university, and then they are introduced to a code that has been put together by me and many former athletes. (See chapter 4 for an in-depth discussion of my rule-setting process.) They are codes that teach the player to be self-disciplined and help her become an elite athlete.

Ten-Mile Run

I have always tried to impress upon my players the importance of class attendance. One April we had an off day the last Friday of the month. Early that April I announced to the team that we would not practice on the last Friday in April, but that they must go to class. Our game schedule was such that we did not play that Saturday or Sunday. Halfway through April, I again reminded the team that we would be off the last weekend but that they must go to class on that Friday. The night before the last Friday, we were returning home from a trip to Iowa and I again reminded them about class attendance the next day. At that time I said, "If you don't go to class, be ready to run 10 miles." We gave our closing cheer and the next morning I sent my assistant to see who was and who was not in class. Seven players decided not to attend class! That Sunday night I called each of those athletes and told them to be at the field the next morning at 5:30 A.M. Monday morning I loaded those seven into my van and drove 10 miles out of town. I dropped them off and said, "See you at practice this afternoon." It has been a few seasons since anyone has missed a class.

It also takes discipline to perform the movements of an athlete. The athlete learns certain motions, styles, and techniques of how to perform no matter what sport she is participating in. For example, in softball the athlete learns what is called a batting position. This position asks the hitter to be disciplined at keeping her eye on the ball, remaining balanced, and many other techniques that lead to successful hitting. This skill discipline is something that is taught using forms of discipline to reinforce the correct action.

In practice I will use jumping jacks, a jog to the fence and back, or sprints as a form of discipline to motivate athletes to develop their skills. For example, we play a hitting game and ask that each hitter perform a certain skill. It might be taking the ball to right field or putting it on the ground. When the hitter is successful, all goes as planned; when the hitter is unsuccessful, she must do an assigned amount of jumping jacks. When she is done jumping she gets another try at performing a hitting skill. The skill takes discipline and I try to reinforce that by disciplining the undisciplined hitter. If the hitter cannot put the ball on the ground in the game when we need it, there will be a negative outcome much greater than jumping jacks.

SUMMARY

Motivating players is vital to the team's success. Each player is different and can be reached through different means. However, certain threads will run through the program. I motivate by doing the following:

- Strengthen a player's focus by using verbal reinforcement.
- Use one-on-one communication to let the athlete know you appreciate her efforts.
- Use token reinforcement as a motivator.
- Set up practices to allow for individual attention.
- Make softball special and fun. Include practice competition drills as a motivator.
- Incorporate goal setting into daily, weekly, and monthly planning.
- Encourage athletes to set performance goals and to reevaluate and adjust goals throughout the season.
- Instead of seeing yourself as providing motivation, think of yourself as giving inspiration. We have the potential as coaches to inspire players to become better athletes with a successful and healthy future.

Chapter 4

BUILDING A SOFTBALL PROGRAM

Many considerations go into building a successful program. These include deciding on a system of play, utilizing and nurturing outside support, setting up rules, and recruiting athletes. I've learned about these ingredients throughout my playing and coaching career. I played under Chuck McCord with the Pekin Lettes for seven years. I then had the opportunity to compete professionally with the Connecticut Falcons. That roster read like a "Who's Who" of coaches in Division I athletics. All of this opportunity happened while I was coaching at Western Illinois University. In 1979 I decided to build my own women's major premier fastpitch team, the Macomb Magic. I began by setting a goal that it would be a professionally run team that would compete against the very best in the country, be exciting to watch with tremendous athletes, and that it would represent our community at the elite level.

Many hours went into this dream and the outcome saw a club that played in two United States Olympic Festivals, twice finished fourth in national tournament play, qualified for five national tournament participations, and won state championships and regional titles as well. All of this occurred in the seven-year existence of the program.

When I decided to put this team on the field, my first obligation was to find the players who would be its heart and soul. This was accomplished by selecting two WIU players, Robin Lindley-McConnell and Jackie Crescio, who were finishing up their senior years. The next player I chose was my assistant coach, Kathy Welter. With these three players, I had the nucleus of talent and desire. The four of us then brainstormed ideas for the vision, the team makeup, and the team image. I rounded out the team with players whom I had coached in the past as well as other players from the Western Illinois team. It was a small squad but one with the ingredients I felt were necessary for success. The team members liked each other and respected each other's talent. They knew my style of coaching and brought to the program solid pitching, strong defensive tools, and offensive power.

With the players on board, I asked my good friend, Kathy Orban, to serve as the business manager. The two of us worked with a tremendous local marketing person, Steve Yeast, who helped us target the professional image we were after. He designed our media guide and helped us with marketing strategies. He also taught us how to link with community members and earn community support. With his ideas and our own we began our fund-raising efforts. From the very beginning we competed with a strong schedule and traveled from coast to coast.

Our main financial support came from gate receipts and sponsorships. The Macomb Magic played evening games and weekend games at home whenever possible, and we drew from area cities and towns. In our seven-year existence, attendance at home games was outstanding.

I have brought many of those ideals that were established with the Macomb Magic into each Western Illinois University team that takes the field. In this chapter I will discuss developing a system, gaining support for your program, recruiting, implementing the system, and instilling pride in your program.

DEVELOPING A SYSTEM

Along with every coaching philosophy comes a coaching style, and from this a certain system or method for playing the game. My coaching philosophy has always been to handle my team in the fairest possible way. For example, all players receive the same amount of work and practice

throughout the year. On a personal level, I try to treat each player differently because their personalities are different. At every practice a lesson of "how to" is delivered to the athletes. These lessons reflect the coaching style, and from there a system is born. I hold five points as the standards within my system: to be myself; to be honest; to give respect; to let the players know they are people to me, not just softball athletes; and to stay positive.

My system and style of play has always mirrored the Macomb Magic teams. I want to find and recruit great ballplayers, athletes who are talented enough to play more than one position. I have always believed that if you can hit, there will be a defensive spot for you. I believe that a player either brings a great bat to the team or a great glove. I want the player who has both, of course, but more often the athlete has more of one than the other. When I recruit I look for the athlete with strong hitting and throwing mechanics. I know I can teach and refine those skills, but I want that strong base to start with.

GAINING SUPPORT FOR YOUR PROGRAM

There are many avenues to pursue to gain support for your softball program, from your school's administration, faculty, and students to other members of your community. Without the friends and families of our players, as well as administrators, faculty members, trainers, and members of the community, we could not be successful. Their support is what we count on at Western, and in the following sections I'll talk about some of the ways I've gained that support. Keep in mind that your number one goal should be to gain people's respect for you, your program, and your athletes.

Administrative and Faculty Support

The softball program is a representative of the university. It's important when making decisions about the team, uniforms, opponents, fundraisers, and other issues that you keep the administration informed and ask for their input. Communication is essential. If you have good communication lines, then it will be easier for

athletic directors, counselors, principals, and superintendents to support you. They do not want to feel left out on big decisions or think that you are trying to go over their heads. Working together will bring about a better relationship.

I want my administration to get to know the softball athletes on a personal level. To that end, I include the administration in many of the events we put together in a social or professional setting.

A Tear of Support

We held the 1996 Conference Championship at our university. We were all hoping that we would clinch the title as tournament champions and all would celebrate. Unfortunately things did not go our way. We lost a close game against DePaul and went on to lose in the bottom of the seventh to Troy State the next day. Troy State went on to beat DePaul and win the championship. In our game against Troy State we went with our starting pitcher. Troy State began hitting her pretty hard so we brought in Becki Warner for relief. Becki had held them scoreless the previous day. Troy's batters came up to the plate to hit the ball and they did. They scored the two runs they needed to win and the game was over and so was our year. We packed up the dugout and said our thanks to our fans.

My assistant and I were walking around trying to fight the "what ifs" when I noticed Becki sitting in the stands, so I went and sat by her. Our athletic director, Dr. Helen Smiley, came over and sat by us. As I told Becki about the good year she had had, she just looked down and shook her head to let me know she was listening. When I turned to talk with Dr. Smiley, she asked me, "What do you say to your players?" When I looked in her eyes to respond, I noticed a tear in her eye. It was then that I realized that she understood how I was feeling, but more importantly, how Becki was feeling. I felt comforted to know that our athletic director felt the loss, and we had a moment to share our disappointment. The memory of the tear is a reminder to me that we are a bigger team than only the people in uniform.

The faculty members see the athletes every day as students in the classroom. I work with my athletes to let the instructors know they are also great athletes. At the beginning of each semester, we prepare a packet that our players hand deliver to their instructors. It contains the schedule, a brochure, and a letter from me introducing me and the program. I point out the days and times we will be away from campus for games and tournaments. In this way the professor can see when the student athlete will be away from class and can assist her in rescheduling quizzes and tests.

My staff and I go to the professors' offices to introduce ourselves and invite them to follow our program. At this time we try to get to know the professors and we sometimes deliver an additional program or schedule of our competitions. It is important that we let them know that we respect and understand the value of our athletes' education. We also dedicate a home competition to them, "professor night," where they are the special guests of the evening. It allows the professors to see the many talented facets of their students. This effort to inform teachers of absences and provide information about the program shouldn't be limited to the college level. In high school, the teachers and students spend more time together and this closeness should lend itself to athletes supporting teachers and teachers supporting athletes.

Student Support

There is nothing like hitting the ball hard and hearing the roar of a big crowd. It's a great feeling to have the stands full of your peers supporting you and your talent. Our staff tries to always inform the student body of our game times and team successes. We also have people working on promotions to entice the students of Western to come out and watch some pretty amazing women playing softball. We involve the crowd with games that go on in the stands and drawings that give them a chance to try to hit a ball over the fence in between games. There are prizes and giveaways and chances to mingle with the athletes after the game, not to mention action-packed softball with diving catches, balls going over the fence, pitches at 65 miles per hour, and headfirst slides into home plate. All these things combined help us gain the support of the students. If we can get them to come out, we bet that they will come back.

Community Support

There are many ways to involve your community in your softball program. For example, to increase community awareness and support for our team, I've launched a fastpitch softball club for fans. I tried to put together a package that would allow fans the opportunity to get to know the players and the coaching staff on a personal level, and to let them experience the various "stories" behind the scenes. I have included an example of our Fastpitch Club's description and benefits in figure 4.1.

We also have a Diamond Club for the young fans that gives them softball experience along with the chance to get to know the players and coaches (see figure 4.2).

We have also been fortunate enough to obtain business sponsorships for our home games to boost our community support. We structured a plan called Community Corporate Teammates (CCT), which works like this: For each of our home games we involve a local community group to assist in both the promotion of the game and in giving away prizes they have donated. For each of the CCTs we do a press release along with radio announcements and newspaper coverage. In exchange for a cash contribution or free products, the CCT receives a press release, a certificate, a picture of the team and the CCT's employees taken in the CCT's establishment, a public address announcement, a program listing, and a list of all the promotions appearing in the local newspapers.

There are countless activities you can organize with corporate sponsors: free squeeze bottles, gift certificates, and magnets from area restaurants; sponsorship of youth clinics by area businesses; prizes from area merchants for returning foul balls; and the list goes on! We've involved nearly 30 community corporate teammates in one season with little expense for them and a win-win situation for all of us.

RECRUITING

At the college level, recruiting is an important part of building any program. Playing softball is like a business in that you want to gather quality people to support your club and make it a success. In doing this you must first evaluate what your team needs to make it successful. Second, investigate where you can find the athletes who have the qualities you seek. And finally, ask what they will need to come and join your team. Recruiting is a full-year project with the evaluation of athletes occurring in the spring and summer for us. We also see some high schools that play their championships in the fall.

When you are first starting a team, write down the physical criteria you want each athlete to meet plus whatever else you would like them to bring into your program. You should already know that you will need an athlete at each position, but you should do some research on what these positions ask for in an athlete. After you have gone through and set the physi-

cal criteria, you must always remember the personality of the athlete. Are you looking for assertive athletes or passive? Or do you want a mixture? It is good to have in mind what you are looking for in a particular athlete before beginning the recruiting process.

Once you know what you are looking for, start collecting athletes' profiles from your comments on watching athletes play, a letter the athlete or her coach has sent to you, or possibly a scouting service, then make a plan of where you're going to see each athlete play in the most efficient manner. When recruiting, be sure to know the rules! NCAA rules are very specific about when and where athletes can be recruited, and by whom. Be sure you are familiar with the rules of your association.

When we return from seeing the athletes play, we send them letters letting them know we were there and asking them if they are interested in

Figure 4.1 WIU Fastpitch Club Information

You are invited to join the WIU Fastpitch Club

Who:
The WIU Fastpitch Club is governed by a Board of Directors and Officers. The membership consists of alumni, friends, and supporters of Westerwinds softball.

Why:
The WIU Fastpitch Club is being formed as a friends group for the Western Illinois softball program. As financial constraints continue to rise in college athletics, support from friends groups such as the Fastpitch Club becomes critical.

In addition to the financial support, members have an opportunity to support and promote the Westerwinds team. Loyal backing from alumni, family, and friends has a tremendous meaning for the student athletes.

Membership Options

Individual— $30 yearly
Student— $20 yearly (high school or college)
Lifetime— $200

Membership Benefits
- The opportunity to promote and support the WIU softball program
- The opportunity to meet and interact with the coaches and players at club functions and games
- Newsletters mailed throughout the year. The newsletter includes updates on the team, feature stories, notes from the WIU coaches, and upcoming club activities.
- Decal, schedule card, poster, media guide, and trading cards
- Acknowledgment in the game program
- Social opportunities such as tent gating, invitation to the "Big Game Breakfast," Fan Van, and postgame socials
- T-shirt

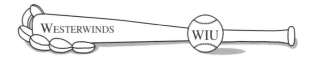
WESTERWINDS   WIU

Figure 4.2 WIU Diamond Club Information

You are invited to join the WIU Diamond Club

Who:
The WIU Diamond Club is open to girls in grades 2 through 8.

Why:
The WIU Diamond Club provides four clinics to help you be the best fastpitch player you can be. You will learn from the Westerwinds softball athletes and coaches. You will be playing with other players in your age group and skill level.

Each clinic will cover all aspects of the game of fastpitch. You will be working with fun equipment and learning from the best athletes around—the Westerwinds!

Membership cost = $70

Note: If you do not wish to join the Diamond Club, but would like to attend the clinics, they are three hours long and cost $20 each.

The cost of joining the club and not attending the clinics is $20.

Membership Benefits
- Free admission to all home games
- The opportunity to meet and visit with the coaches and players at club functions and games
- Four clinics
December 29	1:00 - 4:00 P.M.
January 19	1:00 - 4:00 P.M.
February 15 or 22	6:00 - 8:00 P.M.
April 19	6:00 - 8:00 P.M.
- Decal, schedule card, poster, and media guide
- Trading cards
- Social opportunities such as tent gating and postgame socials
- T-shirt

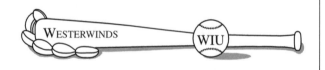

visiting the campus. We then make plans to show them what we have to offer as a university and as a team. Often an athlete will decide within a month or two if she wants to attend your university and play on the team. You usually know if the shoe fits or not, but there are many great universities out there as well as tons of great athletes and everyone likes to shop a little before saying yes.

Once you have signed your team for the next year, you begin this process all over again for the year after that because, unlike a business, you only have your athletes for four years. You are usually saying good-bye as you are saying hello. In saying the good-byes, you have to replace whomever is leaving the team.

IMPLEMENTING THE SYSTEM

Once you have developed your own softball system and have the school and community behind you, you are ready for the final step in building a softball program: implementation. In this step you concern yourself with hiring assistants, establishing team rules, and passing the pride you have in your program on to your players.

Hiring Assistants

It's very important when searching for an assistant that you look for someone who will complement you and the program. Just as you recruit a certain style of athlete for a certain position, you search for a certain type of person to come in and assist you in the coaching duties. Your assistant will bring knowledge, experience, and support to the team. Take your time when looking for an assistant and make sure that she has all the attributes you are looking for. For example, I look for outgoing and personable characteristics in assistant candidates I evaluate. It is crucial that you look at her dominant characteristics and decide if they will mesh with yours. Even if your assistant is a volunteer, you should still make sure you are comfortable with her.

Check into the background of a potential assistant to make sure she is qualified. Talk with former employers and ask about the characteristics you are most interested in. The two most important qualities for me are loyalty and trustworthiness. These two attributes do not develop overnight, but with time and a solid working relationship these feelings begin to grow. Once you feel you can trust your assistant, you begin to relinquish more responsibility to her, and then she is able to give ideas and put more time into the program. Offer her tons of teaching opportunities and room to grow. Remember, no relationship is perfect, but with open communication and trust you should be able to pull through the disagreements.

Establishing Rules

Every organization has a goal or a purpose. To reach our goal I feel we must have guiding principles or rules to help direct us. These rules are ways of governing our team, and they give us an opportunity to discuss how we feel we can best represent our university and play softball at the highest Division I level.

I believe rules are necessary and give unity and an identity to a program. The rules and standards you set for yourself say something about you, your program, and your team. That is why it is important that the team as a whole develop rules and commit to them.

Judi Garman, the great coach at Cal State Fullerton, once told me she has a simple rule, and that is, "If a team member makes another member unhappy, she is asked to leave the team." I have come to realize the importance of this rule and I also use it.

The Rule-Setting Process

When developing rules and setting standards, I provide the athletes with a team handbook. This handbook outlines the student athletes' rights, expectations, softball rules, plays, academic information, and so on. I let the team members give their input on the rules dealing with alcohol consumption and drug use. They discuss what they feel are appropriate standards, I write them up, and then they sign their names to ensure we are all committed. When talking about alcohol use and drug use, we ask each player to stand up and express her feelings and beliefs. This often leads to testimonials from upperclasswomen who have a very strong message for the younger athletes.

I also give each athlete a code of ethics. The purpose of intercollegiate athletics is to provide the opportunity for the athlete to develop her potential as a skilled performer in an educational setting. Following is a list of the ethical considerations for the student athlete:

1. Maintain personal habits that enhance healthful living.
2. Objectively acknowledge your own strengths and weaknesses, and recognize that each person has both.
3. Value your personal integrity.
4. Respect differing points of view.
5. Willfully abide by the spirit, as well as the letter, of the rules throughout all practices and competitions.
6. Uphold all standards and regulations expected of participants.
7. Treat all players, officials, and coaches with respect and courtesy.
8. Accept victory or defeat without undue emotion.
9. Graciously accept constructive criticism.
10. Respect and accept the decisions of the coaches.
11. Be willing to train in order to achieve your full potential.
12. Respect the achievements of your teammates and opponents.
13. Be honest, work hard, and give your all.

Rules are sometimes broken. That is why I get together with the team and together we decide on a discipline for when the rules are broken. Again I set the boundaries so they are neither too harsh nor too lenient. I let the players discuss and brainstorm their ideas, then we pick through them and toss out those that will not work on this ball team. I want the team to feel involved in deciding anything that deals with their health and well-being.

We want the athletes to know the ramifications of their actions and what is expected of them regarding responsibility. I list the team rules they are expected to follow, along with consequences for breaking these rules. I ask them to read the rules carefully, and if they have any questions or concerns regarding these rules, to speak to the team captains or the coaching staff. They are then asked to sign a contract stating that they have read, understand, and are willing to abide by these rules:

- NO drugs or smoking will be allowed during the academic year. If a player is caught smoking or using drugs at any time during the year, the following consequences will occur:
  - 1st violation: One-week suspension from all practices and games.
  - 2nd violation: Three-week suspension from all practices and games; appointments made with a counselor.
  - 3rd violation: Scholarship withdrawn and dismissal from the team.
- If a player is late to practice without a legitimate excuse:
  - 1st violation: Additional running at the end of practice.
  - 2nd violation: Suspension from that day's practice.
  - 3rd violation: One-week suspension from practices and games.
- If a player misses a practice without notifying the coaching staff:
  - 1st violation: Suspension from the next day's practice or game.
  - 2nd violation: One-week suspension from all practices and games.
  - 3rd violation: Reduction of athletic scholarship.

Being a member of the WIU softball team affords the athlete many benefits but also involves many responsibilities. One of these responsibilities includes adhering to high standards of physical training. Being an athlete is a 24-hour-a-day commitment, and as a full-functioning team member, the athlete must be willing to make that commitment. She is asked to obey basic training rules such as these:

- Get eight hours of sleep each night and especially get plenty of rest before a game.
- Eat a balanced diet that includes fresh fruits and vegetables, whole wheat bread, low-sugar cereal, chicken, fish, and low-fat dairy products.
- Drink plenty of water and avoid sugar and high-caloric, low-nutrition foods (candy, chips, etc.).
- Eat a nutritious breakfast.

Where's the Rake?

I once had a player who had a lot of personal problems during her sophomore year. It seemed drinking and fighting were getting in the way of her having a happy, healthy year. She could not obey team rules and was dismissed from the team after our first four games. The following summer she begged to be given another chance. After a few meetings with her, I agreed to let her try out. She then said, "If I make the team will I get to play?" She was so persistent in her demands that I finally stood up and said, "You should be begging me for a chance to rake the infield." On that note, she asked, "Where's the rake?"

I told her where it was and she left the office. Later that night, I drove by the field and noticed my player raking away. The temperature was over 100 degrees that day. That night I called her up and told her she had done a great job on the field. She said, "Thanks . . . that was a chore." I said, "See you at practice." She said, "I'll be there, and if there is anything extra I can do, just ask."

The player who raked the field did earn a uniform that fall. She drew up a contract for herself to make some positive changes in her life, along with helping set up and take down practice each day. She went on to earn a starting spot in the lineup and was the consummate practice player: came early, stayed late, worked hard, and gave her all.

We traveled to our first game that fall, played great, and came away victorious. This player went three for three, had three RBIs, and had a fine defensive game. As we walked over to shake hands with our opponents, the game ball was sitting on the ground. I bent over, picked it up, and found myself looking right into that player's eyes. I handed her the ball and said, "Great game." She took the ball

and immediately brought it in to her body, toward her heart, and tears filled her eyes.

It was in that instant of the softball going to her heart that we both realized the importance of the game to her. Later she told me that she woke up to her clock radio playing "One Moment in Time" by Whitney Houston. That game was truly one wonderful moment in time, and demonstrated the heart of a champion. The player was Venus Taylor, who was selected by her teammates twice as their most valuable player and who then went on to become a professional fastpitch player.

The Unwritten Rules

We were on the bus after a very hard loss and I heard laughter from a few rows away. At first I ignored it, but then it continued. I asked my assistant coach to please let that player know that it was not appropriate to laugh after a loss. The athlete apologized and said she didn't realize that was a rule. My assistant, Mindy Dessert, told her it was an unwritten rule. The next day the athlete again apologized and quietly asked if she could have a list of the "unwritten rules." I realized there are things we expect as coaches but may not

let the athletes know in a timely manner. I now have "The Unwritten Rules" in their handbooks. They are the following:

1. Be five minutes early.
2. Say "Hello."
3. Hustle everywhere.
4. Lend a hand in practice setup.
5. Turn in your uniform immediately after the game.
6. Keep a ball in your glove.
7. Always have your uniform shirt tucked in.
8. If you are not playing, cheer for those who are.
9. If you are going to be late or are going to miss a practice, give 24-hour written notice.
10. Always tell the coaches the truth.
11. If you disagree with something, set up an appointment to meet with the coaches.
12. If you make other people on the team unhappy, you will be asked to leave.
13. Treat equipment with respect.
14. Always run when arriving late.
15. No headphones while in uniform.
16. No laughing after a loss.

The Coach's Input

I believe the coach sets boundaries for several different areas of the program. I try to give my input when I feel that decisions that are being made by team members or by the team are not beneficial to the team as a whole. This does not happen very often. It is a good feeling for the players and me when they make correct decisions because I then feel we are on the same page. When they stumble off that page is when I use my authority to pull them back on.

I give my input only when asked for it. When an athlete comes to me and says, "Coach, what do you think about . . . ?" I tell her what I think. This is my favorite way to give input because it is absorbed better when it is asked for.

Captains

I prefer that the team elect the captains and co-captains. These women are always juniors or seniors and are players to whom the team can turn as a liaison between themselves and the coaching staff. We have captains' lunches every week where the coaches and captains can discuss the status of the team and any issues the captains wish to bring up. This allows a very informal, open sharing of ideas that helps to keep the team healthy. I believe healthy teams talk and this is one forum that we count on each week to work together.

A captain is a leader. She is someone with whom the athletes should feel comfortable talking. The captains should be elected to their positions because their teammates respect them, feel comfortable with them, and know they will do what is right for the team. The chosen captains mediate issues like playing time and practice opportunities between the athletes and coaching staff, and among the team members. They should be able to voice the opinions of their teammates and confront any issues the team might be having.

I feel having captains is vital for the team. It gives the athletes someone to go to with a problem before approaching the coaching staff. If the problem can be worked out without our interference, then everybody gains. The athletes develop a trust in the captains, the captains feel a sense of internal reward for being

able to help out a teammate, and the coaches can carry on with coaching.

There are certain situations when a problem might be too big or important for the captains to try and fix themselves. It is the responsibility of the team captains to make the judgment of when the right time is for them to bring the issue to the coaches. More than likely they will know the right thing to do.

On the field the captains are leaders and teachers. In practice they offer their insight and enthusiasm. During the game they give direction with their actions and create team unity with cheers, talks, and actions. The job of a captain is a crucial one. Thus, it is important for the team members to know all that they are asking from the athletes chosen as well as for the chosen to look inside and see if they can perform all that will be asked of them.

INSTILLING PRIDE

I have a wall of honor behind my desk and on it are pictures of former players who have graduated from the softball program. These are all color action shots, and each year it is bittersweet to put up the recent set of graduates. When prospective student athletes come into the office for a visit they can look at me, or look behind me to see the former Westerwinds. Even after they have signed on, every time they return to the office it is gratifying to watch their eyes as they look at all of the pictures. Our office is covered with pictures: images of the present and memories of the past. We do not keep trophies or plaques in our office—we keep people instead.

The more the players of today know about their tradition and heritage, the more special their role becomes. They are continuing a great tradition of excellence when they wear the purple and the gold and represent the university.

Talent can fail and so can mental toughness at times, but if you have pride in yourself, your team, and the program, you are sure to be able to pull through the tough moments. These moments could be during games, when a team crisis arises, or when the program is being tested by the administration. Your team needs to feel its worth. The players need to know their efforts are appreciated and that they are part of something important. It is the coach's job to build this feeling by showing them that he is willing to stand up for the athlete, the team, and the program.

Former Players

Western has many former athletes who return to the program as great fans, volunteers, and coaches. They always set a precedent with their support and words of encouragement. It is nice for the new team to get the chance not only to meet past women athletes, but to be supported by and learn from them.

Fans in Florida

On spring break in 1996 we took the Westerwinds on a softball-blazing trail and headed down to Tampa, Florida. We were going on a 17-day road trip and were anxious about the upcoming action. When we arrived at our first game in Tampa, I was very excited to see four past Westerwinds sitting in the stands waiting to cheer us on. I knew two of them lived in Tampa, but the other two had flown in from St. Louis. It was a great feeling for me as well as for the team to see former athletes being such great supporters. After the games I invited them to eat dinner with us. I introduced the former Westerwinds to the team, and we all talked for hours about softball. For some people it may seem shocking that these women took their vacation days from work to come watch the Westerwinds. But for me and the Westerwinds, it is not shocking because we all know how great it is to be part of the Westerwinds tradition and to play fastpitch softball.

These types of interactions let our new athletes see the great pride the athletes of the past have in the Westerwinds tradition. As each year passes, each player builds more onto this tradition with her contributions as a student athlete. Although many players see what their efforts do for themselves or their team, not very many of them think about the impact their hard work and actions will have on the Westerwinds of the future. When former athletes come back and visit, the current players get the chance to see what impact they had and continue to have on the program.

I have always felt fortunate to see so many of our past athletes at games. It is nice to bring them down after the game and introduce them to the team. Many of the past athletes come around often enough that they establish friendships with the new athletes. But even former athletes who do not frequent the games as much leave a lasting impression with their presence.

If you are particular about whom you recruit as athletes, making sure they are also good people, you will be rewarded not only in the years that they are part of your ball team but for many years to come.

A Classy Operation

When we put on our uniforms I expect total representation of the university. I want our players to know that they represent something bigger than themselves: the athletic department, the players before them, future players, and the school itself. Players' names may slip from memory as time passes, but the school, community, and program will continue into the future.

I remember one year when the Macomb Magic won 60 games and at one time had recorded 44 wins in a row. We were playing in a tournament in Chattanooga and we all walked into the complex together—I was somewhere in the middle of the group. I realized at that moment that I was exactly where I wanted to be, and I felt so proud to be associated with such tremendous athletes. During that streak I know some people came to see us play, wondering if we were going to lose. When we did lose game 45, we had our usual team meeting highlighting the game, the players changed their shoes, and we all agreed, "Well, it wasn't going to last forever." The players showed me "class."

Every day that you spend with your team you need to remind them that it is a privilege to play intercollegiate athletics. They need to hear that they are great athletes playing a difficult sport at one of the highest levels of competition. I believe they need to know these things because it is easy to have class when you have pride in what you do, who you are, and what you represent. I am always proud of our athletes when I watch them behave with class.

Milestones to Remember

When I reflect on my many exciting moments in coaching, certain milestones come to mind. I can clearly see wins number 300, 400, 500, and 600 as if they just happened. Our final win in 1987 made 299 for me. I felt pretty confident that in 1988 I would hit the 300 mark. At our coaches' convention the winter before the '88 season, a good friend of mine told me to let her know when I won my 300th game. I said, "Margaret, it's going to be against you." She just looked at me sort of puzzled, and I told her that we opened with her team that next spring.

Sure enough, we won the opening game of the year against U.S. International University, which was the first game of a doubleheader. Margaret came over after the game with her lineup for game two and shook my hand, gave me a hug, and said congratulations. I thought that was really classy of her to come over and acknowledge that milestone. She was a new coach herself and is now well on her way up the milestone trail.

Win number 400 came one day after my birthday in a tournament game in Florida against Miami of Ohio. I was fortunate to have my mom in attendance, and we won an extra-inning affair in the bottom of the eighth inning. As the game-winning RBI hitter rounded third base, she grabbed me and had a huge smile on her face as she said, "That one's for you, Coach!" That batter was Lori Tubbs, an awesome hitter, always sending off rockets from her bat. I guess that rocket was for me.

I know in that victory every single one of our players played in the game, from relief pitchers to pinch hitters to pinch runners. As we talked about it afterwards, we all felt so proud to be a part of a tradition. I remember everyone sitting around discussing the game, and there wasn't a dry eye to be found.

Win number 500 was a wet ordeal, but the rain did not wash away the smiles. I have a great picture in my office of all of us, drenched but happy. Some of the athletes are holding up five fingers and some are holding up one. When my assistant suggested we take the picture, I told her we were all wet and funny looking. She said, "That's okay. We'll look back on it and know it was a special day." She was right.

Win number 600 was so smooth. The team played great and we won easily, 9-0. I told the players it was a wonderful thing because we had all made an impact in many of those victories. My assistants had played for me, so some of those wins came from their on-the-field, as well as off-the-field, performances. The freshmen on the team had a certain glow as they wondered what number 700 would bring.

SUMMARY

There are many considerations that go into building a successful program.

- Find and utilize all of the people and groups who can help you succeed, and design your program to incorporate them. They include community members, faculty members, and students.
- Recruit the type of athletes who you want to coach. Be sure you know their character and their skills.
- Hire assistants who are trustworthy and loyal. Encourage them to create and design parts of the program.
- Establish rules that players help write and enforce. Use rule building as team building.
- Work closely with the captains and allow them to communicate team concerns to you.
- Instill pride and run a class program on and off the field.

Part II

COACHING PLANS

Chapter 5

PLANNING FOR THE SEASON

In this chapter we will discuss the importance of careful planning. Some of the topics we will cover are medical screening and insurance, conditioning programs, medical staff, designing a master conditioning plan, planning with your staff, and scheduling fair competition. Some may view the coaching professional as one who conducts practices and games during one season of the year. However, coaching softball is a full-year commitment to planning and preparation. If you have done these two things completely, the season will run smoothly.

MEDICAL SCREENING AND INSURANCE

When we invite athletes to Western for a recruiting visit, we make sure that one stop they make is with our head athletic trainer. We have them go through some simple strength tests and fill out a questionnaire about their current health and any previous health conditions. This is a necessary precaution for us because each athlete is an investment for the team. We also have a medical form that each returning athlete is required to complete at the beginning of each year.

Once an athlete is declared eligible, she must have a physical examination and authorization from a physician at our health center. This must happen before being issued equipment and before being allowed to practice and compete for a WIU athletic team. This precaution ensures that all athletes are in good health and that participating in practice will pose no threat to either their health and safety or to the health and safety of other participants.

It is important for the high school coach to become familiar with the school's insurance plan and then to make sure the parents understand it. Be familiar with the procedure that takes place following an injury—that is, who pays for what and which insurance company is responsible. Let the parents know what to expect well in advance so that when it is time to go through the claims process everyone understands how the insurance coverage works. The institution's (sports program's) insurance is generally secondary and will cover whatever the primary (parents') insurance does not cover. This may vary from school to school. For example, at our institution the athletic insurance will only pay for those injuries that are a direct result of an accident in the intercollegiate sports program. If an athlete is injured outside of practice or a game, she is covered by student health insurance.

PLANNING FOR MEDICAL CARE

I have been very fortunate to have had wonderful athletic trainers who work with the athletes through injury and rehabilitation. The purpose of the athletic training program is to work for the prevention of athletic injuries, care for those that occur, and accomplish complete recovery through rehabilitation so that the athletes can return to competition as safely and quickly as possible. Early detection of a possible problem is essential. The athletes are to report all their injuries, illnesses, cuts, abrasions, and so forth

to a trainer without delay. If an injury occurs during practice and there is no trainer present, the coach must summon one. It's important for everyone to be cooperative at all times for proper treatment to occur.

The athlete must be honest and report any injury so that treatment can begin as soon as possible, and to prevent the injury from getting worse. My responsibility is to allow the trainers the latitude to do their job. I am informed of each player's limitation prior to practice. With this information I can plan for that athlete, whether it be restricted activity or only observation.

When an athlete becomes injured and the injury is beyond the expertise of the training staff, then the trainers arrange an appointment with a physician. Good communication between the training staff and coaches is necessary to deliver proper medical care to the athletes.

At the high school level, and sometimes at smaller colleges, access to a training staff is not available. Whether you have the medical staff or not, it is critical that all coaches take a first aid course to be better prepared to handle minor or major emergencies.

Since most teams below the college level are not furnished with trainers who go everywhere and carry their own first aid equipment, here is a list of some of the items that I think are essential for a first aid kit, or to have handy.

- Full water bottles for each athlete or some source of water
- Adhesive bandages
- Ace bandages
- Sterile gauze and bandages
- White athletic tape
- Rubber gloves
- Peroxide
- Antibacterial ointment
- Sunscreen
- Burn ointment
- Aspirin
- Ibuprofen
- Antihistamine
- Tissue
- Scissors
- Finger splints
- Eye flush

- Antacids
- Anti-diarrhea medicine
- Tweezers
- Fingernail clippers
- Cotton swabs
- Ice bags
- Insect sting kit

CONDITIONING YOUR ATHLETES

A complete conditioning program is vital to softball performance. I believe each athlete needs high fitness and nutrition levels. We want our players to form healthy habits that will last even after their playing days are over. A good overall program will include flexibility, strength building, conditioning, and nutritional fundamentals. The year is divided into preseason, season, and postseason for the coaching staff and athletes. As you go through this section you'll learn different conditioning programs for different times of the year.

Getting Started

Before we begin our winter workouts, we go through a battery of 10 tests. These baseline scores illustrate for us our beginning level of fitness and strength and provide a good way for each player to see her improvement through the training period. Using these scores, we divide our team into mini-teams for other activities. With the help of station workers it's possible to test 20 athletes at all 10 activities in two hours or less. These tests can be done inside or outside. Prior to the tests the athletes do a warm-up run and stretch. We then divide the players into five groups of four athletes. What follows is the first set of tests.

1. Home to home—The athlete starts at the plate with a rockaway foot pattern and sprints from home to home. Two stopwatches are used and the average time is recorded. After all athletes have had one try, they repeat and the best time is recorded for each player.

2. Agility run—From a starting line the athlete runs through cones that are set up in a zigzag pattern. The course is approximately 60 feet long. The foot pattern calls for changes of direction and the finish line is next to the starting line. Two stopwatches are used and the average time is recorded. After all athletes have had one try, they repeat and the best time is recorded for each player.

3. Jump and reach—The athlete measures her standing reach. Then, from a balanced position, she takes one step and jumps up. That measurement is taken and the first measurement is subtracted from the second for the vertical jump distance.

4. Chin-ups—The athlete uses a reverse grip and stands on a chair at the chin-up bar. She does as many as she can and steps down on the chair when she is finished.

5. Chest pass—The athlete sits in a chair with both feet on the floor and a belt holding her hips to the chair. A tape measure is laid out on the floor in front of the athlete and she chest-passes a medicine ball (about 10 pounds) out along the tape measure. Each athlete gets two tries and her best distance is recorded.

The players perform each of the above tests and then rotate as a group to the next station. When these stations are completed, the next series of four tests are explained. A group of five athletes is assigned to each of the four stations as follows:

1. Triceps dip—The athlete places her feet (toes up) on a chair or other support that elevates her lower body parallel to the floor. She is positioned straight-armed between two benches or chairs, supporting herself with her hands on the seats. She slowly lowers her body, keeping her elbows together, and exhales as she pushes up. The on-deck player can hold the benches to keep them stable. This drill is performed for one minute and the number of dips are recorded.

2. Decline push-ups—The athlete places her feet on a bench or chair and her hands on the floor in the push-up position. While inhaling, she lowers her body slowly until her chest touches a cone (about 10 inches high). Exhaling, she slowly pushes herself back to the original position. This exercise is performed for one minute and the number of push-ups is recorded.

3. Flexibility—The athlete sits on the floor at the front of a flexibility box (a wooden box with a ruler extending from the top of the box toward

the athlete) and places her feet against the box. She then reaches forward as far as possible over the ruler. The distance reached is recorded.

4. Sit-ups—The athlete sits on the floor with knees bent at a 90-degree angle and feet flat. A partner holds her feet. The player crosses her arms over her chest, places her hands on her collar, and curls her trunk so that her shoulder blades are off the floor. She does as many sit-ups as possible in one minute. The partner counts and the score is recorded.

These nine tests are done leaving one for the track. We time each athlete one trip around the track, starting seven off at the same time, running three heats. In six or seven minutes all athletes have run.

To score the test I build a spreadsheet with the athletes' names down the left column and all of the tests along the top row. Each test is ranked from the best performance to the lowest performance. One hundred points are assigned to the best score, 95 points to the second best, 90 points to the third best, and so on. If two players tie for one spot, the two scores are added together and divided by two. For example, two players are tied for the first and second best times; that's $100 + 95 = 195 \div 2 = 97.5$. The score of 97.5 is awarded to the two athletes who tied.

Each athlete now has points for all 10 scores, which are added for a total point production. I rank them from the top down and award small prizes for the best five athletes. I then place the athletes in balanced teams that will be used throughout the workouts.

This ranking is similar to seeding a tournament and it provides for four balanced teams with five athletes in each team. This battery of tests is repeated at the end of every four weeks with awards and presentations made and new teams assigned.

Developing a Conditioning Program

The demands on the athlete's skill and stamina must be considered when developing a conditioning program. In this section I present a cross-training program for you that is part of the preseason workouts. It builds discipline, mental toughness, cardiovascular endurance, total fitness and power, agility, footwork, and speed.

Mondays and Thursdays are similar activity days and focus on the arms while Tuesdays and Fridays are similar and focus on the legs (see figure 5.1). Wednesday is an off day with extra stretching assigned, and Saturday and Sunday are optional.

Weight Training

What is the role of weight training in softball? We weight train to prepare for competition, to prevent injury, to rehabilitate, and to produce a better athlete. If we have a player with the highest level of softball technique and skills and couple that with the highest level of development of physical qualities, then we will have the best possible player.

Strength is the main physical factor developed in a weight-training program. An athlete who first undertakes a weight-training program will not only gain additional strength. She will also increase her running speed and her ability to throw and swing the bat faster and harder. Weight training can help prevent injuries, too. The concept of muscle balance states that the closer in strength two opposing muscles are the less likely the weaker of the two muscles will become injured. To prevent or correct such imbalances, training must ensure that all opposing muscles are trained to the same extent. Plus, the weight-training program must consist of exercises which train all major muscle groups.

If a player were only to do weight training for several months with no explosive training mixed in, she would actually lose some of her ability to be quick and explosive in her movements. Therefore, we combine our weight training with explosive (plyometrics type) training as described in figure 5.1.

Flexibility

Flexibility exercises should be done before and after any exercise to maintain complete range of motion and to help prevent injuries. Instruct your athletes on some basic stretches for a softball flexibility program:

• Low back stretch—Lie on your back with your head on the ground, one leg straight and one leg bent. Grasp the back of your bent knee and slowly pull it up to your chest while gently

Figure 5.1 Sample Preseason Conditioning Program

Mondays and Thursdays—Arms

2:45 Team stretch
2:55 Three-mile run (run or walk as needed). I use a route around campus rather than a track.
3:30 Team stretch
3:40 Sit-ups—three sets of 30 crunches
3:50 Weight room—chin-ups, triceps dips, lateral pull-downs, T-bar rowing, and dumbbell flys. On arms days pitchers will be in the training room doing small dumbbell rotator-cuff work for internal and external rotation. They'll also work with therabands in a rowing motion to strengthen their upper backs.

4:05 Jump rope routine—feet together, right foot only, left foot only, side to side, and front to back (all for 30 seconds each); as many as you can for 15, 30, and 45 seconds; end with double jumps for 60 seconds.

4:10 Cones—Do these drills in single-file formation five times (each one taking 75 seconds).

- Three-corner drill (to improve footwork, change of direction skills, acceleration, and deceleration)—Athlete starts in a ready position on first line. Sprints to first cone, plants and drives off the left foot, shuffling right to second cone. At second cone, backpedals to third cone. Once at the third cone, plants left foot and breaks at a 45-degree angle to the right as if she were breaking for the ball. Make sure the athletes use good acceleration while sprinting to the first cone, don't cross their legs on the shuffle step, and stay low on the backpedal.

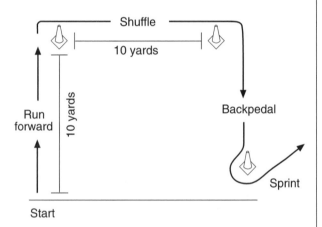

- Zigzag (to improve change of direction skills, footwork, and flexibility in hips)—Athlete starts on the right side of the square and runs forward. At the first cone makes a reverse pivot by throwing the right shoulder clockwise. Grapevines to the second cone. Reverses pivot and backpedals to the third cone. Reverses pivot and grapevines to the finish. Make sure the athletes are facing the proper direction when doing the grapevine, and that they back pivot and have good acceleration and deceleration while sprinting to the cones.

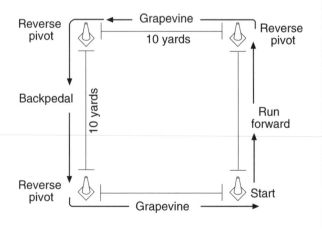

(continued)

Figure 5.1 *(continued)*

- Backward zigzag (to improve foot action and backpedaling)—Athlete starts on the right side of the square and backpedals to first cone. At the first cone, grapevines to the second cone and then backpedals to the third cone. At third cone, grapevines to the finish. Make sure the athletes stay low on the backpedal.

- Combination zigzag (to improve footwork, backpedaling, and change of direction skills)—Athlete starts on the right side of the square and backpedals to the first cone. At the first cone, sprints diagonally to the second cone and then backpedals to the third cone. At the third cone, sprints diagonally to the fourth cone. Make sure the athletes stay low while backpedaling.

4:15　Bats—Do these drills in single-file formation five times (each one takes about 50 seconds).

- Change of direction (to develop quick foot action)—Athlete starts at either right or left side at one end of the bat and runs forward to the other side of the bat. Have player plant her outside foot at the end of the bat, exploding forward toward the other end of the next bat, and continue through all bats. Make sure the athletes push off with the outside foot.

- Forward-backward (to develop quick foot action and high knee action)—Athlete is in a ready position with knees slightly bent, upright torso, head up, and hands and arms away from her body. On command the athlete runs forward to the end of the bat. She then backpedals through the bats to the opposite end, and then forward. Repeats through all bats, ending with a five-yard sprint. Make sure the athletes

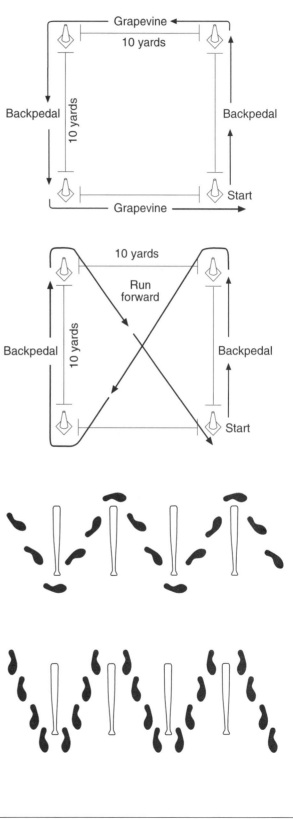

(continued)

Figure 5.1 *(continued)*

stay low throughout drill and that their weight is forward on the backpedal. Encourage them to eliminate false steps when changing directions.

- Zigzag (to develop foot coordination and quickness)—Athlete starts at either right or left side at one end of the bat facing the row of bats. Shuffles diagonally beyond the first bat and then changes direction and shuffles to the end of the second bat. Continues shuffling through all bats. Make sure the athletes stay low throughout the drill and do not cross their feet, but that they do push off with the outside foot when changing direction.

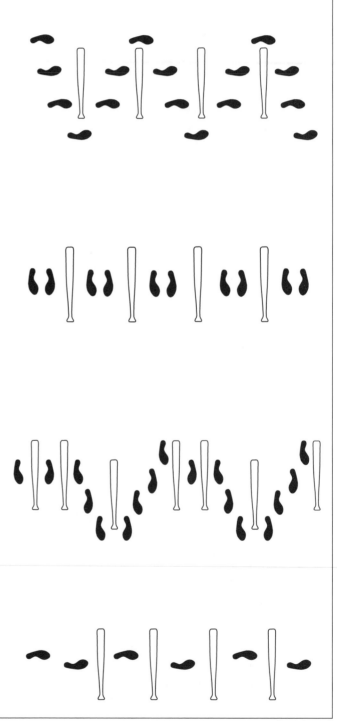

- Bunny hop (to improve hip flexibility and foot quickness)—Athlete laterally hops over the first bat keeping the legs and feet close together. After contact, quickly hops again over second bat and continues hopping over each bat. Make sure the athletes pull knees up high and move feet quickly.

- Combination lateral (to improve footwork and leg drive)—Athlete is in a two-point stance with knees slightly bent, upright torso, head up, and hands and arms away from her body. Runs laterally over the first two bats and then sprints five yards to the third bat and laterally steps over it. Backpedals five yards and laterally steps over bats four and five. She should continue through the bats doing this pattern. Make sure the athletes have good acceleration and stay low during the backpedal.

- High knees (to improve foot quickness)—Athlete starts at either right or left side at one end of the bats facing the row of bats. Sprints to the first bat pulling knees up to her

Figure 5.1 *(continued)*

waist and pumping her arms. Continues through all bats. Make the sure athletes keep their knees high, backs straight, and pump their arms.

4:20 Run 10 60-foot sprints
4:30 Dismiss

Tuesdays and Fridays—Legs

2:45 Team stretch
2:55 Three-mile run
3:30 Team stretch
3:40 Sit-ups—50 crunches
3:50 Weight room—hamstring curls, lunges, squats, hip sled, and jumps. On legs days, all players do the same exercises.

4:05 Push-ups (20)
4:10 Plyometrics—two minutes each

- Double-leg bounding—Athlete begins from a half-squat stance, with shoulders forward and out over her knees, back straight, and her head up. Athlete jumps outward and upward, thrusts with her arms, and reaches maximum height and distance by fully straightening the body. Upon landing, she goes into the next jump.

- Alternate-leg bounding—Athlete starts with knees bent and one leg slightly in front of the other. She drives that leg up and out in front of her, jumping as far as possible. Upon landing, she repeats with her other leg.

- Lateral bounding—Athlete starts in a ready position, one long step from an incline. She pushes off with her outside foot and lands on the incline, then immediately pushes back off of it, trying to gain as much lateral distance as possible.

- Side hops—Athlete sets two 18-inch high cones two feet apart. Starts on outside of one cone with feet together, and jumps sideways over both cones, one at a time. Athlete changes direction and jumps back over the cones, keeping her arms at a 90-degree angle throughout the drill.

- Side jump and sprint—Athlete sets one cone 15 yards from the finish line, and starts in the same position as the side hop. She jumps back and forth over the cone 10 times then sprints to the finish line.

4:20 Medicine ball exercises—two minutes each

- Twist and toss—Athlete starts with ball cradled next to her body at waist level, and feet spaced slightly wider than shoulders. She twists her torso in opposite direction of the intended toss, then quickly and powerfully changes direction of twist and releases the ball with arms outstretched. Make sure the athletes use their hips, shoulders, and arms for this exercise.

- Sit-up throw—Athletes start by sitting on the floor facing each other with feet interlocked. Keeping arms extended, they use their abdominal muscles to both throw the ball with an arc and absorb the shock of the catch by rocking back.

- Ball scoop and toss—Athlete starts in a semi-squat stance holding ball low and between her legs, with her arms fully extended, back straight, and head up. She scoops up the ball and tosses it up using her shoulders, arms, back, hips, and legs, then moves back into a semi-squat position to catch the ball.

- Chest pass—Athletes start by facing each other standing, sitting, or kneeling. One partner holds the ball at chest height with arms flexed and backs of hands touching her chest,

---

Figure 5.1 (continued)

and pushes it outward toward the other partner, fully extending the arms. The other partner anticipates the catch with arms extended horizontally at chest height, and absorbs the shock of the catch by bending her elbows but not allowing the backs of her hands to touch her chest. The catching partner immediately returns a throw in similar fashion.

- Throw—Athlete starts by kneeling on the floor and holding the ball

behind her head with her elbows bent. She slowly leans back then quickly flexes forward using her torso muscles and follows through by throwing the ball as far as possible. Make sure the athletes concentrate on thrusting their arms forward from the shoulders and chest.

4:30   Dismiss

---

lifting your forehead toward the bent knee. Switch legs and repeat. Then bring both knees to your chest as you lift your forehead to meet the bent knees. Hold each position 15 to 30 seconds and repeat twice.

- Quadriceps stretch—Stand with your hips square and bending your right leg back, reach behind and grasp it just above the ankle. Your support leg should be in line with your upper thigh—be careful not to let your weight shift to your support thigh. If you have difficulty keeping your hips square, grasp your ankle with the opposite hand. Hold this position 15 to 30 seconds then switch legs. Repeat twice.

- Sitting hamstring stretch—Sit on the ground with your legs fully extended in front of you, knees slightly bent. Slowly reach for your toes. Hold for 15 to 30 seconds and repeat two to three times.

- Lower back and hip stretch—Lie on your back with your head on the ground, arms out at your sides, and shoulders flat on the floor. Lift your right leg up, bend it at the knee, and gently pull your right knee over your left leg using your left hand. Turn your head toward your outstretched right arm, and continue to pull your right knee down with your left hand towards the floor. Hold for 15 seconds. Switch legs and repeat.

- Shoulder and arm stretch—Face a wall or chain link fence and press against it (or hold onto it) with your right hand at shoulder level. Then bring your left arm around your back and press that hand against the wall as well (or grab

the fence). Look over your left shoulder, keeping it close to the wall or fence as you slowly turn your head. Switch sides and repeat.

- Groin stretch—Sit on the floor with your legs a comfortable distance apart and slowly lean forward, keeping your back straight, quadriceps relaxed and toes pointed toward the ceiling. Keep your hands out in front of you for balance and stability or hold on to something for greater control, and try not to lean forward with your head and shoulders—this will cause your hips to move backward and put pressure on your lower back. Hold for 35 seconds.

- Ankle stretch—Sit on the floor with your legs a comfortable distance apart and pick up your right leg at the ankle. Rotate your ankle clockwise and counterclockwise through a complete range of motion using your hands to provide slight resistance. Rotary motion of the ankle helps to gently stretch out tight ligaments. Repeat 10 to 20 times in each direction for both ankles.

- Standing calf stretch—Stand facing a wall or other solid support and lean on it with your forearms, resting your head in your hands. Bend one leg and place your foot on the ground in front of you, with the heel on the ground and toes pointed straight ahead or slightly turned in as you hold the stretch. Your other leg should be straight behind. Slowly move your hips forward, keeping your lower back flat, and remember not to bounce as you stretch. Hold an easy stretch for 30 seconds, then switch legs and repeat.

• Simple triceps stretch—With arms overhead, hold your right elbow with your left arm and gently pull it behind your head. Hold for 15 seconds, then switch elbows and repeat.

• Simple shoulder stretch—Gently pull your left elbow across your chest and toward your right shoulder with your right hand. Hold for 10 seconds, then switch and repeat.

• Low back and gluteal stretch—Sit on the ground with your arms to the sides and legs together in front of you. Lean forward as far as possible, then have a partner place her hands on your shoulders and hold you in that position. Push back against her resistance for eight seconds, then relax and allow your partner to push forward slowly until you feel a slight discomfort. Repeat two to three times, then switch partners.

• Hamstring stretch—Lie on your back with one leg elevated and the other on the ground, keeping your toes of the ground leg pointed up towards the ceiling. Your partner should position herself so she can block your "up leg" as you try to depress it toward the ground. Hold this position for eight seconds, then relax. Repeat two to three times with both legs, then switch partners.

• Anterior shoulder stretch—Stand with your feet shoulder-width apart, and extend your arms to the sides with elbows straight and thumbs up. Keeping your arms parallel to the ground, reach as far back as possible. Your partner should then grasp your wrists to block any forward motion and gently pull your arms further back in a steady motion until you feel a slight discomfort. While your partner is pulling your arms back in a steady motion, provide resistance by trying to move your arms forward. Switch partners.

Aerobic and Anaerobic Activity

We have two off-season programs, one in July and August and one in November and December. These programs have a stronger aerobic emphasis and use exercises such as distance running. We have two in-season programs, one in September and October and the other from January through May. Our in-season conditioning programs combine both aerobic and anaerobic exercise with a stronger anaerobic emphasis. Softball requires quick, explosive bursts of power, whether it be sprinting to first, sprinting after a deep fly ball, running to the backstop to play a wild pitch, or throwing a hard drop ball.

During the season we design our drills to incorporate speed work and power work. We emphasize technique throughout the year and we always include technique as we condition. Figure 5.2 shows our off-season July and August workout. The distances are in yards and the numbers in parentheses represent the amount of time to rest between runs. For example, if set 1 says 4 × 220 at 40 seconds (2:00), it means to run 220 yards in 40 seconds or less and then to rest for two minutes. Repeat it three more times. 1:3 means rest three times as long you work. The times are recommendations and if the player runs a slower time, that is her time for the rest of the set.

Nutrition

Nutrition is an important component of the overall strength and conditioning program. Food has an enormous impact on the well-being of the athlete, but this fact is often neglected. I believe that sound nutritional habits are important to remain healthy and to have energy for the active lifestyle of the athlete. We teach proper nutritional habits each day. A section of our team

Figure 5.2 Sample 8-Week Off-Season Conditioning Program

Week	Monday	Tuesday	Wednesday	Thursday	Friday	Saturday
Week 1	20-minute run/walk 10-minute stretch before/after	Infielders: 100 ground balls Outfielders: 75 ground balls and 25 fly balls 20 75-foot sprints	20-minute run/walk 10-minute stretch before/after	Infielders: 100 ground balls Outfielders: 75 ground balls and 25 fly balls 20 75-foot sprints	20-minute run/walk 10-minute stretch before/after	Infielders: 100 ground balls Outfielders: 75 ground balls and 25 fly balls 20 75-foot sprints
Week 2	20-minute run 10-minute stretch before/after	Infielders: 100 ground balls Outfielders: 75 ground balls and 25 fly balls 20 75-foot sprints	25-minute run 10-minute stretch before/after	Infielders: 100 ground balls Outfielders: 75 ground balls and 25 fly balls 20 75-foot sprints	30-minute run 10-minute stretch before/after	Infielders: 100 ground balls Outfielders: 75 ground balls and 25 fly balls 20 75-foot sprints
Week 3	Set 1: 4 × 220 at easy (1:3) Set 2: 8 × 110 at easy (1:3)	Infielders: 100 ground balls Outfielders: 75 ground balls and 25 fly balls 20 75-foot sprints	Set 1: 2 × 440 at easy (1:3) Set 2: 8 × 110 at easy (1:3)	Infielders: 100 ground balls Outfielders: 75 ground balls and 25 fly balls 20 75-foot sprints	Set 1: 2 × 440 at easy (1:3) Set 2: 6 × 220 at easy (1:3)	Infielders: 100 ground balls Outfielders: 75 ground balls and 25 fly balls 20 75-foot sprints
Week 4	Set 1: 2 × 880 at easy (1:3) Set 2: 2 × 440 at easy (1:3)	Infielders: 100 ground balls Outfielders: 75 ground balls and 25 fly balls 20 75-foot sprints	Set 1: 6 × 440 at easy (1:3)	Infielders: 100 ground balls Outfielders: 75 ground balls and 25 fly balls 20 75-foot sprints	Set 1: 3 × 880 at easy (1:3)	Infielders: 100 ground balls Outfielders: 75 ground balls and 25 fly balls 20 75-foot sprints

(continued)

Figure 5.2 *(continued)*

Week	Monday	Tuesday	Wednesday	Thursday	Friday	Saturday
Week 5	Set 1: 8 × 110 at 20 seconds (1:3)	Infielders: 100 ground balls	Set 1: 12 × 110 at 20 seconds (1:3)	Infielders: 100 ground balls	Set 1: 16 × 110 at 20 seconds (1:3)	Infielders: 100 ground balls
		Outfielders: 75 ground balls and 25 fly balls		Outfielders: 75 ground balls and 25 fly balls		Outfielders: 75 ground balls and 25 fly balls
		20 75-foot sprints		20 75-foot sprints		20 75-foot sprints
Week 6	Set 1: 4 × 220 at 40 seconds (2:00)	Infielders: 100 ground balls	Set 1: 4 × 220 at 40 seconds (2:00)	Infielders: 100 ground balls	Set 1: 4 × 220 at 40 seconds (2:00)	Infielders: 100 ground balls
	Set 2: 16 × 110 at 20 seconds (1:00)	Outfielders: 75 ground balls and 25 fly balls	Set 2: 16 × 110 at 20 seconds (1:00)	Outfielders: 75 ground balls and 25 fly balls	Set 2: 16 × 110 at 20 seconds (1:00)	Outfielders: 75 ground balls and 25 fly balls
		20 75-foot sprints		20 75-foot sprints		20 75-foot sprints
Week 7	Set 1: 8 × 220 at 40 seconds (2:00)	Infielders: 100 ground balls	Set 1: 8 × 220 at 40 seconds (2:00)	Infielders: 100 ground balls	Set 1: 8 × 220 at 40 seconds (2:00)	Infielders: 100 ground balls
	Set 2: 8 × 110 at 20 seconds (1:00)	Outfielders: 75 ground balls and 25 fly balls	Set 2: 8 × 110 at 20 seconds (1:00)	Outfielders: 75 ground balls and 25 fly balls	Set 2: 8 × 110 at 20 seconds (1:00)	Outfielders: 75 ground balls and 25 fly balls
		20 75-foot sprints		20 75-foot sprints		20 75-foot sprints
Week 8	Set 1: 8 × 220 at 38 seconds (2:00)	Infielders: 100 ground balls	Set 1: 8 × 220 at 38 seconds (2:00)	Infielders: 100 ground balls	Set 1: 8 × 220 at 38 seconds (2:00)	Infielders: 100 ground balls
	Set 2: 8 × 110 at 18 seconds (1:00)	Outfielders: 75 ground balls and 25 fly balls	Set 2: 8 × 110 at 18 seconds (1:00)	Outfielders: 75 ground balls and 25 fly balls	Set 2: 8 × 110 at 18 seconds (1:00)	Outfielders: 75 ground balls and 25 fly balls
		20 75-foot sprints		20 75-foot sprints		20 75-foot sprints

bulletin board is called "nutritional tips," and every other day we present an important concept about nutrition and the choices the players can make. We try to educate our athletes about what makes up a sound diet and how it can enhance their performance.

Making a Master Plan

We strive for a year-round program of fitness, conditioning, and nutrition. A good overall program will consist of aerobic activity, flexibility, strength training, foot quickness, agility, and a strong nutritional base. Our overall plan for the year is broken into summer workouts, fall practice, winter workouts, and preseason and in-season segments (see figure 5.3 for a sample plan).

PLANNING WITH YOUR STAFF

My staff and I plan, well in advance of the season, the responsibilities of each of the staff members. I will delegate certain responsibilities, but I am the one ultimately responsible. I try to be sure my assistants and managers are working in the areas they enjoy and in the areas of their expertise. We discuss our plans and programs throughout the year and continually review all aspects of the program.

Assistants

You cannot run a successful program alone—you need the assistance of a strong staff. Do not be afraid to delegate certain responsibilities and then adjust your assistants' duties depending on their ability to fulfill them. The general responsibilities of my assistant coaches are as follows:

- Individual player academic monitoring
- Scouting reports on opponents
- Team travel curfews
- Team goal chart and locker room bulletin boards
- Summer camp administration

Figure 5.3 Sample Master Conditioning Plan

Month	Emphasis	Description
July–August	Summer training	Running, throwing, fielding
September–early October	Game play	Practice, maintenance
Early October–late October	Time for the athlete	Recovery, rest, no softball activity
November–mid-December	Strength building, nutrition	Weight training, plyometrics, flexibility, finding a healthy meal plan
Mid-December–mid-January	Home training	Athletes on semester break. Self-monitored continuation of weights and running.
Mid-January–late February	In-season training	19-week practice season, weights
Late February–end of May	Game play	Maintenance
June	Off season*	Rest period

*Athletes are encouraged to play summer ball and we adjust their summer workouts to meet their competitive schedules. If athletes do not play on summer teams they begin their training in July.

- Direction of the student managers
- Answering all recruiting mail and phone requests
- Coordination of home game staff
- Maintaining current media file
- Assisting with equipment and uniform checkout
- Cooperation with the booster club
- Team testing and charting
- Recruiting organization

Student Managers

To make any program a success it needs "hired hands" and hearts to work for it. These people are the coaches and others behind the scenes—people who love athletics. One such person who helps the program run smoothly is a student manager. We are usually fortunate enough to hire a student manager to assist us with specific duties.

I have always found that the managers do not have to know everything about your sport to succeed; they just have to be eager to learn about it. They must want to be part of a successful program and to do their part.

When putting together a list of the student manager's duties, I try to look at what could be done without coaches present and what activities would offer us more coaching time if another person were to perform them:

- Assists in all practice setups.
- Assists in practice with drills by picking up balls, running the stopwatch, recording hits, and so on. (Manager plays a key role in the efficiency of the practice.)
- Assists in closing up practice and making sure everything is put away. The athletes will be assigned to certain equipment items; the manager is to double-check that nothing gets left out.
- Learns to use all video equipment—the manager is asked to videotape practices, games, and individual lessons. He is also in charge of setting up videos that will be viewed in the team room. The video equipment is the manager's responsibility at all times.
- If not videotaping, keeps the score book during games. The manager shares this duty with other athletes. It is important that he becomes familiar with the way the team records statistics.
- Makes sure the score book is stocked with all necessary items: pencils, score sheets, lineup sheets, umpire evaluation sheets, and so on.
- Writes up the lineup and turns it in to the officials and the opposing team. Asks for the opposing team's lineup and enters information into the score book.
- When on the road, works with the assistant coach to locate restaurants, motels, locker rooms, training facilities, and laundromats.

The student manager is a valuable resource for the coaches. When he performs his duties well he earns the respect of the team and becomes a part of the experience. I guess I expect the same thing from a student manager that I do from the athletes—a winning effort.

A "Jeff" of All Trades

I once had a volunteer student manager who could do stats, catch the pitchers in the bull pen, videotape, hit fly balls—he even filled in at positions when athletes were injured. The list was endless. All these things were a blessing, but what made Jeff Mison stand out the most was his love for the game. He wanted to learn as much as he could from our program. He traveled with us whenever he could, and besides being our manager, was our biggest fan. His great effort and heart allowed us to get many things accomplished. The second year that Jeff helped out, he went with us to the conference tournament and we won the championship. It was a great feeling for all of us. To celebrate the victory, we ordered conference championship rings. It was very special, as I handed them out to the team, to hand one to Jeff. I hope when Jeff looks at the ring he realizes how his helping hand played a part in all of us being champions.

Scouting

One of our staff's responsibilities is scouting. Because we have two seasons every year that involve competition—the fall and the spring—we will scout as many of our upcoming opponents as possible. The NCAA does not permit us to go to watch our opponents unless we are in the same tournament as they are. In this case we will assign a member of our staff to study our opponents at that tournament. We mostly scout the hitters and the pitchers. We focus on each team's strongest offensive threat and try to give our hitters some insight into their pitching style. A more detailed description of our scouting charts and methods is contained in chapter 14.

Scheduling Fair Competition

It's my responsibility to build a schedule based on fair competition for our squad. In our conference we play four games against each conference opponent in our division, but the rest of the scheduling is left up to the individual institutions. I want to be sure we play teams of the same caliber as we are. We emphasize a strong regional schedule. We play in three or four tournaments each fall and spring. We look to play in tournaments that give our athletes exposure, as well as to play many opponents who are ranked higher than we are. I also want to play as many home games as possible so that our fans have the opportunity to cheer us on. In this way we can build a strong fan base that supports our athletes on and off the field.

Uniforms

The Western Illinois University Athletic Department provides its athletic teams with full sets of uniforms and practice clothes. Since we usually play more than once a weekend, we raise the funds to pay for a couple more sets of uniforms. The uniform should be comfortable and weather-appropriate. Keeping these things in mind, we work with a company in Florida that cuts the uniforms to fit women. Besides the basic shirt and pants, we provide undershirts and sliders that are warm and help protect the skin.

One of the best ideas I had was to ask the soccer program if they wanted to share the cost of some warm parkas; they could use them during their fall season and we would have them during our spring season. They agreed, and we not only saved a considerable amount of money but we were all warmer.

I have always felt it is important to get the athletes' input on uniforms. I make it a point to ask what they are looking for in a uniform as far as comfort and design. They make sound choices and are excited when the new uniforms arrive.

Equipment

Our softball staff works on getting quality equipment for our athletes. We work first on the softball necessities: bats, balls, catching equipment, and so on. The players provide their own gloves, but we have helped them choose ones that are best for their hands and positions. After the necessities are covered, we generate dollars to help us afford tools and apparatus to enhance performances. In some cases we have had companies donate their product to us and we then showcase the product at our clinics and camps.

It is necessary that the athletes have the right equipment. Each athlete will find through trial and error the right bat size and weight and the right glove size for her. It is the coach's responsibility to assist the athlete in discovering what is a right fit for her and to notice when a bat or glove is actually hindering performance.

In your equipment closet you should have some batting Ts. I would suggest having five or six of them. A pitching machine is essential also unless you have a person who can throw tons of pitches all day long. The machine not only offers relief to your pitching staff but allows the batter to focus on a moving ball with her swing. A catch net behind the batter becomes a great ball-retrieving tool when hitting off the T or the pitching machine. Having big buckets of regulation softballs handy will always be needed, but a bucket of tennis balls can also provide you with several different drill opportunities. Finally, we use some specialty equipment in circuit work that helps batters with different aspects of their hitting positions. For example, the short stroke trainer teaches the batter to take a short path directly to the ball, which allows for a quick swing. A visualizer helps train the batter's eye by throwing golf ball-sized Wiffle balls to her, and she tries to hit them with a thin, round stick. Equipment like this adds variety to practices while reinforcing skills.

FACILITIES

Western Illinois has been working along with our softball staff to design a great softball field. We are fortunate enough to have a safe, level field, and this is what is important when looking for a place to practice and play. First and foremost, it should be regulation in design. What I look for in a safe field is regulation fences, dugouts, a level outfield with no holes, and a level infield with smooth dirt. It is always nice to play on a field that pampers the spectator as well. No one ever complains about a field with bathrooms, nice bleachers, and possibly a concession stand. These things are nice but should be second to the field itself.

Dust in the Wind

The Westerwinds often go to a tournament in the fall that has two main fields and four secondary fields. When we were there a few years back, we found ourselves scheduled to play several of our games on the secondary fields. This was not a problem until we realized that these fields were not being watered and that the winds were heavy. We essentially ate a lot of dust that day and it did not make for very fun softball.

Our team received an invitation to play at the same tournament the next year. I liked the competition but could not get the lack of field maintenance out of my mind. I told the tournament director we would only participate if we were guaranteed that there would be proper field maintenance. He agreed and we played, but it rained and we ended up playing on a pitiful little field with no outfield fence. I thought to myself, "These are college athletes and they are playing on a field most high schools would not even practice on!"

When making out the schedule for the next year, we decided on another tournament. I feel it takes away from the game when you have to be worried about the danger of the facilities.

SUMMARY

You can never plan too much for a season. Planning involves much more than just practice schedules. The on-the-field activities are just a small portion of the coach's responsibility.

- Design programs for team development and set goals each week. Each day work to accomplish those goals.
- Plan for medical assistance *before* your athletes begin their first practice.
- Use your assistants in areas that incorporate their strengths. Know that ultimately you are responsible for all aspects of the program.
- Build an in- and out-of-season strength program. Build strength in the off-season, and run a strength maintenance program during the season.
- Don't forget about the essentials for your team: uniforms, equipment, and facilities.

Chapter 6

PREPARING FOR PRACTICES

I have always believed the game is for the player and practice is for the coach. It is very important to list objectives of each day's practice in terms of what you want to accomplish and what skills need to be refined.

I want practice to be quick paced, challenging, in small groups, and with players and coaches knowing what is to be accomplished. For example, if we are hitting off a T, I want to teach the drill so that the player knows what her focus should be, such as knob to the ball, short stride, and so on. It is important to save every practice's notes and make additional notes on them after practice so that a great practice can be repeated.

PLAYER PREPARATION

Before your team begins the practice they need to be prepared for the practice mode. Something often overlooked but very important is practice attire. Your players need to be in comfortable practice clothing, suited to the weather. Some schools have the luxury of having an assigned uniform, but if you don't, make sure they wear clothes suitable for practice. For example, let your players know that they will be expected to slide in practice the next day. Some athletes will prefer to wear pants rather than shorts in this situation.

Players with injuries not only should talk to the coach ahead of time about what type of participation they will be allowed, but they should also get all their injuries treated before practice time. Colleges and universities usually have a training room where trainers will be available to treat the athletes who need it. In some special cases the player might be late, but again this is to be brought to the coach's attention before the practice hour.

The player also needs to begin the practice in the correct frame of mind. I post the day's practice plan one hour before practice on the bulletin board outside the locker room. This helps the athlete review what will be expected in practice. I always tell my players that when they walk on the practice field they should shed their problems as they shed their jackets. I usually get about two hours of practice a day; because of this, I need the athletes to be focused on the tasks at hand, not on their car problems, tests, or an argument they had. Two hours in a

24-hour period is a minimal amount of time. I have worked with my assistants to make these two hours a valuable experience for the athletes, so I expect them to respect our efforts and to put 100 percent of themselves into the practice. I do realize that 100 percent on one day might be different on another and I take this into consideration.

To help the athletes get focused I usually give them a motivational quote or talk about something that I feel will motivate them for that day. I have also used video as a tool in motivating. Once I showed a video about a friend of mine who played women's pro softball and later was struggling with a debilitating disease. When the video was over there wasn't a dry eye and everyone grabbed her glove and headed out to practice. I wasn't sure how practice was going to turn out but was pleasantly surprised at how driven they were. I thought that they should all know how lucky they were to have their talent and the opportunity to play. I have also used videos of the nationals and world series games. I want them to want to be there and this seems to work well also.

Conditioning in Practice

I am always looking for a new and challenging way to condition during practice. I like to have

our drills serve a dual purpose:(1) to develop skill and (2) to condition the athlete. One of the plans I like the best is called "Fitness 15" and involves a 15-minute workout that is packed with activities and events. We do the Fitness 15 every other practice throughout the preseason. It serves a different purpose than the preseason workouts because it ties in all of the softball athletic movements as well as isolating specific skills. A pretest and a posttest is conducted with our players, and I have been very impressed with the improvement in strength, speed, and agility. This circuit of drills accomplishes many things: a tremendous cardiovascular workout, development of foot speed along with leg power, development of agility, and training in softball skill technique.

You can tailor this circuit to meet your needs by inserting different activities for variety and specific problem areas. It utilizes space the size of a basketball court and can be done indoors or outdoors. The Fitness 15 is composed of 15 stations at one minute each, with a changing period of 15 seconds, allowing the athletes to go from one drill to the next. This is the only time they can walk or get a drink. I have them take their water bottle or cup with them so that they can get a drink during the changing time.

In this circuit the name of the station is written on a 3×5 index card and placed on the floor at that station. I also use very small cones to help lay out the activities. There are five exercises for leg workouts, five for softball skills, and five for agility. Figure 6.1 shows the Fitness 15 layout.

You may want to substitute other activities for variety, such as push-ups, sit-ups, medicine ball throws, or wrist roll-ups. Keeping the format of five stations each for three skills allows you to maintain balance and an organized tracking system. We also play upbeat music during the Fitness 15, and when the music stops after one minute the athlete moves to the next station. You may not be familiar with my terminology for the stations so a brief description is presented here.

- Cone jumps—Place a 12-inch-high pylon 40 feet away from a base. The athlete stands next to the cone and jumps sideways over the cone for 10 jumps. After the last jump she sprints to the base, then jogs back and repeats.

- Soft hands—Use a soft hand paddle and a wall. The athlete stands about 15 feet from the wall and makes low throws to the wall. As the ball rebounds from the wall, the athlete makes the catch and throws the ball back.

- Forward-backward—Place seven markers about five feet apart in a staggered diagonal (see figure 6.2). The player starts at the end marker, sprints forward and touches the next, sprints backward and touches the next, and keeps going forward and backward until all seven are touched, then jogs back and repeats.

- Straight sprints—Place a starting base and a finishing base about 60 feet apart. The athlete begins at the starting base in the rockaway leadoff position and sprints through the finishing base, then jogs back and repeats.

- Balanced bat swings—Player uses a line or a board on the floor and swings using her perfect technique while staying balanced.

- Four dots—Four dots or low cones are placed on the floor about five feet apart to form a square. With feet together the athlete jumps from dot to dot, making an imaginary box. This drill is done rapidly for the full minute.

Figure 6.1 Fitness 15 setup.

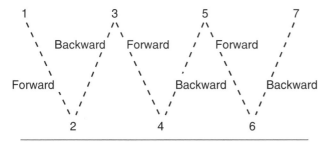

Figure 6.2 Forward/backward Fitness 15.

• Jump rope—The athlete does a prescribed rope-jumping pattern such as jumping on the left leg only for 30 seconds; jumping on the right leg only for 30 seconds; jumping while moving the feet sideways; or jumping in quick time, and so on.

• Pop flys—Remember how much fun these were as youngsters? Outside or inside, players throw pop flys to themselves either with or without a glove.

• Power out—The athlete is in her defensive ready position, as if to field a ground ball in front of her. A target cone or marker is 10 feet in front of her. From her ready position she sprints quickly forward as if to field the imaginary ground ball, then jogs back and repeats.

• Skips—Skips are great for ankle, calf, and quad workouts. They also develop the arm to drive up, working to get the elbow high. The athlete drives the right knee up to help lift the left foot off the ground and reaches for the sky with her left arm, slightly bending the elbow. Then she repeats with the opposite leg and arm. She performs these actions in a constant motion, skiping down 40 to 50 feet and back.

• Five dots—Four dots or low cones are placed on the floor about five feet apart. Place a fifth dot or cone in the center. The athlete starts with her feet apart at the back two dots, jumps feet together at the center dot, jumps feet apart at the front two dots, lands and then jumps and turns in the air to face back to her starting direction, jumps to the center dot, to the end dots, jumps and turns in the air to face back to the dots. Repeat pattern for the full minute.

MAKE PRACTICE FUN

Most of your players love to play because they are competitive and love a challenge. It is your job to make each practice day just that—a challenge. By challenging I do not mean having players merely survive practices but instead, having them face some type of competition built into practice. I do this by creating a segment of each practice where players go head-to-head. I make the competition worthwhile by offering an external reward to go along with the natural internal reward of winning. You can be very creative in what you offer. It can be not having to participate in sprints or a team run, or it can be a sticker for the player's locker, and so on.

This type of challenge in practice is very effective because the majority of the athletes want to win and give it their all. They are preparing, without concentrating on it, for game situations.

Small groups work best. This gives the group a chance to work as a team and focus on each other's strengths. They strategize about how to win and then in the end celebrate their win with a handshake and gained respect. The groups that don't win lose together and seem to bond and make fun threats about winning the next time.

COVER ALL THE BASES

Coaching is teaching and every teacher wants to make sure she covers all the material needed before the test. The same situation applies in game play; you cannot expect your athletes to perform well on a sacrifice bunt play if you have never gone over it with them in practice.

To make sure she hits all the key points, a coach will want to make a list of essential skills to cover (see figure 6.3) and keep track of what is being accomplished at each practice session so that she will be sure to cover every aspect of defensive and offensive play before the first scheduled game. The amount of sessions devoted to each fundamental and the time spent on each should be determined by the coaching staff. This will depend entirely on the experience level of the team as well as that of the individual position players.

Weather is a factor in our sport and unfortunately it can necessitate changing our plans. I always hate to cancel practice, so, on bad weather days we move into our indoor area and scale down the practice to fit the space allowed. As coaches we have to be flexible and creative at

Figure 6.3 Practice Checklist

DEFENSE
Infield

- Sacrifice bunt defense
  - runner on first
  - runner on first and second
  - runner on second
  - runner on third
- Running slap-bunt defenses
  - runner on first
  - runner on first and second
  - runner on third
  - no runners on base
- Slap-bunt defense from the right side
  - runner on first
  - runner on first and second
  - runner on third
- Holding runners
  - runner on second
  - runner on third
  - hold and get the out
  - check and hold the runner
- Fake throws
  - runner on third, ball hit to the third baseman
  - runner on second, ball hit to the short-stop
- First and third situations
- Rundowns
- Squeeze bunt defense
- Steals of second and third
- Pickoffs at first, second, and third
- Fundamentals of fielding ground balls
- Fundamentals of catching fly balls
- Defensive situations with ground balls to infielders
  - runner on first, force play at second
  - runners on first and second, force play at third
  - runners on first and second, force play at second

- bases loaded, force play at home
- runner on second, hold and go to first
- runner on third, hold and go to first
- Runner interference on ground balls
- Wild pitches and passed balls
- Pitchouts

Outfield

- Defensive situations with balls hit to the outfield
  - runner on first, fly balls to right, center, and left
  - runner on second, fly balls to right, center, and left
  - runner on third, fly balls to right, center, and left
  - runner on first, single to right, center, and left
  - runner on second, single to right, center, and left
  - runner on third, single to right, center, and left
- Fundamentals
  - grounders
  - angles
  - diving
  - playing the fences
  - lanes
  - sun balls
  - balls over their heads

Team Defense

- Balls hit between
  - outfielders
  - infielders
  - infielders and outfielders
- Communication priorities
  - on all bunts
  - on all fly balls
  - between infielders
- Cutoffs
- Relays

(continued)

Figure 6.3 *(continued)*

OFFENSE
- Hitting fundamentals
- Bunts: sacrifice, base-hit, push, slap, and squeeze
- Hit-and-runs
- Sacrifice flys
- First and thirds
    - cut when runner on third breaks for home
    - cut when you can pick off runner on third
    - cut if throw is wide at second
    - cut and flip to shortstop
    - ball goes through to second base, runner on first in rundown
    - ball goes through to second base and back to catcher
- Hitting behind runners
- Baserunning
    - leadoffs
    - sliding
    - steals
    - tagging up at bases
    - rundowns
    - running to bases

these moments. We still accomplish our objectives for that day's workout.

Figure 6.4 includes a detailed practice checklist for each defensive player and the defensive skills required for that position. You can put down whatever defensive skills you wish to cover with each position. Next to the skill, record the date and time spent on each particular item. When game time is getting closer, pull out your checklist and make sure you have covered all the important aspects of each position.

Everyone knows the feeling of being "unprepared." You never want to go to practice without something written down to follow. You might make adjustments once practice starts, but you still should have some outline of what you want to cover and how much time should be allotted. I schedule activities in the same order when planning my practices. For example, we always stretch, run, and throw in the first half hour so that we are physically warmed up and prepared to do other drills. Following is a list of the basics we cover at practice with suggested time frames.

1. Pitchers and catchers report early for a half-hour workout prior to team stretch.
2. Team stretch (10 minutes)

Figure 6.4 Individual Defensive Skills Checklist

Catcher
- Shifting technique
- Handling low balls in the dirt
- Handling pop-ups
- Tag and force plays at the plate
- Fielding bunts
- Giving signs to the pitcher
- Pitchouts and intentional walks
- Framing the pitch
- Runners on first and third
- Bunt defenses
- Pickoff plays
- Suicide squeeze
- Throwing to second and third
- Using the cutoff player
- Rundowns
- Throwing ball from the backstop

Pitcher
- Bunt defenses
- Suicide squeeze defense
- Double play situations
- Backing up bases and the plate
- Covering home plate
- Fielding ground balls
- Fly ball communication
- Ground ball communication
- Rundown responsibilities
- Intentional walks
- Pitchouts

First Baseman
- Fielding bad throws
- Cutoff responsibilities
- Bunt defenses
- Double steal plays
- Pickoff plays
- 3-6-3 double play
- Playing the fence on pop-ups
- Ground ball communication

- Fly ball communication
- Rundowns

Second Baseman
- Back-up throws from the plate
- Covering second on steals
- Cutoff responsibilities
- Double steal plays
- Bunt defenses
- Pickoff plays
- Making tag plays
- Tandem relays
- Rundowns
- Fly ball communication
- Ground ball communication

Shortstop
- Back-up throws from the plate
- Covering second on steals
- Cutoff responsibilities
- Double steal plays
- Bunt defenses
- Pickoff plays
- Double play situations
- Making tag plays
- Tandem relays
- Fake throws
- Rundowns
- Fly ball communication
- Ground ball communication

Third Baseman
- Covering third on steals
- Cutoff responsibilities
- Double steal plays
- Bunt defenses
- Pickoff plays
- Double play situations
- Making tag plays
- Playing the fence on pop-ups
- Fake throws

(continued)

Figure 6.4 *(continued)*

- Rundowns
- Fly ball communication
- Ground ball communication

Outfielders

- Using cutoff players
- Using relay players

- Throwing to bases
- Playing the fence
- Fly ball responsibilities and communication
- Backing up bases
- Rundowns

---

3. Conditioning run (10 minutes)
   - Jog laps
   - Line jogging—All players jog single file around the field; the last player in the line sprints to the front. When she is almost to the front of the line, she yells "Go" to repeat the sequence.
   - Progressives—Sprint to first. Sprint from home to second. Sprint from home to third. Sprint from home to home.
   - Interval runs—Sprint a certain distance and then rest. Repeat.
   - Fitness 15
4. Plyometric drills (10 minutes)
5. Baserunning drills (15 minutes)
6. Warm-up throwing (15 minutes)
   - Loosen up—Partner catch
   - One-hop drill—Partners throw one-hop ground balls back and forth.
   - Short fly drill—Partners throw lateral fly balls back and forth.
7. Infielders, pitchers, and catchers (15 minutes)
   - Coach works with infielders on ground balls and specific situations.
   - Pitchers and catchers throw back and forth in the bullpen, or pitchers take ground balls from coach and catchers take balls from infielders.
8. Outfielders—Fundamentals (15 minutes)
9. Team defensive drills (15 minutes)
10. Hitting drills—Circuit training (45 minutes)
    - Toss stations
    - T stations
    - Machine station
    - Live pitching station

11. Alternate hitting and fielding to maximize either skill
12. Scrimmage days

Figure 6.5 is a practice template that helps you organize and keep practice structured. It is simple to use and yet flexible enough to incorporate the skills and drills you want to stress that day.

For some coaches, getting started is the hardest part of organizing practice. To make it simple we prepared your first five practices, as shown in figure 6.6. They utilize one softball field with some adjacent space. The time allowed is two hours with 15 players. It is important on the first day to cover all basics of hitting, catching, and throwing techniques, and to instruct the players in your method of skill development so that you can begin to correct any errors in their technique.

SUMMARY

Planning your day-to-day practices asks for a great deal of your time. You need to make sure that you are organized and that you begin by covering the basics. When you conclude all of your practices, you want to ensure that you have hit all of your checkpoints. Here are some ideas to help get you there efficiently:

- Make sure your players are fully prepared for practice, both physically and mentally.
- Make conditioning a part of every practice, emphasizing skill development and getting in shape.
- Have a checklist you can go to, to know what you have and have not covered.
- Ensure that you spend the amount of time needed for certain activities by having a template to follow. Use flexibility with the times planned, but try to stay on course.

Figure 6.5 Practice Template

Date_____

Outdoor _____   Indoor_____

Session number _____

Primary objectives:

1. _____

2. _____

3. _____

1. Announcements (5 minutes)

2. Stretching (10 minutes)

3. Conditioning drills—circuits (15 minutes)

4. Baserunning drills (5-10 minutes)

5. Introduce new skill or concept (10 minutes)

6. Defensive work (30 minutes)

7. Offensive work (30 minutes)

8. Team play or special situations (30 minutes)

9. Stretching (5 minutes)

10. Review and put away equipment (5 minutes)

Figure 6.6 5-Day Sample Practice Plan

Day One

3:00   Announcements
3:10   Jog and teach stretching, then stretch
3:20   Hitting circle—teach hitting fundamentals (players form a circle around the coach to copy her hitting motions)
3:25   Teach Fitness 15
3:45   Hitting circuit (demonstrate) with players in five groups of three for five no-ball drills (see chapter 8 for drill descriptions)

- Hip Turn
- Plumb Bob
- Balance Beam
- Stride Box
- Wall Swings

4:10   Demonstrate catching techniques
4:15   Practice catching techniques using the wall

4:20   Demonstrate throwing techniques
4:25   Practice throwing techniques with a partner
4:30   Drink break
4:35   Demonstrate fielding techniques
4:40   Practice ground balls—fielding mini-drills (see chapter 11 for drill descriptions)

- Soft Hands
- Worker-Helper

4:50   Baserunning—third to home
4:55   Stretch and review tomorrow's agenda
5:00   End

Day Two

3:00   Stretch
3:05   Fitness 15
3:25   Throw
3:35   Hitting circuit (demonstrate) with play-

(continued)

Figure 6.6 *(continued)*

ers in five groups of three for five still-ball drills (see chapter 8 for drill descriptions)

- Stride, Stop, Swing
- Deflated Volleyball
- Inside-Outside
- Target on the Fence
- Two Ts

4:00 Baserunning—first to second
4:10 Drink break
4:20 Triangular Ground Balls drill for three players
4:30 Reaction Fielding drill
4:40 Range drill
4:55 Pack up

Day Three

3:00 Stretch
3:10 Partner throw and pitchers throw to each other
3:20 Tracking and Recognition, or Take the Pitch drill
3:40 Pitch Recognition and bunt drills (two different groups are doing each at the same time)
4:00 Sprint workout
4:10 Baserunning—second to third
4:20 Make four teams and play Over the Line off a T

Day Four

3:00 Five-minute jog
3:05 Stretch
3:10 Fitness 15
3:30 Drink break
3:35 Tracking and Recognition, or Take the Pitch drill
3:45 Hitting circuit (demonstrate) with players in five groups of three for five tossed-ball drills (see chapter 8 for drill descriptions)

- Bounce in Front
- Reverse Tracking
- Figure Eight
- One Hand, Small Bat

- Drop Toss

4:30 Baserunning—third to home
4:40 Range drill
4:55 Pack up

Day Five

3:00 Stretch
3:05 Sprint workout
3:15 Hitting circuit (demonstrate) with players in five groups of three for five combination drills (see chapter 8 for drill descriptions)

• Take the Pitch	• Inside-Outside
• Drop Toss	• Stride, Stop,
• Balance Beam	Swing

Note: To ensure that all of our players get equal time in the batting cage, we make it part of a circuit of drills where each group has time allotted in the cage.

4:15 Baserunning—home to first
4:25 Defensive circuit—It is best in groups of two. To make this work you could have two stations of Soft Hands and so on. Or, you could have groups of three where there is one inactive athlete. (see chapter 11 for drill descriptions)

- Soft Hands
- Triangular Ground Balls
- Worker-Helper
- Reaction Fielding
- Short Hop

4:55 Pack up

Hints

- You do not need to throw every day in practice. This gives the players' arms rest.
- Give your drills a name so you can refer to them by that name and do not have to review them every time.
- Let pitchers take part in the first day like the rest because they need these fundamentals.
- Always give a drink break.

Part III

COACHING OFFENSE

Chapter 7

OFFENSIVE FUNDAMENTALS

The most important skill in offense is the ability to score runs through the use of all offensive weapons. I believe that situation hitting—moving a runner when necessary by going with the outside pitch or hitting the long fly ball with a runner on third—is key to run production. Another key to scoring runs is bunting, which places runners in scoring position where a clutch hit can drive them home. We also want to coach smart base runners who are aggressive and who understand the offensive play in progress: runners who know how to execute the hit-and-run or the double steal. Ball games are won through proper execution of a well-placed bunt, smart baserunning, and a timely hit.

In this chapter I touch on the key concepts in hitting: the mechanics of the swing, how to correct hitting errors, teaching all types of bunts, and understanding hitting situations. Baserunning principles and strategies are discussed in chapter 9.

Key Concepts in Hitting

I believe the key to being an effective teacher and coach is to develop a simplified, comprehensible approach to instruction. When working on batting skills, my goal is to develop hitters who understand the key concepts in hitting. What follows is a summary of those concepts, starting with the mechanics of the swing: stance, stride, swing, position at contact, and follow-through.

Stance

The stance may vary from player to player, but there are some characteristics of the stance that have general applications. The feet should be about six inches wider than shoulder-width apart (see figure 7.1). A stance that is too wide will inhibit weight transfer and hip rotation; if this occurs the batter will lack power. One that

Figure 7.1   The batting stance.

is too narrow may produce too long a stride, which will cause too much head movement and poor ball tracking. The knees should be slightly flexed, with the upper torso bent forward at the waist. The head is turned toward the pitcher with both eyes level and the chin is near the front shoulder at the start of the swing.

There are three types of stances: square, open, and closed. The square stance is the most workable because it gives the hitter the best plate coverage without any disadvantages. In the square stance the feet are the same distance away from home plate, and weight is evenly distributed on the balls of the feet.

In the open stance, the hitter is turned 30 to 60 degrees on the balls of her feet toward the pitcher so that her front foot is about two or three inches further from home plate than the back foot. The weight is distributed evenly on both feet. In this stance the hips are more open to allow for a shorter swing. Hitters should use this stance when they are having difficulty making contact, when a pitcher is throwing predominantly inside, or to cut back on a big swing. The disadvantage of the open stance is that it limits plate coverage on the outside third of the plate.

In the closed stance, the player's front foot is moved about two to three inches closer to home than the back pivot foot. Hitters should use this stance when they pull their head or step away from the ball. The hips are closed, allowing for more hip rotation. In this stance the right-hander can drive the ball to right field. The disadvantage of the closed stance is that it prevents the batter from reaching pitches on the inside of the plate.

Proper plate coverage is an important aspect to consider. It is important that the hitter have good coverage of her strong areas of the strike zone. The further back she is in the batter's box, the more time she will have to read the pitch, and when facing a power pitcher, hitters should move to the back of the box. Moving up in the box is advantageous, though, when facing a control pitcher who does not throw hard. Therefore, the depth in the batter's box depends on the nature of the hitter and the type of pitcher throwing. A player with great bat speed can move up in the box, while the hitter who does not possess great bat quickness might achieve more success by positioning herself further back in the box.

A player's grip on a bat is equally important: a grip that is either too tight or too loose will reduce power and bat speed. The hands should be set near the back shoulder and should be no more than three to six inches from the body. The lead shoulder is pointing at the pitcher or is slightly closed in the stance. The bat should be held in the fingers of the hands with the grip placed in the top hand from the base of the index finger to the heel of the hand. The second knuckles of each hand are aligned when gripping the bat.

When the hitter is in her stance, her focus is soft with her eyes relaxed and looking at something on the pitcher's jersey. As the pitcher's hands come apart, the batter should change the focus to the pitcher's knee (a hard focus). We all know what it feels like to stare with a hard glare at something. That is a hard focus.

Stride

As the pitcher is moving toward the release, the hitter is beginning to initiate some preparatory movement—the stride, which does little more than move the front foot to establish some momentum into the pitch. The stride should not be more than eight inches. Simultaneous with the stride, most hitters will cock their hips and also have some movement with the hands. The hip cock is the inward turn of the front hip. The front shoulder also slightly turns in as the front hip turns in. The hips remain parallel during this cocking action and the front shoulder should be slightly lower than the back shoulder (see figure 7.2). The front knee turns in slightly and points at home plate, and the back knee remains firm but flexed.

As the hips and shoulders are turning, the hands are moving as well. Just after the stride, the hitter's top hand turns slightly so that it is closer to the pitcher than the bottom hand. As the pitcher is releasing the ball, all preparatory movement, including the stride, should be completed. As the stride is completed, the hitter's weight is back on the inside of the rear foot. The hands should be in the hitting position, just off the rear shoulder as the ball is released. The knees should be flexed and ready to initiate the swinging motion.

Figure 7.2 The stride should be short and balanced.

Swing

The swing begins with the legs and hips (the hands and shoulders stay back). The hitter pushes off the ball of the back foot as the softball approaches the plate. The back knee will begin to move in and the hips begin to rotate. During rotation the hips remain parallel to the ground. During the movement of the legs and hips, it is vital that the head and eyes remain level and still. As the hands begin to move the knob of the bat toward the ball, the hitter does not allow the bat head to fall below the hands. The lead arm maintains a 90-degree angle. (see figure 7.3). This method of approaching the ball ensures a shorter arc and a more compact swing.

One of the most important body parts is the front shoulder. Stress to the hitter to drive the front shoulder to the ball. If the front shoulder pulls away from the ball, the following problems might happen.

- The head will come out of the proper position and eye contact with the ball will be reduced.
- The back shoulder will drop down, which creates an unlevel position for the shoulders in their approach to the ball.
- The hands will drop, creating a loop in the swing.
- The back leg will collapse and eliminate any positive hip action in the swing.

The batter should allow the front shoulder to track the ball from the pitcher's hand to the contact zone. As the bat is approaching the ball, the arms remain bent. If the arms are extended too early in the swing, the swing arc will be too large and the hitter will sacrifice bat speed and power. As the hands move closer to contact, the top hand begins to rotate so that at contact the palm is nearly facing up. The hips continue to rotate as the hitter approaches the contact point. The back leg continues to drive into a now firm front leg, and the back toe begins to turn toward the pitcher.

Position at Contact

The hitter's body position at contact may vary slightly for pitches in different parts of the strike zone. What follows here is the position with regard to pitches in the middle of the strike zone. At contact the hips and shoulders should be parallel to the front edge of the plate. The stride leg is firm and straight. The back leg should be slightly flexed at the knee and driving into the firm front side.

The back foot pivots with the toes facing the pitcher, and the front foot is not open to more than a 45-degree angle to the front edge of the batter's box. Because of the hip rotation and drive, the weight will be on the outside part of the front foot.

For an inside pitch, the hips must open early to allow the bat head the freedom to come around quickly and make contact with the ball when it is in front of the plate. At this point, remember the front shoulder is still driving to the ball. The outside pitch requires the hips to stay closed until the swing is made and the back hip comes through on contact. On the outside pitch the athlete does not pivot the full way through because of where the bat makes contact with the ball, so a good pivot is not necessary in driving this pitch to the opposite field with authority.

The lead arm is nearly straight with the back arm bent at the elbow at contact. The palm of the bottom hand faces the ground while the top

Figure 7.3 A balanced, compact swing.

hand is nearly palm up in a position facing the pitcher. The ball is hit slightly in front of the plate and across from the front foot.

An illustration I use to get a player to understand the hand position at contact is to have the player use her top hand to throw a rock so that it will skip across the top of a pool of water. If the wrist rolls too early, the rock goes down. Just as with the rock, if the wrist rolls too early the ball will be hit into the ground. If the wrist rolls too late, the bat will drop and the hitter will fly out.

The hitter's head should be bent slightly down and toward home plate when the bat meets the ball. When the bat makes contact with the ball, the arms should be almost fully extended, forming a V, with the bat being the extension of the point (see figure 7.4).

Follow-Through

After contact the hitter must concentrate on hitting through the ball. The bat continues to move in the direction the ball is hit. A full weight transfer occurs with the majority of the hitter's weight over the firm front leg. This weight transfer helps ensure a long, full follow-through and a quicker time to first base. After contact is made and the follow-through is complete, the hitter's weight is balanced between both feet

with the hitter's ear, back shoulder, hip, and back knee in line with one another (see figure 7.5). I have never seen a hitter in a good finish position make a bad swing. The finish position is a critical part of the complete swing that must be learned.

When players make good swings, consistent hits are automatic. Balance, tempo, and rhythm take on a new level of importance and greatly improve when players focus on swinging to a good finish position.

What's the Problem?

After you've watched your hitters' swings, you may detect some problems. Chapter 8 contains not only detailed descriptions of a variety of individual and team offensive drills to improve your players' skills, but also a drill finder that will help you quickly locate specific drills for your hitters' technique problems. As a coach you may also need to correct hitting problems quickly in game situations. Notice in figures 7.6a and 7.6b how the athlete has made important adjustments in her swing during the same game based on her coach's feedback. You can also refer to figure 7.7 for a checklist of the most important mechanics at each stage of the swing.

Figure 7.4   Position at contact.

Figure 7.5 Proper alignment at follow-through.

a

b

Figure 7.6 a-b Hitting problems can be corrected in game situations. Note how the hitter's back leg is collapsing along with her front leg (a), and how she is able to correct this later in the game by hitting off a firm front leg with a strong back leg drive (b).

Figure 7.7 Mechanics of the Swing Checklist

Stance

1. Eyes and head are level.
2. Eyes are focused on pitcher's jersey.
3. Position is comfortable and balanced.
4. Chin nearly touches the front shoulder.
5. Grips bat with the pads of the fingers.
6. Looks over the front shoulder.
7. Muscles are relaxed.
8. Front shoulder is pointed at the pitcher and slightly closed.
9. Middle knuckles are lined up.

Stride

1. Stride is soft, short, and soon enough.
2. Front side is closed.
3. Stride is short so the center of gravity doesn't move.
4. Body remains balanced. Picks up the front foot and steps out toward the pitch (less than eight inches).
5. Head remains steady with little or no movement.
6. Hands stay back.

Swing

1. Body forms a triangle.
2. Buttocks are up, putting weight on the balls of the feet for balance.
3. Hips rotate toward the pitcher and remain level.
4. Front hand pulls while the back hand "throws" the bat.
5. Base is wide and the knees are flexed.
6. Turning action is started in the lower half of the body.
7. Lead arm stays flexed.
8. Bat head stays above the hands.
9. Front elbow is relaxed and pointed toward the ground.

(continued)

Figure 7.7 (continued)

Contact

1. Hits the ball with the meat of the bat.
2. Wrists do not roll on contact, only after.
3. Takes the knob of the bat to the ball.
4. Hits behind a firm front leg and side.
5. Front shoulder is slightly higher than the back shoulder.
6. Back leg is in an L position.
7. Lead arm is one solid piece down the bat.
8. Uses a strong pivot on the back foot.

Follow-Through

1. Weight is on the outside of the front foot, near the heel.
2. Front knee is straight.
3. Thighs are close together.
4. Ball of foot is on the ground with shoelaces finishing toward target.
5. Rear hip is toward the target.
6. Hands and arms are relaxed and elbows are folded.
7. Bat has swung on an arc behind the back to the shoulder blades.
8. Overall appearance is balanced, relaxed, and in control.

DEVELOPING STRENGTH AND BAT SPEED

Here are four exercises that can strengthen the bat swing. Do these daily and build them into your hitting drills. The athlete can use a bat that is a comfortable weight or one that is a little heavier. Do three sets of 10 three times a week.

Windshield Wiper

Strengthens: Wrists and forearms

1. Hold bat straight out in front with both hands and the barrel pointing up.
2. Move the head of the bat to the right and to the left.
3. Keep the arms extended and the grip at shoulder level.

Pull Overs

Strengthens: Triceps, forearms, and wrists

1. Stand in a balanced position and grip the bat with the barrel directly overhead and slightly behind.
2. "Throw" the bat head over your head, directly out in front.
3. Keep the elbows in.

Wrist Circles

Strengthens: Wrists

1. Grip the bat and hold it at shoulder height directly in front of you.
2. Circle the end of the bat, clockwise and counterclockwise.

Bat Raises

Strengthens: Hands and wrists

1. Grip the bat in your right hand with your palm facing toward the back and hold it down to your side.
2. Use your wrist only to extend the bat backward so that it becomes parallel to the ground, then return the bat to its original position.
3. Rotate your wrist so the palm is facing toward the front.
4. Use your wrist only to extend the bat forward so that it becomes parallel to the ground, then return the bat to its original position.

DEVELOPING A FOUR-WEEK HITTING PROGRAM

It's amazing that with hitting being so important and with so many available qualified hitting experts, we have so few specific programs designed for hitting improvement. Some coaches teach hitting in a hit-or-miss fashion. Usually they observe in batting practice and then offer suggestions for improving mechanics. I have always felt a need for a more systematic method of developing hitting potential.

We use a four-week hitting program that has yielded excellent results at Western Illinois University. Both the players and I feel that the program eliminates much of the guesswork from hitting instruction. This program is simple to administrate and it allows for a concentrated instructional effort.

Procedure

The materials for this hitting program include

- videotaping equipment with slow-motion potential;
- a pitching machine;
- clipboards and pencils; and
- batting criteria forms.

We start by explaining and defining each of the criteria items (see figure 7.8) to the team and informing them of the procedure for the four-week program. Four weeks seems just right for maintaining optimal motivation and for covering all of the essential facets of the program.

We videotape on Mondays, Wednesdays, and Fridays and take traditional batting practice on Tuesdays and Thursdays. The taping is done in a hitting cage off to the side of the main practice area to avoid interfering with other drills. The camera is positioned on a tripod at the end of the batting cage behind the pitching machine with a protective screen in front of it. A TV and VCR are located near the batting cage. Each player steps into the cage and loosens up with 5 to 10 swings at pitched balls. We then videotape five consecutive swings. On Mondays and Fridays we look at down-the-middle strike swings. On Wednesdays we look at location pitches, such as outside, inside, high, or low. Then, the player and I review the slow-motion replay of the five swings, while the next hitter is taking her warm-up swings in the batting cage. The athlete and I try to reach an agreement on the errors of the five swings. These are checked on the criteria sheet and referred to in noting improvement at each of the remaining sessions.

Suggestions for corrections come from both coach and player. The player is instructed to work on her flaws in every hitting drill leading up to the next videotaping session. We also try to have some live hitting every day to work on hitting skills.

The entire procedure takes about 5 to 10 minutes. Once the routine is established, an entire squad can be taped and analyzed in approximately one and a half hours. We are able to do this by having some players report early, so as not to interfere with our usual two-hour workout schedule.

All of the charts are made available at every subsequent session in order to determine progress and discern trends. Once the season begins and we are playing games, we will videotape the hitters who are having real problems. Otherwise, we may freshen up our normal routine with a once-a-week videotaping session.

Figure 7.8 4-Week Video Program Criteria Form

Name: _____ Week/Day: _____

Proper technique	Pitches	1	2	3	4	5
Setup:						
1. Eyes are level in stance and focusing on release point.						
2. Head is level—looking over front shoulder.						
Stride:						
1. Swings at a good strike pitch.						
2. Stride is consistently 6 to 8 inches toward the pitcher.						
3. Hands stay back over back foot.						
Hitting position:						
1. Swing starts with lower muscle groups.						
2. Body has formed a triangle with top hand closer to the pitcher and the hands over the back shoulder.						
3. Bat head is above the hands.						
4. Lead arm stays flexed.						
5. Loose bat (loose muscles are quick muscles).						
6. Back leg forms L and front leg is firm.						
Contact:						
1. Strong pivot on back foot.						
2. Hits behind the front leg.						
3. Lead arm is one solid piece down bat.						
4. Top hand is palm up; bottom hand is palm down.						
5. Wrists roll after contact.						

This depends on how we have been hitting in the actual games.

BUNTING

No team's offensive arsenal is complete without the bunt. The bunt can alter the outcome of many games each season. The entire team should know the importance of the bunting game. Stressing the idea that a hitter will not be called upon to bunt unless it is important can help in the team's understanding of this strategy. A well-rounded team has players who take pride in their bunting skill. Just as in hitting, the degree of success in bunting will depend on mechanics and good pitch selection.

The bunt is a good offensive weapon because it can put pressure on the defense by catching them off guard or by forcing them to make an error as a result of a hurried play. The bunt can also get the swift runner to first base or move a

runner into scoring position. Probably the most exciting play in fastpitch softball is the suicide squeeze bunt! The game could be won or lost with proper or improper execution.

Bunting must be practiced in game-like situations. Bunting stations with lines drawn or targets established to emphasize good bunts can be a tremendous help. Most bunting practice occurs during batting practice. Mix bunts into batting practice by having the hitter swing away a few times, then bunt, then swing away, and then bunt again. See chapter 8 for bunting drills.

I will discuss five types of bunts: the sacrifice bunt, base-hit bunt, push bunt, slap bunt, and squeeze bunt. The goals of each bunt are similar in some ways, mainly to pressure the defense to make a perfect play and to get runners on base or to move runners. They are also very different. The base-hit bunt is designed to get the batter to first base without giving up an out, and to advance any runners who are on base safely. The sacrifice bunt gives up an out by the batter not reaching first base, but advances other runners. A spin-off of the sacrifice bunt is called the push bunt, which is performed by "pushing" the ball past the pitcher and first baseman or the pitcher and third baseman. This bunt functions as a base hit while using sacrifice bunt techniques. The slap bunt is designed to drive the ball toward

and through the middle infielders. If done by a left-handed batter, the batter will run in the box, plant her left foot, and swing. If done by a right-handed batter, she will set up like a sacrifice bunt and then quickly draw the bat back and swing (left-handed batters can also utilize this method).

Sacrifice Bunt

In a sacrifice bunt situation we are giving up the batter in order to advance a runner or runners. While it is important not to be too perfect in the placement of the sacrifice bunt, it is generally accepted that with a runner on first base the bunt should be placed down on the first-base side of the infield. With a runner at first and second, or second only, the ball should be placed on the third-base side of the infield. One other detail—the pitch has got to be a strike.

To execute the sacrifice bunt, the hitter does the following.

1. The batter positions herself in the front of the batter's box to increase the chances of the ball going forward and fair.
2. The batter should not attempt to make a base hit out of a sacrifice bunt unless the defense allows her to do so. The

coach does not want the batter to step on the plate.

3. The batter shouldn't give the bunt away too soon. The correct time to move into the bunt position is when the pitcher separates her hands and the ball is in the downswing position of her pitch.

4. I like the batter to pivot and open her hips toward the pitcher. Her feet are still in a forward-backward position. The hitter pivots on the heel of her front foot and on the toes of her back foot (see figure 7.9a).

5. At the time of the pivot, the top hand moves up the barrel and grips the bat above the tape. The bottom half of the bat should meet the top half of the ball.

6. The barrel must remain higher than the hands at all times, and to reach a low pitch, the batter drops her hands down and bends at the knees (see figure 7.9b).

Base-Hit Bunt—Left-Hander

The ability to bunt for a base hit can add 25 to 50 points to a hitter's average. I allow players to base-hit bunt on their own, with no one on base.

If the player believes the infield is not expecting a bunt or the corners are positioned near their bases, the surprise tactic will work in her favor. It is important to wait for a good pitch and then to get the ball on the ground, dropping it near the foul line. The left-handed batter may begin making a motion toward first base when the ball is halfway to the plate. The most successful pitch to bunt is a low strike.

To execute the base-hit bunt by a left-hander, follow these steps.

1. The batter begins with her head, eyes, and shoulders level, and she has a hard focus on the ball. The left leg is pushing and the right foot has picked up and started to go. Her hands are up on the barrel and separated for control.

2. As the batter continues the bunt, her right foot is driving and pushing off the ground and her left leg has come around and is ready to plant (see figure 7.10). Her head, eyes, and shoulders are level. She uses soft elbows to cushion the rebounding effect of the bat. Her hands are lower than the barrel and split to ensure the ball going down.

3. As the batter completes the bunt, her eyes have tracked the pitch and follow

a   b

Figure 7.9 a-b Two key steps in the sacrifice bunt: the bunter separates her hands and pivots her feet (a) and keeps the barrel higher than her hands when making contact with the ball (b).

Figure 7.10 The left-handed base-hit bunt.

the contact to the ground. Her left leg is firm and planted and the right leg has begun the run. The bunter and the ball are in front of home plate. Her hands have controlled the bat and have directed the ball down, while the hips are open to begin the run to first.

Base-Hit Bunt—Right-Hander

The right-handed batter can drop a bunt for a base hit as well. The technique is quite different because she must wait until the ball nearly gets to the strike zone before her attempt. For the right-hander to be effective, she must maintain her batting stance until the last possible second. No movement occurs until the ball is five to eight feet from the plate.

To execute the base-hit bunt by a right-hander, follow these steps.

1. The batter keeps the left hand on the bat and slides the right hand to above the grip (see figure 7.11).
2. She brings the knob of the bat into the center of her body near the belt buckle.
3. She keeps the barrel above the knob.

4. At the same time as the hand transfer, her feet move into a forward-backward position. The right foot goes forward (toward first base) about six inches and the left foot goes back about six inches. This foot placement aligns the hips, knees, and toes with first base.
5. The batter strikes the top of the ball with the bottom of the barrel so as to drop the ball straight down. The ideal ball position is three to six feet in front of the plate.

Push Bunt

The push bunt is used when the batter can push the ball between the pitcher and the third baseman or between the pitcher and the first baseman. It must be hard enough to get by the pitcher, yet soft enough that the second baseman or shortstop must charge in to field the ball.

The batter must get the barrel out, firmly extending the bat toward the ball, and then push the ball toward a point between the pitcher and the corners. The location of the

Figure 7.11 The right-handed base-hit bunt.

pitch will dictate the location of the push. For a left-handed batter, an outside pitch should be pushed toward the shortstop and an inside pitch should be pushed toward the second baseman. Right-handed batters should attempt to push a ball over the plate toward the second baseman or the shortstop, to push an outside pitch toward the second baseman, and to push an inside pitch toward the shortstop.

As the ball is released, the batter should move the top hand up above the top of the grip in a similar grip with other bunts. The body position is the same as in the sacrifice bunt.

Slap Bunt

The right-hander and left-hander will execute the slap bunt differently. The slap bunt is an alternative for the left-handed batter to produce a hit in an RBI situation or to get on base when a bunt may not be appropriate. This tool catches the infielders in a shifting position, having to either commit to a bunt or commit to a hard ground ball. This technique was designed to add confusion to the responsibilities of the infield-

ers. They must decide, with no one on base, who covers first on this would-be bunt or ground ball. It is the responsibility of the second baseman to cover first on bunts, yet it is the responsibility of the first baseman to cover first on routine ground balls.

The challenge continues for the infielders with runners on base. The shortstop may now be called on to field the slap, or to cover second base, if there is a runner on first base. Probably the most difficult responsibility is for the shortstop to cover second on a possible steal and the batter to slap the ball to the glove side of the third baseman.

What the slap must do is pull the defensive players away from their assigned positions and force them to try to field and throw the ball under the pressure of a very quick batter running to first base. A left-handed slap bunter is a triple threat: She can drop and drag a bunt, she can push the ball between infielders, and she can slap the ball in the gaps for base hits.

What follows is a pictorial summary of the key techniques of the left-handed slap bunt. In step one (figure 7.12a) you'll notice the following:

1. Slapper has opened and stepped on the right foot.
2. The left leg continues the run to open the hips.
3. The eyes remain perfectly level.
4. Barrel of the bat remains back.

In step two (figure 7.12b) you'll notice the following:

1. Left leg is planted.
2. Eyes remain perfectly level.
3. Right hip and hands are ready to drive the ball.
4. This slapper uses a choke position with both hands together.
5. Barrel of the bat is ready to be driven forward.

In step three (figure 7.12c) you'll notice the following:

1. Contact is made.
2. Left arm is extended and the barrel is an extension of the arm.
3. Left foot is planted.
4. Left hip is open and driving the ball.
5. Head and eyes are perfectly level.

The slap bunt technique for right-handers is slightly different. As the pitcher starts her delivery, the hitter must look like she is going to hit. When the pitcher's hands come apart, she quickly squares around to show bunt. As the pitcher's arm is at the top of the backswing, the batter must quickly get her hands back to the hitting position. No motion change with the feet occurs except for a slight pivot as in a sacrifice bunt. We are attempting to move the infielders on the show of the bunt and to create some holes which a hitter might be able to take advantage of with a ground ball. It is now the hitter's job to drive the ball hard and down.

Fake Bunt and Slap

This offensive tool is used when the defense is either playing in very close in a bunt situation or the defensive players are moving early to cover

a

b

c

Figure 7.12 a-c   The left-handed slap bunt: the slapper opens up and steps on her right foot (a), plants her left leg and begins the swing (b), and then drives the ball, keeping her left arm extended (c).

particular areas of the infield to defend the possible bunt. This is also an excellent hit-and-run tactic. If the corner infielders are charging on the pitch, the fake bunt and slap can be an excellent offensive tactic. Also, if the shortstop and second baseman are moving to cover first, second, or third base, chances for success are excellent. The technique is the same for left-handed batters and right-handed batters.

1. The batter squares around just as the pitcher separates the hands to deliver the pitch.
2. As the body is pivoting, the top hand slides up the bat to above the grip.
3. The batter sets up as if to bunt the ball so as to make the defense react to a possible bunt.
4. The batter then brings the bat back quickly, as little time is allowed for a full rotation or full swing.
5. Batter utilizes a good, short, compact swing to drive the ball on the ground, as the infielders may be slightly out of position.

Squeeze Bunt

There are two types of squeeze bunts, the safety and the suicide. Both are used with a runner on third base. In the suicide squeeze, the base runner is going on the pitch, whereas in the safety, the base runner goes to the plate when she is sure the ball has been bunted down.

In the safety squeeze bunt the batter can be selective on the pitch and bunt a good strike. This skill is very much like the sacrifice with one important difference: The batter delays squaring to bunt until the ball is on its way to the plate. The longer the batter can wait, the more the element of surprise for the infielders. The base runner must get a good jump off third, in anticipation of a strike and the bunt.

In the suicide squeeze the base runner leaves third base on the pitch. In essence, she is stealing home. For the batter, everything is exactly like the safety squeeze except that she must put the ball on the ground, *fair* if at all possible. Two problems that need to be avoided are committing to bunt too soon and not putting the ball on the ground.

SITUATION HITTING

The hitter must take into consideration the game situation when going to the plate. A team with good pitch selection and discipline jumps on mistake pitches. Teach your players to use the time in the dugout when waiting to bat to study the pitcher for types of pitches thrown, what she throws when she is ahead in the count, what she throws when she is behind, what her best pitch is, and so on. Time spent teaching hitters to prepare mentally for what they must do at the plate will add runs to the final score.

Hitters can watch the pitcher for patterns. Does she follow certain pitches with other pitches, such as throwing a change-up after a rise ball or a change-up after the batter pulls a long foul ball? Hitters can also learn to detect the type of pitch thrown by the grip the pitcher uses.

The Count

Hitting to the count is important. Each count presents a different hitting challenge. Sometimes the advantage is with the pitcher and sometimes it is with the hitter. By knowing what to expect, the hitter gains the edge. To establish discipline, the hitter must take into account the count. Every hitter loves to be ahead in the count at each at bat. The pitcher has to throw a pitch over the plate and usually that pitch is her best control pitch. The prepared hitter will know what type of pitch the pitcher generally throws when behind and when ahead in the count. Pitchers will establish some type of pitch pattern during the game, and the smart hitter looks for certain pitches in the various ball-strike counts. Here are some key things to look at regarding the ball-strike count.

Hitter Is Well Ahead in the Count

When the count is 3-0, 3-1, 2-0, or 3-2 the hitter is ahead in the count. Therefore, the pitcher must get the ball over the plate for a strike. Even the 3-2 count is to the hitter's advantage since the pitcher must throw a strike to avoid walking the batter. The hitter should look for a pitch in this situation that the pitcher has good control over. If the pitcher has a good off-speed pitch, this is an excellent count to throw the change-up.

Hitter Is Well Behind in the Count

With the 0-2 count the hitter must stay disciplined and not swing at a bad pitch in her effort to protect the plate. She should look for a pitch in the strike zone with which she can make good contact. The pitcher will try to pitch out of the strike zone and will attempt to throw waste pitches. The pitcher may miss with a location pitch and bring it too close to the strike zone.

Hitter Is Behind in the Count

On the 0-1, 1-1, and 1-2 counts the pitcher has a distinct advantage over the hitter. On these counts the pitcher will try to get the hitter to chase a bad pitch. With the 1-2 count, the pitcher will try to strike out the batter. The hitter should look for a ball that moves down and out hard or up and in hard. Teach hitters to stay disciplined and not to expect to get a good pitch to hit with these counts.

Pitcher Is Trying to Even the Count or Prevent Getting Behind in the Count

On the 0-0, 1-0, 2-1, or 2-2 counts the pitcher is trying to even the count or to keep from throwing a ball that will put her behind the hitter on the count. The 0-0 count is placed in this category because a strike thrown on the first pitch will quickly put the batter at a disadvantage. Hitters shouldn't look for a pitch down the middle; this is where the in-out or up-down location for a strike comes into the picture. An off-speed pitch is also an effective pitch thrown in these counts.

Discipline

A hitter who swings at the pitcher's best pitch when she (the batter) is ahead in the count is committing a serious hitting error. If she takes one of the pitcher's poor pitches when ahead in the count, she is committing the same type of error. The better the pitcher, the more the hitter must practice good pitch discipline. For example, if a pitcher possesses an excellent drop, a hitter must lay off that pitch with less than two strikes unless the pitcher happens to throw the drop into her hitting zone. Since the good pitcher will throw less mistake pitches than the average pitcher, the hitter cannot afford to take any mistake pitches. If a pitcher does not possess a "strikeout" pitch, the hitter can afford to have two strikes on her.

The plate umpire is a factor in pitch selection and discipline. The nature of her strike zone will dictate what the batter can and cannot do with a particular pitcher on the mound. For example, if the umpire is a high-pitch umpire, the hitter must take this into consideration when evaluating the pitch on its way to the plate. With two strikes, she needs to protect the high part of the strike zone.

An umpire with a "small" strike zone affords the hitter the opportunity to practice much better discipline than if the umpire has a "big" strike zone. Hopefully, the umpire will establish his strike zone early in the game and will maintain that zone throughout the game. If the strike zone constantly changes, then the hitter needs to protect the plate a little more when she has two strikes.

"Happy Zone"

Every hitter has a certain area of the strike zone that she likes to hit the ball in—the "happy zone." But there are also areas of the strike zone where the hitter has a tough time making solid contact with the ball. Hitters need to realize that even great hitters have a difficult time making good contact in certain parts of the strike zone. They also need to realize that some hitters can make good contact on pitches outside the strike zone, while other hitters need to have the ball in the strike zone. Every hitter is different and every hitter must understand her limitations and capabilities. To become a successful hitter, the batter must make adjustments and understand her hitting zones. Hitters can improve their averages by being selective while still maintaining their aggressiveness.

Pitch Selection and Discipline

Each at bat during the course of a game has its own unique set of circumstances. In the following sections I will take you through some of these game situations and the hitting strategies that should be considered. For a summary of additional game situations, please refer to the chart in figure 7.13.

Leadoff Hitter in the Inning

The leadoff hitter in the inning must try to find a way to get on base. The easiest way is to draw a walk or to hit one of the pitcher's mistake

Figure 7.13 Game Situations and Pitch Selection Chart

Situations	Outs	Objectives	Pitch to look for
Runner at 2nd	0	Move the runner	LH: a pitch to pull inside or off-speed RH: an outside pitch to drive to the right side
Runner at 3rd	Less than 2	Score the runner	LH: off-speed to produce a fly ball; inside to drive to the 2nd baseman RH: off-speed to produce a fly ball; a good pitch to hit hard through the infield
Double play possibility	Less than 2	Avoid the double play and move the runner	LH: inside or off-speed to hit between the 1st and 2nd baseman RH: outside or off-speed to hit between the 1st and 2nd baseman
Sacrifice bunt	Less than 2	Avoid a pop-up	LH and RH: low in the strike zone
Squeeze bunt	0, 1, or 2	Score the run	LH and RH: batter must get ball down or foul
Tying or winning run at 2nd late in the game	0, 1, or 2	Discipline and going after good pitches	LH and RH: pitcher may attempt to pitch around batter to get to the batter on deck; drive a good pitch into left center or right center
Tying or winning run at 1st late in the game	Less than 2	Discipline, drawing a walk, or moving the runner to 3rd	LH or RH: strikes and an up pitch to drive for an extra-base hit
Hit-and-run	0	Use when the batter has good bat control and the runner has average to above average speed	LH or RH: count is 1-0, 2-0, or 2-1; can be run on any ball/strike with less than 2 strikes and less than 2 outs; hit to the right side LH: an inside pitch RH: an outside pitch
A great hitter at the plate with the opportunity to win the game	0, 1, or 2	Disciplined strike zone; the opposing pitcher may be throwing around the strike zone	LH or RH: something in your hitting zone
The team is behind late in the game		Get on base!	LH or RH: draw walks; the pitcher will be throwing strikes to avoid walking batters

pitches. The leadoff hitter for a team should be a hitter with good discipline along with a high on-base percentage.

Runner at First Base With No Outs

If the leadoff hitter has gotten on, then a right-handed number two hitter should have the ability to drive the ball to the right side of the infield. A left-handed number two hitter should have the ability to pull the ball to the right side of the field. If the defense is playing the left-handed batter to bunt or pull the ball, the hitter must be able to drive the ball to the left side of the infield. However, it is more difficult for the defense to complete a double play on the right side of the infield than on the left side. The hitter must be disciplined to look for a pitch in her hitting zone, one that she can drive to whichever area will provide a better chance of staying out of a double play.

Runner at Second Base With No Outs

This situation forces the hitter to practice great discipline so that she can react to a pitch that can be hit hard to the right side of the field. The right-handed hitter should look for a pitch from the middle of the plate to the outside corner of the plate. She must stay disciplined and not swing at an inside pitch because hitting this pitch may result in a ground ball to the left side of the infield, preventing the runner from advancing. The left-handed hitter must look for a pitch that she can pull while knowing that the smart pitcher will keep the ball away from the lefty. A coach may sacrifice bunt in this situation if the batter does not have the ability to move the runner to third.

Runner at Third With Less Than Two Outs

In this situation the hitter must look for a pitch she can hit hard somewhere. With less than two strikes she should look for a "mistake" pitch. However, if the pitcher gets two strikes on the batter, the batter needs to concentrate on making contact. In this situation a hard ground ball will have an excellent chance of getting through the infield. The hitter must make every effort to get a good pitch to hit when she has less than two strikes.

Runners at First and Third With One Out

With runners at first and third and only one out, the hitter should make every attempt to avoid an inning-ending double play. If the runner on first has started on the pitch, the hitter must exercise good discipline to take advantage of the infielder's movement to cover the steal. The hitter should go to that side of the field if the pitch allows her to do so.

SUMMARY

Hitting is a challenge; thus, basics and fundamentals must be taught and practiced continually. There are no quick fixes, but by having an awareness and proper mind-set, the hitter can perform much more consistently. A softball coach must spend a great deal of time in practice sessions teaching the hitting phase of the game, since hitting is a tough skill to learn and execute.

The good hitting coach must analyze a hitter who is having a difficult time making solid contact, and then offer suggestions for correction in a way that the athlete can understand, so that adjustments can be made. When the hitter evaluates her at bats, she should build for success by hitting the ball hard and working to understand the challenges of situation hitting.

When the hitter is having success in hitting the ball hard, it is best to allow her the chance to stay with her swing even though her hitting mechanics do not fit the classic picture of proper fundamentals. If the hitter is not having good success, be able to assist her to get the maximum out of her potential as a hitter.

What are hitting mechanics all about? The hitter wants to minimize her movement to maximize her efficiency. The hitter must be as quick and as efficient as possible from the launching position to the contact point. In chapter 8 you will see some fresh ideas on hitting drills to help you develop a more productive hitter.

- Teaching aggressive hitting is critical to success. The hitter must have the mentality that every pitch thrown will be a strike.
- The hitter must be thinking "yes—yes—yes." It is much easier to not swing if the pitch is not a strike than it is to suddenly make up your mind to swing. Bear in mind that most pitchers will throw a strike on one of the first two pitches.
- Hitting is a very difficult skill, one that takes a lot of repetition and a lot of practice. The more the hitter can swing in practice, the better she will be in the game.

Chapter 8

TEACHING HITTING SKILLS

When it is time to begin teaching hitting skills keep in mind the following: The opposing pitcher is throwing up to three hundred pitches each day. For the hitter to be successful, she must have the opportunity to train at an equal level. Because hitting is a reactionary skill, numerous repetitions are vital. In this chapter I present a number of hitting drills, broken down into the following: no-ball drills, still-ball drills, tossed-ball drills, machine-ball drills, and pitched-ball drills. There are also drills designed for challenge and competition—games where players compete individually or as a team—as well as some bunting drills. In all drills, the batter should execute a complete swing and swing only at good tosses or good pitches because swinging at bad pitches in practice will carry over into the game. The no-ball, still-ball, tossed-ball, and machine-ball drills can all be performed for three to five minutes at a time, while the pitched-ball and challenge drills can take as long as is necessary to execute. This chapter begins with a drill finder that lists several common hitting errors and the drills in this chapter that will correct them. The use of drills for the coach and player can greatly enhance technique evaluation.

Problem	Drill	Page
Dropping the barrel Result: missing the ball or popping up	Barrier Behind	88
	Towel	89
	Wall Swings	89
	Down on One Knee	89
	Regular T	90
	Swing Over the Top T and Hit the Second T	90
	Two Ts	91
	Partner High Toss	93
	Soft Toss—Off Back Knee	94
	Pepper Game	98
Pulling the ball Result: hitting ball foul	Inside-Outside	89
	Target on the Fence	90
	Reverse Tracking	94
	No Pull	96
	Hit 'Til You Drop	97
	Over the Line	98
Wrist rolls too soon Result: ground ball	Lead Arm Extension	92
	One Hand, Small Bat	92
	One-Hand Soft Toss	93
	Paddle	93
	Reverse Tracking	94
	Partner Fair Ball	96
Weak lead arm Result: no power and slow swing	Barrier Behind	88
	Draw a Line	88
	Wall Swings	89
	Drop Toss	92
	One Hand, Small Bat	92
	One-Hand Soft Toss	93
	Paddle	93
	Snap Backs	94
	Very Fast Pitching Machine	96
	Toss Game	98
Lack of hip rotation Result: slow swing and loss of power	Hip Turn	88
	Advanced T	89
	Bat Paddle	91
	Hip Rotation	92
	Standing Toss	94
Pulling the head Result: missing the ball	Mirror	88
	Shadow	88
	Regular T	90

(continued)

Problem	Drill	Page
	Front Toss	92
	Tracking	96
	Move the Runner	98
Slow hands Result: lack of power and hitting to the opposite field	Draw a Line	88
	Drop Toss	92
	One Hand, Small Bat	92
	Snap Backs	94
	Soft Toss—Off Back Knee	94
	Very Fast Pitching Machine	96
Big stride Result: swinging under the ball	Mirror	88
	Plumb Bob	88
	Shadow	88
	Stride	89
	Stride Box	89
	Deflated Volleyball	89
	Stride, Stop, Swing	90
	Balance Beam and Ball	91
	Front Toss	92
Balance Result: weak ground ball and loss of power	Balance Beam	88
	Isometric	88
	Deflated Volleyball	89
	Stride, Stop, Swing	90
	Partner Low Toss	93
	Situation Hitting Practice	96
No trigger Result: late swing	Look at Pitcher, Then Hit	90
	Bounce in Front	92
	Drop Toss	92
	Two-Ball Toss	94
	Tracking and Recognition	97
Hand-eye coordination Result: mis-hits and not hitting the center of the ball	Drop Toss	92
	Figure Eight	92
	Reverse Tracking	94
	Two-Ball Toss	94
	Colored Ball	95
	Game-Like Batting Practice	96
Poor pitch selection Result: weak hits and swings and misses	Standing Toss	94
	Colored Ball	95
	Drop Ball	95
	Rise-Ball Pitch	96

(continued)

No-Ball Drills

Balance Beam

Purpose: To get the proper feel of balance during a swing.

Procedure: The batter stands on a low balance beam made from a 2×8 piece of lumber. The beam is placed on the ground in the batter's box, and the batter takes her normal swing while trying to stay on the beam. Her goal is to not lose balance and step off the beam.

Barrier Behind

Purpose: To emphasize taking the hands directly to the ball and keeping the barrel up.

Procedure: The batter's rear foot is parallel to the side of a batting cage and in contact with the net. The batter swings by taking her hands to the ball and keeping the bat barrel up. The bat should not touch the barrier on the swing.

Draw a Line

Purpose: To practice moving the hands to the ball and to develop speed and a strong lead arm.

Procedure: The batter assumes her stance without a bat and with her lead hand in its normal position with the thumb up. The hitter draws a line across her chest and then extends to the ball.

Hip Turn

Purpose: To practice opening the hips and driving the back hip into the swing.

Procedure: The batter places the bat behind her back and wraps both arms around the bat at the elbows. Without taking a step, the batter whips the hips open.

Isometric

Purpose: To practice a complete swing and follow-through.

Procedure: The batter assumes her stance while her partner stands behind and holds the top of the bat with both hands. The partner offers resistance as the batter strides and swings all the way through.

Mirror

Purpose: To develop a picture-perfect technique.

Procedure: Batter assumes batting stance in front of a mirror with or without a bat and swings, focusing on length of stride, hip rotation, and contact point.

Plumb Bob

Purpose: To practice keeping weight centered.

Procedure: The batter grasps the knob of the bat with the lead arm and lets the bat hang in front of the midline of her body. The batter then takes her stride; with a correct stride, the bat will not move.

Shadow

Purpose: To stop any extra head movement and swaying.

Procedure: The batter positions herself with her back to the sun, then assumes her stance. A partner places a cap on the shadow's head. The batter goes through her swing keeping her head in the cap. The batter should feel her weight stay centered if there is no head movement.

Stride

Purpose: To emphasize keeping the hands back while taking a soft, short step.

Procedure: The batter assumes her normal stance and takes a low, soft stride forward, while the hands remain back.

Stride Box

Purpose: To concentrate on keeping the front side closed during the stride.

Procedure: Construct a stride box by forming an L from two 12-inch lengths of 2×4s. Lay the stride box on the ground where it will serve as a gauge as to how far the batter's foot should move during the stride and where it will make sure that the front foot stays closed. The batter assumes her normal stance with her lead foot about three to six inches from the front of the L. She then goes through her normal swing, trying not to step on the stride box.

Towel

Purpose: To practice keeping the lead elbow down and the barrel up.

Procedure: The batter takes a towel and places it under the lead arm, then takes a swing while keeping the towel in place until the follow-through. The batter must keep the elbow down and the hands out on the swing.

Wall Swings

Purpose: To avoid casting the barrel in a long, sweeping swing.

Procedure: The batter stands facing the wall, about a bat's length away. She assumes her batting stance and swings. The bat should not touch the wall if the hands are going to the ball. If the batter has a long, sweeping swing, the bat will hit the wall.

STILL-BALL DRILLS

Advanced T

Purpose: To learn muscle memory by performing the swing the same every time.

Procedure: The batter is in her normal position at a T. Her partner places the ball on the T. The batter hits one, then closes her eyes and hits again.

Deflated Volleyball

Purpose: To emphasize keeping the knees together with a short, balanced stride.

Procedure: The batter assumes normal position at the T with a deflated volleyball placed between her knees. The batter then swings through the ball while remaining balanced and gripping the volleyball with her knees.

Down on One Knee

Purpose: To concentrate on keeping the barrel above the hands to hit the high pitch. The only way to hit the high pitch is to tomahawk the ball.

Procedure: The hitter is down on the back leg with the front leg extended straight. The ball is on a T above shoulder level when the batter is on one knee. The batter keeps her hands down and the barrel up, tomahawking the ball.

Inside-Outside

Purpose: To emphasize taking the same stride, regardless of the pitch location.

Procedure: One T is placed on the inside corner of the plate (in front of the plate), and the second T is placed on the outside corner of the plate (even with the plate). While using correct mechanics, the batter alternates between hitting the inside ball and the outside ball.

Look at Pitcher, Then Hit

Purpose: To practice refocusing from the pitcher to the point of contact.

Procedure: The batter at a T looks out at an imaginary pitcher and then refocuses on the T and takes a normal swing.

Regular T

Purpose: To practice keeping the head down and the barrel up.

Procedure: Place the T in the strike zone so that the barrel stays up. The batter should drive the front shoulder to the outside corner of the plate. After contact the batter should look inside the T. This ensures that the head stays down (see figure 8.1).

Coaching points: Be sure to locate the T in front of the plate where contact is made.

Stride, Stop, Swing

Purpose: To practice keeping the hands back in the hitting position and remaining balanced throughout the swing.

Procedure: The batter is at a T and takes her normal stride. She holds her stride position for a split second and then swings.

Swing Over the Top T and Hit the Second T

Purpose: To emphasize keeping the barrel above the hands.

Procedure: Position two Ts one in front of the other with the rear T three inches higher than the front T. A ball is placed on the front T. The batter assumes her normal stance and swings over the higher T to hit the ball on the front T.

Target on the Fence

Purpose: To practice a smooth rhythm and follow-through.

Figure 8.1   Regular T drill.

Procedure: Place a target on the fence and a T about 15-20 feet in front of the target. The batter tries to hit the target.

Two Ts

Purpose: To concentrate on hitting to and through the ball on the sweet spot of the bat with a line drive contact.

Procedure: Two Ts are placed at the same height one directly in front of the other with a ball on each. The batter tries to drive the bat through the ball on the first T and into and through the ball on the second T (see figure 8.2).

TOSSED-BALL DRILLS

You can use tennis balls or baseballs for these drills. These smaller balls make softballs appear much larger and easier to hit. The batter must really see the ball to make solid contact. The tosser's role is vital! The toss should be made to the proper bat contact location. In all of these drills the batter can hit into a net, the fence, or the open field. The partner usually stands facing the batter about six feet away. The tosser and the batter have their shoulders squared toward each other. Sometimes the tosser will be positioned like a pitcher in relation to the batter. If this is the case, the tosser is in front of the batter.

Balance Beam and Ball

Purpose: To develop balance as well as a firm front leg and a powerful back leg.

Procedure: The batter stands on a 2×4 and hits a ball off a toss. She takes her normal swing and tries to remain on the board during the swing. The partner stands facing the batter about six feet away and tosses the ball into the contact position.

Bat Paddle

Purpose: To develop hip turn and rotation.

Procedure: Tape a paddle to the barrel of the bat so that it extends beyond the barrel. The batter places the bat behind her back so that the paddle extends beyond her back hip and grips

Figure 8.2 Two Ts drill.

the bat with both hands. The hitter assumes her batting position and her partner stands in front of her about 10 to 12 feet away. The tosser pitches the balls underhand across the plate. The batter takes a full hip turn trying to hit the ball with the paddle.

Bounce in Front

Purpose: To practice the hitting rhythm and the trigger and to learn to hit the ball at the top of the bounce.

Procedure: The partner stands six feet to the side and three feet in front of the batter and tosses a tennis ball that bounces up into the strike zone in front of the plate. As the ball bounces the batter "triggers" and gets her hands started into the swing. She waits until the ball is at the height of the bounce before swinging and driving it into a net.

Drop Toss

Purpose: To develop hand speed to the ball.

Procedure: The batter assumes her stance with a partner facing her with the ball held at shoulder height. The batter tells the partner when to drop the ball. The partner releases the ball and pulls her arm up away from the strike zone. The batter takes a full swing.

Variations: The partner can stand on a chair or on the bleachers, which will add a challenging tracking test.

Figure Eight

Purpose: To develop a quick adjustment to the ball.

Procedure: The batter is in her stance, and a tosser is down on one knee with a ball in each hand. The tosser is six feet away facing the batter. The tosser tumbles both balls around each other and then tosses one or the other to the batter. The batter then takes a full swing and hits the ball into the net. The batter does not know which ball will be released.

Front Toss

Purpose: To emphasize swing techniques utilizing proper mechanics.

Procedure: Place a screen 10 to 12 feet in front of the plate with the tosser standing behind it. The tosser throws underhand and can control pitch location while the batter takes a normal swing (see figure 8.3).

Hip Rotation

Purpose: To practice hitting the ball hard using only hip rotation.

Procedure: The hitter stands three feet from the fence or screen with a tosser. The tosser stands six feet from the hitter facing her and tosses the ball into the contact area. The hitter hits the ball hard into the fence using only hip rotation. The bat is held in the starting position and the arms and wrists are not used.

Lead Arm Extension

Purpose: To emphasize the shoulder unlock, the elbow unlock, and the wrist unlock.

Procedure: The hitter kneels on her back leg 10 feet from a screen or fence and the tosser positions herself four feet in front and to the side of the hitter. The hitter hits the ball hard using only the lead arm (left arm for right-handed batters and right arm for left-handed batters). The batter starts with both hands on the bat, holding it in proper position. A full swing is taken.

One Hand, Small Bat

Purpose: To emphasize the top hand movement by having the hand cock the wrist for full extension; the top hand grips the bat "like a hammer" and swings through the ball.

Procedure: The batter assumes her stance using a small bat (25 to 28 inches) which she can control with the top hand. A helper tosses balls that the batter hits with the small bat.

Figure 8.3 Front Toss drill.

One-Hand Soft Toss

Purpose: To emphasize loading the lead arm in sequence: shoulder, elbow, and then wrist.

Procedure: The batter is down on the back knee with the front leg up and grips the bat with only the bottom hand. The tosser stands six feet from the batter and tosses the ball out in front of the batter's lead arm. The batter swings only at strikes and drives the ball into a net.

Paddle

Purpose: To concentrate on unlocking the lead arm in sequence: shoulder, elbow, and then wrist.

Procedure: The batter positions herself with her back knee on the ground and her front leg up. She uses a short paddle (pickle ball paddle or table tennis paddle) and holds it in the lead arm at the set-up position. The tosser makes a routine toss with a Wiffle ball and the batter makes contact using only the lead hand.

Partner High Toss

Purpose: To practice keeping the barrel above the hands with the weight transfer through the ball.

Procedure: The tosser stands about six feet to the side and facing the hitter. She tosses a firm chest-high toss into the hitting area in front of the plate. The batter hits into a screen.

Partner Low Toss

Purpose: To concentrate on a soft, short, and balanced stride.

Procedure: The hitter stands 10 feet from a screen or a fence and the tosser positions herself four feet in front and to the side of the hitter. When working on the inside pitch, the hitter closes her stance and the ball is tossed to her front hip. When working on the outside pitch, the hitter slightly opens her stance and the ball is tossed to the front hip across the center of the plate. The toss should be low and firm (not a lob) and the batter hits the ball hard and into the screen.

Reverse Tracking

Purpose: To practice tracking the ball and keeping the hands inside the barrel.

Procedure: The ball is flipped from behind the hitter on an inside-out plane. The hitter can slightly turn her head to track the toss. As the ball comes forward the hitter must hold her power angle until contact. The hitter must wait on the ball and then drive it with authority into the center of the net. The hitter needs to fully extend before rolling her wrists (see figure 8.4).

Snap Backs

Purpose: To develop quick hands, a small stride, and forearm and wrist strength.

Procedure: The partner stands six feet from the batter and tosses balls in rapid succession to the contact point of the strike zone. The hitter is standing up and drives one ball after another into a net by taking her swing and snapping the bat back to the starting position in preparation for the next toss.

Soft Toss—Off Back Knee

Purpose: To concentrate on hitting down on the ball.

Procedure: The hitter kneels on her back knee and the tosser stands about six feet to the side and facing the hitter. The tosser tosses at the hitter's contact position. The object is to drive the ball into the center of the net while working on hand speed. This drill eliminates the lower body and emphasizes hand quickness (see figure 8.5).

Standing Toss

Purpose: To practice pitch selection and swing technique.

Procedure: The batter is in position at the plate with a tosser, standing, facing her about six feet away. The tosser tosses the ball in front of the plate at the contact spot in the strike zone and the batter takes a normal swing (see figure 8.6).

Two-Ball Toss

Purpose: To practice keeping the hands back until the last possible second.

Procedure: The partner stands about six feet to the side of the hitter and holds two balls in the same hand. The tosser tosses both balls at the same time and commands the batter to "hit the top ball" or "hit the bottom ball." The batter hits into a screen.

Figure 8.4   Reverse Tracking drill.

Figure 8.5   Soft Toss—Off Back Knee drill.

Figure 8.6   Standing Toss drill.

MACHINE-BALL DRILLS

Unless stated otherwise, the machine is at normal distance for the batter and on normal speed.

Colored Ball

Purpose: To practice visual tracking as well as taking the pitch.

Procedure: Red and black colored quarter-size dots are painted on four sides of the balls. The hitter is instructed to hit the black balls and to take the red balls. This drill can be done in a batting cage or on a field with fielders.

Drop Ball

Purpose: To practice hitting a drop ball.

Procedure: Position the pitching machine on a short stand, about six inches off the ground. The pitched ball will then come from an elevated position to a low strike position. The batter must swing at only strikes. This drill can be done on the field with fielders or in a batting cage.

Game-Like Batting Practice

Purpose: To concentrate on proper techniques and execution.

Procedure: The feeder at the machine gives an offensive signal to the batter, who must execute the play as if it were a game situation. The feeder uses all plays, such as the hit-and-run, bunts, and squeezes. This can be done in a batting cage or on a field with or without fielders. Base runners are used when fielders are present.

No Pull

Purpose: To emphasize keeping the front side closed throughout the swing.

Procedure: Set the machine at normal speed to throw to the outside corner of the strike zone. The first baseman, second baseman, and right fielder are at their positions for the right-handed batter, as are the third baseman, shortstop, and left fielder for the left-handed batter. If the ball is hit to the right (or left) side of second base, the defense returns the ball, but if any ball is hit elsewhere, the batter must run and get it. Each player takes one turn and goes to the end of the line. Base runners are practicing going from first to third and second to home.

Partner Fair Ball

Purpose: To practice hitting off the machine on a field with fielders.

Procedure: The pitching machine is on the mound and set on the hitting speed and location for that day. All players have a partner and they take turns hitting off the machine. One hitter hits until she hits a fair ball. Then it is the

partner's turn. A prescribed amount of time is allotted for each pair combination. Fielders and base runners can be used.

Rise-Ball Pitch

Purpose: To practice hitting a rise ball.

Procedure: Take the legs off the pitching machine and position the machine on the ground. The pitched ball will then come from a low position to a high position. The batter must swing at only strikes. This drill can be done on the field with fielders and base runners or in a batting cage.

Tracking

Purpose: To develop hard focus and pitch location discipline.

Procedure: Set the speed so the hitter is practicing correct technique. The batter tracks the ball all the way from the machine to the backstop without swinging.

Very Fast Pitching Machine

Purpose: To emphasize a short, soft stride and quick hands.

Procedure: Move the hitter very close to the machine or set the machine on high speed. The batter just tries to make contact with a regular swing. This can be done on a field with fielders and base runners or in a batting cage.

PITCHED-BALL DRILLS

Situation Hitting Practice

Purpose: To practice offensive plays.

Procedure: The coach gives an offensive signal and the batter must execute the play. The coach can utilize the hit-and-run, the bunt, or the squeeze or slap bunts. This drill is done off of a machine or with a live pitcher. Defensive players are at their positions and base runners are used. All swings taken must be purposeful, because swinging at bad pitches in batting practice sessions will carry over to the game.

Coaching points: Situation hitting in batting practice sessions provides the hitter and coach the opportunity to evaluate the hitter's discipline and pitch selection.

Variations: Play an intersquad game using different counts or place the hitter in a certain count each time she steps to the plate.

Target Hitting

Purpose: To develop the right-handed batter's skill of hitting an outside pitch to right field and an inside pitch to left field, and vice versa for the left-handed batter.

Procedure: In batting practice the batter must hit into an assigned area of the field. For example, the first pitch a right-handed batter hits must be to right field. She will need to be sure to wait for an outside pitch. On her next swing she must try to pull the ball, thus looking for an inside pitch. This drill can be done with or without fielders and base runners.

Tracking and Recognition, or Take the Pitch

Purpose: To develop tracking skills and to recognize strikes.

Procedure: A pitcher is on the mound with a catcher behind the plate. The pitcher throws pitches and the hitter stands in the batter's box. The batter takes her normal stride and tracks the ball as well as recognizing spin on the ball, such as drop, rise, or change-up spin. The batter does not swing at the pitch but calls out the type of pitch that was thrown.

Twelve Strike

Purpose: To enable the batter to see live pitching and to practice swinging at strikes.

Procedure: A pitcher is on the mound with a full-geared catcher behind the plate, and the hitter is in the batter's box. The batter gets 12 strikes. A strike is called when a pitch considered to be a ball is swung at, when a pitch is swung at and missed, and when a pitch delivered in the strike zone is not hit. The batter keeps hitting until she has had 12 strikes. The next batter comes on deck after 10 strikes. This drill can be done with fielders and base runners.

PLAYER COMPETITION AND CHALLENGE GAMES

Grand Slam

Purpose: To practice proper swing technique and hitting the ball to score points.

Procedure: Players can be grouped individually or in teams. Each player is awarded 10 swings with the object being to score as many points as possible in those 10 swings. Areas of the batting cage are assigned points: four points for hitting the back of the cage; three points for hitting it in power alleys; two points for hitting certain areas of the cage; one point for hitting a ground ball in front of a certain line. Zero points are given for swings and misses and for not getting the ball across the line. The machine is set at a normal speed.

Hit 'Til You Drop

Purpose: To enable the batter to see many pitched balls in a short amount of time.

Procedure: The game can be played with a live pitcher or a pitching machine. A full defense is in place and players are partnered up according to hitting ability (strong with strong and weak with weak). Base runners can be used. The partners get five minutes together to bat one at a time. The batter keeps her turn until she hits a foul ball or swings and misses a pitch. The players continue to alternate until the time elapses and the score is kept by the number of balls hit into play.

Move the Runner

Purpose: To emphasize offensive play execution to move the runner.

Procedure: The game is played with a live pitcher or a pitching machine. A full defense is in place. The players are partnered weaker with stronger. One partner starts on first base and the other is at the plate. The object of the game is to score your partner in less than three outs. The hitter can employ any strategy or play to move her partner. The hitter does not run out the play.

Over the Line

Purpose: To concentrate on pitch selection and hit placement.

Procedure: Set up the field as diagrammed in figure 8.7. The game can be played with three or four players per team. When three outs are recorded the teams change from offense to defense and vice versa. The inning begins with a tosser tossing for a hitter who attempts to hit a line drive over the line. If the ball lands over the line, a single is recorded, and if the ball lands over the deepest line, a home run is recorded. Outs are recorded in the following manner: (a) a fielder catches the ball in the air, (b) the ball bounces before the line, or (c) the ball lands outside the field of play. After three outs teams change sides. Any number of innings can be played.

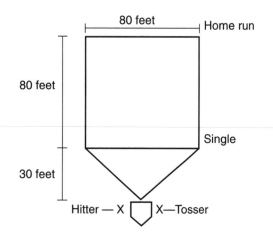

Figure 8.7   Over the Line drill.

Pepper Game

Purpose: To emphasize putting the ball on the ground.

Procedure: Set up a hitter and a line of four or five fielders 20 to 30 feet away. The fielders toss underhand to the hitter, and if the fielder catches a line drive she gets to advance one position. If a fielder misses a ground ball on her glove side, she goes to the end of the line. The batter is out (and gets only one out) if she pops up or a line drive is caught, or if she hits the ball over the fielders, swings and misses, or hits a ball foul. The fielders toss in order. When the batter is out she goes to the end of the fielding line and all other fielders move up one spot.

Toss Game

Purpose: To concentrate on solid contact and good swing mechanics.

Procedure: A game is played with infielders, outfielders, and the catcher. The coach stands 10 feet down the first baseline for the right-handed hitter and down the left-field line for the left-handed hitter. The coach tosses to the hitters and they run out their batted ball. Each player hits once in each inning while the defense clears the bases every three outs until all batters on the opposing team have hit.

Variations: The coach can tell the hitter where to hit or what offensive situation to play.

BUNTING DRILLS

Drop Everything

Purpose: To practice the squeeze bunt.

Procedure: A protective screen is set up in the middle of the pitching area. This drill has two pitchers and two catchers. Pitcher 1 is in front of the protective screen and throws to home plate. Pitcher 2 is behind the protective screen and throws to second base. Each pitcher has a full bucket of balls, and each catcher has an empty bucket. Hitter 1 is at the plate and bunts the first pitch and runs to first base, while at the same time, hitter 2, who is at a plate where second base was, bunts the first pitch and runs to third base. Then both hitters jog to the ends of the opposite lines. If the ball is not contacted by one of the hitters, she runs to the center-field fence, touches it, and sprints to the end of the next line.

Get It Down

Purpose: To practice sacrifice bunts and bunt placement.

Procedure: A rope is placed 15 feet from home plate and in a semicircle stretching from one sideline to the other. The pitcher and catcher are at their defensive positions with base runners on the base paths. The pitcher has a full ball bucket, and the catcher has an empty ball bucket. All the hitters are at home plate. Each hitter bunts the ball and tries to keep it inside the rope. The hitter gets two chances to contact the bunt. If the first or second ball is bunted, the hitter runs to first base. If the hitter misses both balls, she runs all the bases before returning to the end of the line.

Slap Them In

Purpose: To improve on the slap-bunt technique.

Procedure: All infield defensive positions are filled and there is a runner on third base. The hitters are at home plate. The pitcher has a full bucket of balls. The catcher has an empty bucket. Each hitter slaps the ball and tries to put it on the ground toward the second baseman or the shortstop. The runner at third is going either on the pitch or the throw to first. This is decided by the batter through a signal she gives to the runner. After the slap execution the hitter goes to third and the runner goes to the end of the line at home plate.

Slot Shots

Purpose: To practice the push bunt.

Procedure: The pitcher, catcher, third baseman, and first baseman are in their defen-sive positions with base runners. The pitcher has a full bucket of balls and the catcher has an empty bucket. All hitters are at home plate. Each hitter push-bunts the ball and tries to push it in the slots between the pitcher and the third baseman or the pitcher and the first baseman. The hitter gets two chances to push the bunt in the slot. If the first or second ball is bunted, the hitter runs to first base. If the hitter misses both balls, she runs all the bases before returning to the end of the line.

HITTING PRACTICE

Now what? You have all these drills to help develop your hitters. How do you make the pieces of the puzzle fit into a practice plan? I like to spend two days with no-ball drills, then two days with still-ball drills. We then progress to two days of tossed-ball drills before we go into three days of machine-ball drills. When I feel our hitters have established the basics and our pitchers are ready we will progress into pitched-ball drills. When batters have specific problems you should start them with the no-ball drill solutions in the drill finder and then work them up to more complex drills.

After several weeks of practice when the players have had a chance to work through all of the drills in the progression and to become familiar with them, you may want to try taking a five station approach to practice with an equal number of players at each station. I like to put athletes in the same group who have similar technique problems. I use this station plan in the preseason as well as in the regular season, but on a less frequent basis.

You can utilize a facility a little larger than a basketball court, along with all kinds of balls: Wiffle balls, tennis balls, "real soft" balls, and real balls. Set up five areas and use one or two drills in each area. By organizing the drills in the station approach and keeping track of "decks of drills," you can add interest to your hitting practices. Imagine numbering each drill in this chapter (by type of drill) and putting each one on a 3×5 index card. Now put all the drill cards in five different decks as follows:

- Deck 1: no-ball drills
- Deck 2: still-ball drills

- Deck 3: tossed-ball drills
- Deck 4: machine-ball drills
- Deck 5: pitched-ball drills

You have five decks of such drills and five stations. Take a drill from each deck and put it at each station. For example, on one day of practice you might do the following:

- Station 1 (no-ball)—deck 1, drill 1
- Station 2 (still-ball)—deck 2, drill 1
- Station 3 (tossed-ball)—deck 3, drill 1
- Station 4 (machine-ball)—deck 4, drill 1
- Station 5 (pitched-ball)—deck 5, drill 1

Another day of practice might look like this:

- Station 1 (no-ball)—deck 1, drill 2
- Station 2 (still-ball)—deck 2, drill 2
- Station 3 (tossed-ball)—deck 3, drill 3
- Station 4 (machine-ball)—deck 4, drill 2
- Station 5 (pitched-ball)—deck 5, drill 2

You may be using special apparatus and this can constitute one of the stations. Let the specialty items be station 5 instead of pitched-ball drills. If you have any special coaching or teaching items, I suggest they be utilized at station 5 or a new station. Bunting drills could also be utilized at another new station. That format would look like this:

- Station 1 (machine-ball)—deck 4, drill 3
- Station 2 (still-ball)—deck 2, drill 3
- Station 3 (tossed-ball)—deck 3, drill 4
- Station 4 (variety)—deck 1, drill 1
- Station 5 (specialty)—deck 5, drill 1

What should the timetable look like?

Number of players on your team:　20

Number of stations:　5

Players per station:　4

Minutes per station:　8

Minutes to pick up balls and move to next station:　2

Total amount of time:　50 minutes

With this plan, in 50 minutes each batter will be at five different stations and experience five different drills. If each athlete gets 10 to 20 swings at each station, this plan would allow for 50 to 100 total swings in 50 minutes.

SUMMARY

We have looked at five categories of batting drills: no-ball drills, still-ball drills, tossed-ball drills, machine-ball drills, and pitched-ball drills. These drills are categorized in these groups because learning is accelerated when drills follow a progression from the simple to the complex. The batter must first establish muscle memory during a simple task before including variables such as still, tossed, or pitched balls. These drills help the batter pattern the swing and enable her to learn perfect techniques.

- The best practices are those that have fast-paced activities and include small groups.
- When pairing your groups for drills, remind the athletes of the importance of the partner in each drill. The nonhitting partner plays a vital role in the drills that call for one. The partner can be a coach or a teammate. Her job is to make sure the batter gets as many quality swings as possible and to help direct the hitter so that she is performing proper technique.
- Praise and positive reinforcement are vital.
- With these drills and player competitions and challenges, the hitters have a better chance of matching the pitcher's three hundred balls a day.
- Take these drills as a basic outline for developing your own hitting program based on your resources. There are enough drills to focus on technique, while including challenge and variety.

Chapter 9

OFFENSIVE STRATEGIES

My ideal offense is one that can execute the fundamentals correctly and execute them under pressure. I want to be aggressive, and in doing so, I am willing to make some outs. I want our batters to be great base runners and to think about a double every time they hit a single. I do not want to limit them to first; rather, I want them to go as far as they can until the defense stops them. The strategies in this chapter are written with this in mind.

BASERUNNING PRINCIPLES

Softball games are won and lost many times on the base paths, and a coach needs to spend time in practice perfecting baserunning skills. A team that has an aggressive baserunning game can have a devastating effect on the defense, causing them to make errors on routine plays. The principles we look at in this section include getting a good leadoff, tagging up, staying in the base path, and sliding.

I allocate 10 minutes each day to teaching and practicing baserunning. The base runner must be taught to think for herself and to know where the ball is at all times. With these skills she will be able to take advantage of defensive mistakes. I also want our runners to learn to run efficiently with correct mechanics; therefore, in each practice we combine conditioning work with baserunning skills. We also incorporate baserunning in all game-like situations and batting practice.

Leads

A base runner's leadoff stance will vary from base to base. I like the rocker step, or the sprinter start, at first and second base (see figure 9.1). In this position, one foot is on the base and one foot is behind. The base runner rocks back as the pitcher is in the downswing of the pitch. I want the runner to time leaving the base when

Figure 9.1   The rocker-step leadoff.

the pitcher's heel has left the rubber. This cue lets her think about runner's foot and pitcher's foot. On third base we use a traditional baseball start with one foot on the base and the other in front of the base because I believe it opens up the entire field to the runner's view.

The length of a base runner's lead is determined by her ability to get back to the base. The quicker the base runner's ability to get back to first base on a dive, the farther from the base she can get on her leadoff. If the infield area where the runner leads off is firm and in good shape, the runner will be able to get back to first with greater ease. If the dirt is loose or wet, the runner's lead will have to be shortened.

The coach needs to spend quite a bit of time with the players on perfecting their turns at all bases. In the ideal turn, the runner takes an abbreviated turn without losing too much speed on her approach to the base. Most runners begin angling out for their turn when they are about 20 feet from the base. Once they start angling out they should not decrease their speed. The length of the angle away from the base should be no farther than seven or eight feet. Once the runner has reached her ideal angle away from the base, she must begin angling toward the base gradually, so she can maintain as much speed and balance as possible. By dipping the left shoulder in toward the infield and contacting the inside corner of the base with the right foot, the runner is put back on a straight line with the next base (see figure 9.2).

Tagging Up

There are times when a runner will be tagging up at a base to advance to another on a fly ball that is caught. If she feels that there is any chance the ball will not be caught, she must be as far away from the base as possible. One exception to this rule is made for a runner on third and a fly ball (see specific instructions later in this chapter).

When tagging up the runner must watch the catch herself. This prevents any problem in the communication between the player and the coach. The only way a runner can clearly see the ball while tagging up is to have the correct foot on the base, which will give her full sight of the ball as it touches the outfielder's glove. For example, if the ball is hit to the left fielder, the runner on third puts her left foot on the base and

Figure 9.2   Turning at the base.

her right foot about a foot in front of the base. The timing is very important so that the runner does not leave the base too early. If it is going to be a close play, she must leave the base at the exact time the ball touches the fielder's glove.

The coach might give advice while the ball is in the air as to what she wants the runner to do on the catch (this is especially true with a runner tagging up at third base). This would be one of three commands: You're going to go, make a fake, or halfway.

Stay in the Path

The runner should stay in the path of a thrown ball on the bases. Anytime a runner can legally interfere with the throw from one fielder to another, she should do so. However, she does not want to reduce her time to the next base by changing her course on the base path. For example, with the runner at first base and a ball hit well to the second baseman's left, the runner needs to stay on the outside of the base path. With a runner on second and a ground ball hit to the shortstop's right, the runner should run directly toward the third baseman's glove, forcing a difficult throw from the shortstop to the third baseman.

Another example occurs when the runner is at third base and the third baseman fields the ball going close to the line. In this situation the runner should stay in the inside of the base path as she runs toward home plate, making a very difficult throw for the third baseman to the catcher. If the third baseman catches the ball in foul territory, then the runner would stay on the outside of the base path. The runner can never obstruct the view of the player fielding the ball by throwing up her arms or hands or by going out of the baseline.

When the runner advances to second base on a ground ball to the right side of the infield, she must avoid being tagged by the second baseman. If the runner can get by the second baseman, she should make every attempt to do so. If she cannot get by, she must make the infielder come toward her to make the tag. The runner can run out of the baseline to avoid the tag if this will give the batter base runner a better chance to reach first and avoid a double play.

Sliding

The desire and the ability to slide are two important facets of aggressive baserunning. Sliding must be taught so that it will be an asset in reaching the next base and so that poor techniques will not result in injuries. There are three reasons to slide:

1. To reach a base going full speed without going by it.
2. To avoid a tag at a base.
3. To break up a double play attempt.

Once the runner decides to slide, she must slide. When in doubt, she must slide. I will describe four slides: the bent-leg slide, the pop-up slide off the bent-leg slide, the hook slide, and the headfirst slide.

Bent Leg Slide

The bent leg or straight in slide allows the runner to go directly into the base. Either leg can be bent with the lower leg of the bent leg crossing under the knee of the straight leg. The bent leg remains parallel to the ground in the slide. The cleats of the shoe that is underneath should be facing out away from the ground. The straight leg is extended forward with the knee slightly bent and the foot is 5 to 10 inches off the ground. The buttocks remain fully on the ground with the upper body extended back to where the shoulder blades almost touch the ground. The neck is arched forward with the chin toward the chest. The arms are bent and the hands are up in the air (see figure 9.3).

Pop-Up Slide

The pop-up slide is very similar to the bent-leg slide except that the runner finishes the slide by standing on the base and being ready to advance to the next base. The runner starts the slide about eight feet from the base with the upper body remaining in a sit-up position. The body weight is on the bent lower leg and extended back to the buttocks (see figure 9.4a). The extended leg is slightly bent and raised three to five inches off the ground, and the bag is contacted by the instep of the extended leg. As bag contact is made the leg straightens and the upper body moves forward. This movement should be enough to carry the runner back to the upward position (see figure 9.4b).

Hook Slide

The hook slide is used to avoid a tag. In this slide the ball has beaten the runner to the base but may be off target. When sliding to the right side, the outside of the right calf and thigh should

make contact with the ground first. The right leg is bent while the left leg is relatively straight with a slight bend in the knee. The inner part of the lower leg contacts the ground with the bottom of the foot pointed out while the toe is pointed forward. The bag is contacted by the shoelaces. The player's weight should be on the right part of the buttocks with the upper body in a flat position with the head up. Both hands and elbows should be kept off the ground (see figure 9.5). On a slide to the left side, the procedure is reversed.

Headfirst Slide

The headfirst slide allows the base runner to get to the base quicker than any other slide. The disadvantage of the headfirst slide is that it takes longer for the runner to come to her feet and continue on to the next base. I do not recommend sliding headfirst into a tag play at home when the catcher is blocking the plate or when attempting to break up a double play. The slide is not a dive or a leap, but rather should appear as if the runner were gliding on the top of water. Her arms should be stretched forward with a slight bend in the elbows and the head should be up to see the base. Her legs, chest, and arms are all in one parallel plane to the ground. Contact with the ground is made with

Figure 9.3 Bent leg slide.

a   b

Figure 9.4a-b   Pop-up slide: sliding with the weight on the bent lower leg (a) and straightening the extended leg to stand up quickly (b).

Figure 9.5   Hook slide.

the forearms, chest, and thighs, all at the same time (see figure 9.6).

THE FIRST RUN

So much of game strategy is designed to get the first run. We have to score at least one run to win any ball game. So my first intention on offense is to get that run. But I need to know when it is a good time to take a risk and when it is a good time to play it safe. For instance, if I have the leadoff batter on base and she is one of our quicker players, I might choose to have her steal second, rather than use a sacrifice bunt. This is a slightly higher risk play, but I feel it leaves a greater opportunity for our team to score because we now have a runner in scoring position with no outs instead of one out. A little later in this chapter we will look at a comparison of the steal and the sacrifice bunt.

Figure 9.6 Headfirst slide.

Once we get that runner in scoring position we believe we can increase our chances of winning by continuing to pose a threat to the defense. The best way to do that is to put the ball into play. Making contact makes things happen by making the defense handle the ball. We teach our batters to go with the pitch and to become efficient slappers. The more contact, the more plays, and the more likely the defense will be to make a mistake. I often call upon my batters to hit a ground ball in the slot with a runner on third. When the batter takes a full swing, the infielders tend to stay back and we can score on the pitch. In a situation like this, I have to trust my batter to execute, and if she is successful we are rewarded with a run. After we have the first run, we work on the second by continuing to put the ball in play.

I have heard the statistic that the home team (the one with last bats) wins 55 percent of the time. This is true because when you come to bat in the bottom of the seventh inning you know exactly how many runs you must score to win the game.

If the game is tied or if I am ahead by one run and I am heading into the last three innings, I play for one run. By this I mean I move a runner into scoring position at the expense of an out. In the later innings, a two-run lead forces the opponent to score three to win.

Regardless of whether we are home or away I want us to score first and to maintain the lead. However, I do not gamble by trying to be too aggressive on the bases and have the first potential run thrown out at third or home.

GOING TO FIRST

Baserunning starts with the crack of the bat, and upon contact with the ball, the hitter must not concern herself with where she has hit it. She must use the first five or six steps to build up acceleration. She needs to stay low out of the box and sneak a peek over her left shoulder a few steps down the line. That peek allows her to find out if she will be rounding first base or running through it. This is done by tilting the head slightly toward the infield without slowing down. After picking up the flight of the ball, the runner must direct her attention to the bag itself.

I instruct the base runner to make the decision as to whether to check the coach before going to second base or not by the position of the hit. On anything hit up the middle and over to the right-field foul line, the runner makes her own decision. On anything hit to the third-base side of the shortstop, she must look to the first-base coach. This strategy allows the runner to react on her own without losing a step. When necessary, the coach should communicate visually and vocally to the runner whether she should run through the base, take a turn, or go for second base.

Every sure single must be considered a possible double. The runner must make the defense stop her in her effort to get to second base. Only when the defense makes the play does the runner go back to first base. There are many advantages in being at second base, such as being able to score on a single and to avoid the double play. If a coach is going to allow the players the opportunity to make many of their base-path decisions, she must spend time discussing baserunning philosophy. Some factors the runner must concern herself with are her speed and the condition of the base path, the inning and the score of the game, the number of outs, who the hitter at the plate is, and who the defensive player throwing the ball is and the distance of the throw.

When the runner has reached first base and the play is over, she must immediately review the outs, the inning, the score, the hitter at the plate, and the location of the outfielders. She must pick up the signal from the third-base coach quickly and continue to do so after each pitch.

RUNNER AT FIRST

My first thought in this situation is to steal second if we can. It is my first choice if the runner is quick and the catcher is average, slightly above average, or below average. We do not steal second if the catcher is excellent. By teaching the runner to leave on the pitcher's heel release from the mound and to use a headfirst slide, I feel we can be at least 90 percent successful. After a stolen base our chance of scoring is very high.

If we want something less risky we consider the sacrifice bunt. We want the sacrifice bunter to square up on the sacrifice and to keep all options open. The batter needs to be able to read the defense and act accordingly. In practice we work on four types of bunts: the soft sacrifice, the push bunt, the slap, and the fake slap. If the middle infielders commit early and are playing back, a slap is very effective. If the corners are aggressive and charge, look to execute a push bunt. If the corners and middle infielders are at a regular depth, look to fake slap and bunt or hit away.

Fake and Delayed Steals

The fake steal will allow the coach to see how the middle infielders react when the runner makes a break for second base. If he sees one or both of them shifting their position toward second, then they will be susceptible to the hit-and-run play. The fake steal might open up a hole for the batter if one or both of the middle infielders shift toward second base.

In the delayed steal the runner conceals her intent to steal and then breaks for the bag when the catcher throws the ball back to the pitcher or to the first baseman. The delayed steal is not a called play. I tell my team who I believe is a delayed steal threat. The player with good game sense, quick foot speed, and quick reaction is the one who is the delayed stealer. Those designated must study the pitcher and the catcher. A pitcher who looks lazy, does not pay attention to the runner on every pitch, or gets upset with her pitching or the umpiring is a likely candidate to steal on. The catcher who gets into a routine and throws the ball back to the pitcher with very little thought of the runner is also a candidate. I want my designated stealers to think about the delayed steal as soon as they reach first, second, or third base, but they must be students of the play and study the pitcher and catcher throughout the game to learn their rhythm. An aggressive catcher is also a candidate because she will try to pick off the runner at first. My runner can set up that play by appearing to be too far off the base on the leadoff, and when the catcher tries to pick her off, BOOM, she's gone.

Runner at First and a Fly Ball

Too many times we see base runners not being aggressive on fly balls to the outfield. If the outfielder drops the ball, the runner is not in a good position to advance to second and possibly third base. The runner should get well off first base when the ball is in the air and focus in on the outfielder. Once the ball is caught the runner makes eye contact with the outfielder, forcing her to throw to first base. A simple rule of thumb is this: The farther the runner is from the fly ball, the farther away from first base she should be. If the ball is hit very deep and there is the possibility of a tag and advancement to second base, the first base coach yells "Tag up" and then makes the decision to send the runner on the catch. The runner must tag up on any foul ball hit in the air and if other base runners are tagging up. At no time should the runner tag up on a fair ball when there is a question of the outfielder being able to make the catch. If the runner is tagging up, she is doing so with the intent to advance to second base or to make the defense think she is by faking and drawing a throw.

GOING TO SECOND

The runner leaving first base should be completely aware of where the softball is. As is the case with the runner rounding first base, I want the runner to make the decision whether to slide into second, round second, or go to third base. I want the runner to pick up the third-base coach when the ball is hit behind her or in a location where she cannot easily see it in play, for example, on

- any ball hit from right center to the right-field line,
- any ground ball hit behind the runner heading for second base, or
- a hit-and-run when the ball is hit behind the runner.

It is important that the runner pick up the coach's signal about 15 to 20 feet from second base. I find it helpful to do one of three things to signal the runner:

- Hold both arms high in the air to tell the runner to round the bag and find the ball
- Wave both arms in a circular pattern to bring the runner to third base
- Point at second base to let the runner know to take a turn but to stay near the base

RUNNER AT SECOND

As soon as the runner reaches second base, she must quickly review the outs, the inning, the depth of the outfielders, and the hitter at the plate. As soon as this is done, she should check the third-base coach for a sign and continue to check after each pitch. The runner should take an explosive jump off the base on each pitch, selling a stolen base attempt. It is important that the runner get a good jump and continue on only if she believes she was off on the pitch.

Second base is the "keystone": When we get there we must think about scoring. Can we steal third? I think this is the easiest base to steal for the following reasons: The catcher's vision and throw is blocked by the batter in the batter's box, the communication between the shortstop and third baseman on who is covering and when is very difficult, and the batter can decoy the third baseman and shortstop to confuse their coverage of third. I want to know if my runner can beat the shortstop to the base, if we can decoy the third baseman and pull her up with a fake bunt, if we can fake slap and freeze the shortstop, or if the shortstop cheats toward third base.

One option for us is to send the runner if she can beat the shortstop to the bag. I have the batter in her normal stance until the ball is nearly to the plate. She should then attempt a fake bunt at the last second by putting her bat over the ball as it crosses the strike zone. This will pull the third baseman in by a few steps and the base runner can beat the shortstop to third.

Another option, if we are going to steal and the shortstop is cheating toward third base, is to have the batter square to bunt to draw in the third baseman, and then pull back, swing, and miss. This will freeze the shortstop and the foot race to third is on. On the other hand, if the shortstop knows better than to freeze, she will try to cover third base and may overcommit. This is the time to hit the ball on the ground to the shortstop area because she will not be there; she is breaking to cover third. This is our slap-and-steal or our hit-and-run play.

Runner at Second and a Fly Ball

When reacting to a fly ball from second base, the runner must quickly decide whether or not to tag. Most of the time the decision will have to be made by the runner, but there are some general rules I teach. They are as follows:

- Tag up on any foul fly ball. If there is any doubt if the ball is fair or foul, treat it as being fair. If the ball is caught in foul territory, the runner will make the decision about advancing to third base.

- Tag up on all deep fly balls that are catchable in the outfield. Don't tag on second when there is any chance the ball will not be caught.

- On a fly ball that the outfielder has a play on the runner going to third base, make every effort to get to third base on the catch. However, with one out be more conservative as we don't want to make the third out at third base. If the runner decides she cannot tag and advance, she should get as far away from second as she can and still be able to return to the base if the outfielder makes a throw to second. If there is a possibility that the outfielder will not make the catch, the runner should never be tagging at the base.

- With runners at both second and third base or first, second, and third, and a routine fly ball is hit to the outfield, runners should tag if there is a chance the runner on third can score on the catch. On a throw to the plate, the runner on second will tag and advance to third. If the outfielder making the catch has no play on the runner from third, it is the decision of the runner on second to attempt to advance to third on the catch. If the runner on second sees that the runner on third is not going to tag on a catch, she must come down the base path toward third as far as possible to still be able to return to second if the play is made there.

Runner at Second and a Line Drive

After getting a good jump on the pitch, the runner at second will advance to third on any batted ball with two outs. The runner should never be doubled up unless the ball is a direct shot at the shortstop or second baseman.

Runner at Second and a Ground Ball

This represents one of the biggest decisions the runner must make and we spend a lot of time giving the runners the opportunity to tune their instincts. Here are some general rules to follow when there are less than two outs and the runner is not forced to advance.

- If the ball is hit behind the runner after her primary lead, she should be able to advance to third.

- If the ball is hit in front of the runner after her primary lead, she must stay balanced and advance only after the throw is made to first base. This delayed advancement is made only if the runner knows she can beat the return throw to third.

- On a ground ball going toward the shortstop, if the runner can get over the ball and put it behind her, she can continue to third. The runner's speed, the jump she gets, and the defensive ability of the shortstop must be taken into consideration on a ball hit in the area of the shortstop.

- When the runner has to go to third because of a force play, I encourage her to run directly toward the third baseman's glove or the shortstop's glove if she is covering third base.

GOING TO THIRD

The runner leaving second base is responsible for her actions until signaled to by the third-base coach. I like to move out of the coach's box toward the plate so that I can make good eye contact with the runner rounding third and to give myself a little more time to decide what I want the runner to do. If the ball is in front of the runner as she approaches third base, she can use her own judgment on whether or not to advance to the plate.

With a ball hit behind the runner, the third-base coach will be making all of the decisions on advancing to the plate, rounding the base and holding, or stopping at third. The runner should always think about scoring as she heads toward third, and then she can make the adjustment if held up. I use the following signs for the runner approaching third base:

- Waving one arm in a circular motion—I definitely want the runner to score on the play.

- Holding both arms high in the air—I am telling the runner I do not want her to score. I want her to aggressively round the base and then to find the ball as she continues with a shuffle step toward the plate. The runner needs to locate the ball after contacting third and now is responsible for the next decision.

- Yelling "Back"—I use this command when the runner has aggressively rounded the base and is heading for the plate. I yell "Back" and that conveys to the runner to immediately stop and return to third base. The runner must be prepared to dive back into the bag.

- Getting down on one knee and bringing both arms down toward the ground—I want the runner to slide; there is going to be a play made at third. The runner is responsible for finding the ball if it gets by the third baseman.

RUNNER AT THIRD

Once the runner reaches third, she must review the game situation, such as the outs, score, and inning. I review with the runner what I want her to do on various ground balls, fly balls, and passed balls. She must check for signs each time she returns to the base.

The runner should assume the catcher will make a play on her every time the catcher receives the pitch. When this happens, the runner should return to third inside the diamond to restrict the catcher's view and possibly cause the catcher to throw into her.

I always tell the runner it is her call on a passed ball or wild pitch. By this, I mean if she has a good lead and is leaning toward the plate and sees the ball get by the catcher, she decides whether she can beat the play to the plate.

As soon as I can, I tell the runner to stay on the bag on a fly and to take off on a fly blooper. I also let her know when to go on a ground ball in the slot, score on an error, or go on an instinct ground ball. An instinct ground ball is a ground ball that the runner believes she can score on, taking into consideration her speed, the speed of the ground ball, and the depth of the defense. With a fly blooper I say "Get off the bag, get off the bag" and we score when the ball hits the ground. When a ground ball is hit in the slot (the area between the corners and the pitcher), I want the runner to score. When there's an error,

I coach my runners to read the play and try to score. In the final analysis they use their instincts, and would score on a ground ball that pulls the corners way out of position or on a play in which the corners go down on the ground to field the ball. They may also be able to score on the throw from the third baseman to the first baseman.

The on-deck hitter is the coach of the runner trying to score. As soon as the ball is hit, she must position herself in a direct line with the runner attempting to score. She gives the same signs as the third-base coach: arms up and yelling "Up, up, up" or getting down on one knee and motioning with both hands to the ground and yelling "Hit it." Once she informs the runner to slide, she must stay with the signal even though the play might not develop. The on-deck hitter must be sure she is not too close to the plate where she might be struck by the ball.

Runner at Third and a Fly Ball

The runner must quickly respond from her lead to a fly ball beyond the infielders. I believe there is time for communication with the runner on fly balls and I follow these rules when reacting to fly balls:

• Foul ball—I want my runners to tag up on any foul ball hit in the air. If there is any doubt the ball might be fair, they should treat it as fair. If the ball is foul, I will have the runner watch the catch. As the ball is coming down toward the fielder, I will make the decision on whether to score or not. I will say "We're going to go" if I want them to score, or "Not going to go, draw the throw." When they're drawing the throw, I want them to go halfway down the line, keep balanced, and watch the throw coming to the plate. If the ball gets by the catcher they must read the play and decide to score or return to third.

• Routine or deep fly—The same cues are given as in the above situation. I want the runner watching the ball and leaving exactly as the ball touches the outfielder's glove on a possible play to the plate. I will send the runner if the fielder is moving either back or laterally on a routine fly ball.

• Short fly ball—The runner should not tag

up on a short fly or any other ball that looks like it will not be caught by the outfielder. When this type of hit is in the air, my cue is "Get off the bag." The only exception is if the infielder was going out toward the outfield and would be making the catch while running away from the plate. If this was the case, the runner should get back and tag since she might have a chance to score.

Runner at Third and a Line Drive

On a line drive with less than two outs, the runner must freeze when she sees it come off the bat. There is never any reason for a double play on a line drive with a runner at third unless the ball goes directly to the third baseman.

Runner at Third and a Ground Ball

When there is the possibility of a ground ball with less than two outs, I will tell the runner my gambling options prior to the ball being pitched. Depending on the situation I tell them any one of the following:

- Not going to go on a ground ball but draw the throw.
- Going on a ground ball in the slot.
- Going on any ground ball anywhere (we will do this if there is another runner on second base).
- Instinct ground ball (they will attempt to score if they see an error or any infielder falling while fielding the ball, or on a ground ball they got a great jump on, or on a slow ground ball).

Runners at Second and Third

We are going to send the runner to the plate on any ground ball to the infield. The runner at second must get to third base on the ground ball and the batter base runner, after reaching first, must quickly locate the ball and possibly get to second base. The runner on third will be going on any ground ball anywhere. By sending the runner to the plate this forces the infielders to field the ball and make a good throw under a lot of pressure, and the catcher must execute a good tag. If we are out at the plate, the worst that can happen is that we will have runners at first and third.

Suicide and Safety Squeeze

There are two types of bunts that attempt to score the runner from third, the safety squeeze and the suicide squeeze. On the safety squeeze the runner does not go until the ball is obviously going down toward the ground. This necessitates the runner waiting a split second to be sure the pitch was not missed or was popped up. I do not like to use the safety squeeze because I feel we reduce our chances of scoring the runner by the delay. I use the suicide squeeze.

In the suicide squeeze my runner is going on the pitch as if she were stealing home. I want her to "trust a strike," meaning for her to anticipate the ball going into the strike zone where the batter has a good chance of executing the bunt. If the runner sees the pitch going well out of the strike zone as she is breaking for the plate, this may give her the opportunity to scramble back if the ball is not contacted. It is a play to call only with the batters whose bat control you trust. I like to use it when the corners are playing a little deep and we have less than two outs with a solid bunter at the plate and an above average base runner.

The Big Bunter

We had a big, new secret weapon in 1996. We were a little short on pinch hitters, but the one we did have was six foot three and intimidating. The best part of it all was that we would bring her in the game with a runner at third. The opponents would see her and try to size her up for the at bat. We would have her take the first pitch as if she were going to hit. Then on the next pitch we would put on the squeeze play. We were over 90 percent successful with this play. Her size said big, but her touch was soft and accurate and scored runs.

Suicide Hit-and-Run

This is another play with the runner on third going on the pitch. The batter must execute a ground ball. This is a great play against a team that overplays a possible bunt or keeps their middle infielders slightly deep. The pressure is on the batter to put the ball on the ground.

SPECIAL PLAYS

We do not have trick plays in our offense. But there are times when the bats will go cold and we must create runs or manufacture an offense. The score, inning, batter, and base runner are all factors that will be considered when determining which of these plays to use.

First and Third

This is a play that often trades an out for a run. I send the runner from first to second at a full-speed run, selling a straight steal but stopping about 20 feet from second base. She will stop in a balanced position to see where the ball is. If the ball is at second base, I want her to quickly retreat and get into a rundown. If the ball has been cut off or was not thrown to second base, she will have the opportunity to continue to second. With the runner on third I call one of three plays: not going to go, but draw the throw; going on the throw "down" toward second; or going on the throw "through" to second.

On the first play, the runner on third gets a big jump forcing the catcher to pay attention to her and letting the runner steal second. On the second play, the runner on third is going to the plate on the catcher's throw down toward second base. The only question the runner on third has to ask is "Is the ball going past the pitcher?" If the ball goes back to the pitcher, the runner on third must scramble back to avoid getting picked off at third. This should give the runner on first the opportunity to get to second easily. The third play takes the most work for the runner at third base. She will attempt to score on the catcher's throw *to* second base. She is looking for the ball to go "through" the pitcher and "through" the cutoff person.

This has been a high percentage play for us.

The runner going to second must sell the steal and be able to stop in a balanced position. The runner on third must be familiar with the terminology and understand exactly what is expected on each of the options.

Hit-and-Run

This play would be better named "run-and-hit" because the runner is going on the pitch and the batter is looking to put the ball in play. I teach the batter to swing at a big strike while attempting to hit a hard ground ball. A big strike is any ball close to the strike zone. You can use this play when the runner is at any of the bases.

Push Bunt

On this play the batter will push a sacrifice bunt beyond the charging corners. The right-handed batter needs to direct an inside pitch toward the shortstop and an outside pitch toward the second baseman. The left-handed batter needs to direct an inside pitch toward the second baseman and an outside pitch toward the shortstop. This is a tremendous play to advance the runner and to get the batter base runner safe at first. I find this play very effective with the runner on second base as well as the one on first.

Sacrifice Bunt

On the sacrifice bunt we are giving up the batter in order to advance a runner or runners. It is important for the bunted ball not to be fielded by the catcher, and for it to be bunted toward the baselines on the ground. The pitch has got to be a strike when the bunt is on. An intelligent pitcher in a bunt situation will throw a high pitch. This is a difficult pitch to bunt, so the batter should either take the pitch for a strike or bunt the top of the ball. When the runner is advancing to third, I prefer to have the bunt directed toward the third baseman. If the batter makes the third baseman field the ball fair, the batter has done her job, as long as it is a soft bunt. However, a bunt down the first baseline will work just as well, as long as it is well placed and away from the catcher.

Slap-and-Steal

This play is very tough on the middle infielders, as it forces them to cover two bases at the same time. The shortstop must both cover second on a steal and field the ground ball. The second baseman must cover first on a possible bunt or cover second on a ground ball double play from the left side of the infield. On the slap-and-steal the runner goes on the pitch and the batter shows a bunt, but then slugs the ball on the ground. It is important for the batter to go with the pitch. For example, a left-handed batter would slap the outside pitch toward the shortstop. This is clearly a play that can advance the runner and possibly have the batter safe at first base.

Bunt-and-Steal

This is a play where we can advance the runner two bases on a bunted ball. In this play the batter is instructed to drop a soft bunt toward the third baseman, forcing her to field it. If the runner starts at first base, she will go to second on the bunt down and steal third on the infielder's throw to first base. This is an instinctive play where the runner rounds second base and picks up the action at third base. If the third baseman has fielded a soft bunt, the runner will have a good chance to get to third before the pitcher, catcher, or left fielder can cover the bag.

BASERUNNING DRILLS

All Bases

Purpose: To improve the mechanics of baserunning and the player's overall conditioning.

Procedure: Athletes are lined up at home plate. The head coach is in the third-base coaching box, and the assistant coach is in the first-base coaching box. The runner sprints to first base and jogs to home plate. Repeat one time. The runner sprints to second base and continues to round the bases by jogging to home plate. Repeat two times. The runner sprints to third base and jogs to home plate, repeating three times. Then the runner sprints from home to home.

Coach Communication

Purpose: To improve and familiarize the player's reaction to the coach's verbal cues.

Procedure: The team is divided into two groups. One of the groups is in a line at home plate and the other is in a line at second base. One coach is at first base and one coach is at third base. Upon a signal given by one of the coaches, the first person in each line runs to the base ahead of her. The runner looks to pick up the coach's physical and verbal cues on whether to stay at that base, advance, or any other baserunning situations. When both runners have finished their route, the next two runners will begin when given the signal. This sequence continues for as long as desired.

Independent Runner

Purpose: To allow the players to experience game-like baserunning situations at three different bases.

Procedure: All defensive positions are filled. There are base runners at home, first, and third. A coach is at home plate with a ball and the pitcher is on the mound with a ball. The pitcher pitches the ball to the catcher, the runners get their jumps, and when the ball hits the strike zone the assistant coach fungo hits her ball into the field of play. The runners track the batted ball and react accordingly. The defense can be instructed to play on any one of the runners. Each runner plays as if she is the only runner on the field.

Line Jogging

Purpose: To improve the player's speed.

Procedure: The team is divided into two groups. Each group forms a line with one player behind the other. The drill is conducted within the boundaries of the softball field. The first line of players starts to jog with equal distance between the players. Upon a signal given by the first person in line, the last player in line moves out of formation to the right and sprints to the front of the line. The sequence continues for as long as desired. When there is adequate room, the second line of players starts to jog.

Rabbit

Purpose: To improve the player's explosive power off of a base.

Procedure: Runner 1 is at first base, while runner 2 is 10 feet from first base and in the direction of second base. On the head coach's signal, runner 1 tries to catch runner 2 before runner 2 reaches second base.

SIGNS AND SIGNALS

I have always been the coach in the third-base coaching box and have initiated all offensive signals. It is the hitter's responsibility to pick up the third-base coach for a possible sign, as she walks to the batter's box. Once the ball is caught by the catcher, and while she is throwing it back to the pitcher, the batter must again pick up the coach for any signal. All base runners pick up the signals from the third-base coach right after the pitcher has received the ball back from the catcher. I do not want the runner to look at me while the ball is in flight in case of an overthrow. Therefore, the hitter looks at me prior to the base runner, which gives me a chance to establish eye contact with the hitter and then with the runner before flashing signs. This way I can give one quick set of signs to both players.

If a player needs to have the signs repeated, she gives the repeat sign by circling her hands in front of her body. When teaching the suicide squeeze bunt, I have the batter give a sign back and the runner acknowledge the sign so that all parties know the squeeze is on.

Our signals are learned and practiced as often as possible. We have the following:

- Suicide squeeze
- Slap-bunt or push bunt
- Sacrifice bunt or base-hit bunt
- Bunt-and-steal
- Steal
- Slap-and-steal
- Hit-and-run
- Repeat play
- Take off or clear
- Take
- Fake bunt and slap
- Swing and miss
- Swing away

We give an indicator first and then the signal. For example, touching my cheek is the indicator, and the sign that follows touching my cheek is the one to execute. If the play is on for the next pitch, I will give the repeat play sign. We also have a take off signal to tell all parties the play is off. Of course, my favorite signal is the home run hit! That signal can keep you successful for a very long time.

SUMMARY

In this chapter we reviewed ways to score runs. We looked at baserunning principles such as leads, tagging up, staying in the base path, and sliding. My ideal offense is one that can execute fundamentals correctly and under pressure. Keep these tips in mind when planning your offensive strategy:

- Don't underestimate the importance of the first run.
- Execute signs and signals to add to run production.
- Teach baserunners to know where the ball is at all times.
- There are three reasons to slide:
  - To reach the base going full speed
  - To avoid a tag at the base
  - To break up a double-play attempt
- Practice coach and player communication at practice so athletes are familiar with coaching cues.

Part IV

COACHING DEFENSE

Chapter 10

DEFENSIVE FUNDAMENTALS

Games are won because the defense prevents runs from scoring. The game can be won with one run on offense because the defense has held or prevented the opponent from scoring. Where the offense strives to create runs, the defense tries to thwart that creativity by making great plays of its own. We have all heard a player bemoan the fact that "she was robbed" because a defensive player made a great catch of a would-be hit, and we have all seen the double play end a run-scoring chance. The offense is full of schemes. That is why the defense must be polished and tight; it must be the one thing we do correctly 90 percent of the time. In this chapter we will look at what it takes to play each position on the field. Because of the importance of pitching, I have committed chapter 13 to the teaching of that position.

CONSTANTS: PITCHING AND DEFENSE

It takes a combination of hitting, pitching, and defense to win a ball game. Because in hitting we are successful at best three or four times out of 10, we will be failing 60 to 70 percent of the time. However, in defense, we are striving for a success ratio of over 90 percent. Thus, defense must be our constant strength. Defense and pitching are the two elements we can control. Softball and baseball are the only sports where you are on defense when you have the ball. It is true that offense wins games, but defense wins championships!

SOFTBALL: A GAME OF CATCH

Softball is a game where the defensive success relies on the players' abilities to throw the ball back and forth. The thrower must execute with accuracy, location, and speed. The receiver must execute catching the ball, positioning it for a throw or a tag, and preparing for another throw. This is simply a game of catch with pressure in the execution. Even at the Division I level we teach throwing skills all year long and throughout our players' careers. Throwing is an area that must not be undercoached and that is vital for the health and safety of the athlete and the success of the team. The coach must keep stressing the basics of the skill and correct any errors in technique immediately.

Basic Throwing Mechanics

A throw usually starts with a catch. We want our athletes to bring the ball to the cradle position at their chest. We then teach our athletes to grip the seams of the ball with their thumb and middle finger (see figure 10.1). If the index finger can catch hold of a seam, it adds to ball stability and control. The ball should be raised off of the palm and there should be an equal distance between each finger. The thrower now goes to the "star" position: The glove pocket opens toward the target along with the glove shoulder, and the right instep is in line with the target, which puts the body into a sideways position. When sideways, the athlete pulls the ball out of the glove and positions her arms like pendulums, throwing the lead elbow toward the target, as shown in figure 10.2. While keeping the angle of the back elbow, she raises the forearm. The back elbow should lead the arm right over the ear with the ball raised above the head. The ball should be pointed behind and the back of the hand should be pointing toward the target (see figure 10.3). She then pulls the arm through and releases. I teach a very complete follow-through with the throwing arm crossing the body and making contact with the opposite thigh, as shown in figure 10.4).

Maximizing Warm-Ups

During warm-ups similar position players throw with each other—that is, pitchers with pitchers, corners together, middle infielders together, and outfielders together. They are paired together because they make similar throws and it is

Figure 10.1   Gripping the ball for the throw.

Figure 10.2   Approaching the star position.

Figure 10.4   Completing the throw with a full follow-through.

Figure 10.3   The ball is positioned above the head.

easier for the coach to evaluate them. We throw for 12 minutes broken into four segments. For the first three minutes we are about 45 feet apart and work on a full range of motion. For the next three minutes we are about 60 feet apart and work toward a strong throw to a target. For the next three minutes we drop back to 75 feet and continue the full range of motion with a smooth delivery and complete follow-through. The last three minutes may take us to 90 feet apart or to 60 feet again, depending on the time in the season. (Early in the season we will return to 60 feet.) During these 12 minutes I work with each athlete, correcting form and technique.

POSITIONS

Each of the nine defensive positions requires special skills. I want the best nine defensive players on the field, knowing that each position requires different talents. Once I have selected each position, I use drills from chapter 11 to help the athlete improve.

Outfielders

An ideal outfielder must have

- speed and agility,
- a strong throwing arm, and
- the ability to anticipate and to get a jump on the ball.

The left fielder should be a right-handed thrower so that she can cover and throw balls that go down the left-field line. However, this is not the most important concern when placing the outfielders. The left fielder has only one long throw to make and that is to the plate, so the left fielder should have the weakest arm. Since most hitters are right-handed, the left fielder will have fewer problems on balls that slice away from her. Other than the strength of their arms, the left and right fielders' fielding skills should be equal.

The center fielder should be the quickest since she has the most area to cover. She must be the most instinctive when reacting to the batted ball along with being the most aggressive. She should be the all-around best defensive player of the three. I believe I can sacrifice a powerful arm for an accurate one in my center fielder, but I do not want to sacrifice speed and the ability to get a jump on the ball. She is in charge of the outfield and makes the decisions on who should catch the ball. She should have first chance on catching every outfield ball.

The right fielder should preferably be a left-handed thrower so that she can cover and throw balls hit down the right-field foul line. The strength of her throwing arm must be the number one consideration since she will have two long throws to make, one to third base and one to home plate. The right fielder must be an experienced outfielder because balls hit by the right-handed batter will have a tendency to slice toward the foul line.

Standard Outfield Positioning

The outfielder's own ability is probably the number one factor in positioning in the outfield. In deciding where to play the hitter at the plate, the outfielder must take into consideration her own arm strength and ability to go left, right, up, or back. In a few cases the coach will move the outfielder if she feels the fielder is too far back or forward.

If the field has a deep fence, the outfielders need to play deeper to avoid a long run to the fence if a ball gets by. If the fence is short, the outfielder can play closer to the infielders. If the foul-line fence is very close to the line, the outfielder can play a few steps away from the line.

If the infielder in front of the outfielder can go back quickly on balls, then the outfielder can play a little deeper. Similarly, if the infielder has a difficult time going back on fly balls, the outfielder can position herself a few steps in.

Ready Position

The outfielder should be in a comfortable semicrouch stance with both arms out in front of the body and should rock forward on her toes on each pitch (see figure 10.5). She should catch fly balls above her chest just above eye level with both hands on the throwing side of the body.

Catching Balls on the Run

We want our players to pump their arms when they run and not to hold their glove out. This will enable them to run faster. They should run on their toes and keep their heels off the ground. It is critical for them to hustle for the fly ball and

Figure 10.5   An outfielder in ready position.

to wait for it to drop into their gloves. We have established drills that help the outfielder run back on fly balls without backpedaling, locate and touch the fence, and then come back to catch the ball. Communication with each other is critical; outfielders must call loudly and clearly where the other outfielder should throw the ball on plays to bases. We want the player to go all out to make the play on tough chances late in the game when it means stopping the winning or go-ahead run.

Fielding Ground Balls

The majority of errors made by outfielders occur on ground balls. This is why it is so important for the coach to spend adequate time on proper mechanics. The outfielder must attempt to field the ground ball on the high hop or short hop so they do not get caught between hops. By taking the proper angle the outfielder can keep the ball in front of her. There are four types of ground ball plays:

• Down and block—I teach the outfielder to go down on the knee opposite her throwing side and to field the ball with two hands in front of the body (see figure 10.6). It is important to block the ground ball when there are no runners on base, the play is made on a rough surface, it is not a gambling situation, and the throw after fielding will not result in a possible putout.

• Infield style—When a play might have to be made to the infield, I want the outfielder to field the ground ball like an infielder would (see figure 10.7). It is important that the outfielders realize that this style should be used only when the ball is not hit very hard.

• One-handed pickup—This style of fielding is only used in the late innings when the tying or go-ahead run is attempting to score. The ball is played in front of the glove foot in a scooping manner. Both knees must be bent to allow the upper body to get over the ball (see figure 10.8). The ball is fielded as the glove-side foot lands and then a step is taken toward the target. The outfielder then crow hops off the throwing-side foot. If in doubt about her ability to field the ball cleanly, the outfielder should field the ball infield style. This is an emergency play and should not be used unless absolutely necessary.

• In the gap or down the line—When two outfielders are in position to field a ground ball

Figure 10.6   An outfielder blocking the ground ball.

Figure 10.7   An outfielder fielding a grounder infield-style.

in the gap, the one in the best position for the throw should make the catch. When an outfielder is chasing a ball down the line, or is off balance when fielding the ball, she should first take the steps necessary to get balanced and under control before attempting to throw.

Figure 10.8   An outfielder fielding using the one-handed pickup.

Fielding Fly Balls

The proper technique to catch a routine fly ball involves the outfielder moving to the position where she believes the ball will land. I want her to "hurry" under it and then position herself to catch it. The proper position is one where she is behind the ball, her glove fingers are pointed up, and the catch is made about one foot above her head on her glove-shoulder side (see figure 10.9). The arms are away from the body and give a little on impact. Both hands are used for the catch and she must look the ball into the glove. I want the outfielder to get to the fly ball or line drive quickly and be in a position to make a strong and accurate throw.

On a ball hit over the outfielder's head she should utilize a drop-back step. For example, on balls hit back over her throwing shoulder, she would take a strong step with her right foot back toward the fence (if she is right-handed). This opens her hips for her next step to cross over, going toward the fence. She can then turn her back on the ball, check the flight path of the ball with one or two quick glances, and make the catch. As shown in figure 10.10, she must attempt to make the catch with two hands whenever possible and to position the glove away from the body.

Figure 10.9   Outfielder positioning correctly to catch a fly ball.

Diving for Balls

If the outfielder must leave her feet to catch a fly ball in front of her, she should use a bent-leg slide to keep the ball in front of her (see chapter 9). When catching a sinking line drive or soft hit, the outfielder should reach slightly for the ball. Most dive plays occur on short fly balls in front of the outfielder. I want the outfielder to attempt these dives because the ball will not go very far behind the outfielder if it is uncatchable. It is very risky for the side outfielders to attempt to dive after line drives between themselves and the foul lines. There is no backup if they do not come up with the ball.

The Outfielder's Throw

An outfielder must make a lot of overhand throws in practice because long throws for distance help build and strengthen the arm. On long relay

Figure 10.10   Outfielder using two hands to catch a ball hit over her head.

plays the outfielder must throw 60 percent of the distance because they are better prepared to throw long. Infielders shouldn't go out too far to try to make the long throw.

The outfielder should grip the ball with three fingers on the seam and throw with backspin, meaning the ball will spin off her fingers back towards her (in a clockwise direction if you were looking at it from the side). This will keep the ball in the air longer and carry it farther. The ball will also take a high bounce when landing, allowing the catcher or baseman to have an easier time at fielding the throw. It is important that the outfielder closes her throwing position to generate the force necessary for a long throw. This means to go from the star position to a complete shoulder and hip turn more quickly (see figures 10.11 and 10.12).

Catchers

An ideal catcher must possess

- a strong arm,
- quick feet,
- soft hands, and
- great agility.

The catcher plays one of the most important positions on the field. It is a specialty position as is the pitcher's. The role of catcher has many parts: physical skills, team leadership qualities, and the ability to be an emotional companion to the pitcher. All defensive plays initiate from the catcher, who gives signals and lays the foundation for a trusting relationship with the pitching staff. The catcher must encourage and nurture many different pitching personalities on a team.

The catcher has more jobs on the field than any other player. They include giving signals, receiving the ball, blocking bad pitches, throwing to bases, picking off runners, calling plays, handling force and tag plays at the plate, catching pop-ups, and fielding bunts. I describe these skills in more detail below:

- Basic stance—In the basic catching stance the feet should be about shoulder-width apart, with the right foot (for a right-handed catcher) one to two inches behind the left foot and the body weight distributed over the entire foot or toward the inside of the foot; the weight should never be completely on the heels or toes. With a runner on base the right foot should be three to four inches behind the left foot and more weight should be shifted to the balls of the feet

Figure 10.11   Outfielder preparing to throw.

Figure 10.12   Outfielder releasing the ball for the throw.

to allow for a quicker throw. The glove is semi-extended in front of the body, with the bare hand behind the right knee when no one is on base and behind the glove in an extremely relaxed position when there is a runner on base (see figure 10.13).

• Giving signals—When giving signals, usually to the pitcher, shortstop, or second baseman, the catcher assumes a comfortable stance with her trunk up and her head facing the pitcher. The right-handed catcher can rest her left forearm on her left thigh with the wrist held up at the top of the knee. Her glove rests gently along the knee with the pocket facing the other knee so as to hide the signals from the opposing coach at third base. I like the catcher to signal the second baseman for a pickoff at second or at first, as well as signal the first baseman for the pickoff at first and the shortstop for a pickoff at third. I will call the play as well for any pickoffs and the first and third play.

• Receiving the ball—The catcher must catch the ball firmly with the arms and hands away

Figure 10.13   Basic catching stance.

from the body and let the ball come to her with a relaxed semi-extended glove. She should hold the ball in the strike zone for the umpire to see. I also want the catcher to frame the pitch, which involves keeping the borderline pitch within the strike zone. To frame an inside pitch on a right-handed batter, the catcher receives the pitch and turns her glove in toward the plate (clockwise). To frame a pitch at the top of the strike zone, the catcher receives the pitch and curls her glove down toward the plate. On a low pitch the catcher receives the ball and curls her hand up toward the strike zone. On an outside pitch the catcher receives the ball and quickly slides the glove into the strike zone.

• Shifting techniques—When the ball is just out of the strike zone, the catcher must move the hips, legs, and arms, but not the feet. When the ball is farther out of the strike zone, the catcher performs a single-step shift to the left or the right, pushing off in the direction of the ball, and supporting her weight with the opposite leg. When the ball is even farther out of the strike zone, she takes a full step in the direction of the ball and uses the opposite leg to push off the ground to shuffle her feet and transfer her

Figure 10.14 Keeping the ball in front of the body using the blocking position.

weight to shift in front of the ball. When the ball is in the dirt, the pitch must be blocked, not caught, and kept in front of the body (see figure 10.14).

• Throwing to bases—I want the catcher to release the ball with backspin, that is, a spin that moves from the top of the ball to the bottom of the ball back toward the throwing hand. The glove must be brought back with the ball to the throwing position. The wrist should cock slightly back with the elbow bent at a 90-degree angle. The ball is thrown overhand and at the release point the left shoulder is pointing toward the target. The catcher should pivot and push off the right foot and stride in the direction of the target with the left foot (for right-handers).

• Calling plays—The catcher is in a great position on the field for calling the base for bunted balls fielded by the pitcher or the corners. She has the entire field in front of her and she should yell "One—One" and so forth depending on where the play should be made. Her communication is also vital on cutoff and relay plays. If she wants the throw to the plate to be cut, she would yell "Cut two" or "Cut three," for example. If she wants the ball to come to her, she would not say anything and prepare for the thrown ball.

• Force plays at the plate—In a force play with a chance of a double play at first, the catcher needs to position herself about one or two feet behind the plate facing the fielder and provide a clear target. Once the ball is thrown, the catcher moves forward and steps across the plate with her left foot and drags the right foot across the plate. As the foot drags she should jump pivot to face first base and make a throw. On a force play with no chance of a double play, she would position her body facing directly toward the fielder with the ball of her right foot located at the middle front corner of the plate. She should provide a clear target by holding both arms in the air and calling for the ball. If there are runners at other bases, she should fake the throw to first base, possibly allowing her a chance to pick off the runner.

• Tag plays at the plate—When the catcher has the ball, she must move her left foot to the left corner of the plate or further forward if she has time. Her left leg will be facing toward the runner and her chest should be resting against her thigh. To make the tag she should push the ball and the back of the mitt against the lowest

Figure 10.15   Catcher making a tag play.

part of the oncoming runner's leg, and transfer her weight forward as the tag is applied (see figure 10.15). She must not reach out to make the tag.

• Catching pop-ups—Generally with a right-handed batter a popped-up inside pitch will move to the catcher's left and an outside pitch will move to the catcher's right. She should remove her mask and hold it in her right hand while slowly scanning the sky. As soon as the catcher finds the ball, she should toss the mask in the opposite direction, away from the ball (see figure 10.16a). I want the catcher to be on the balls of her feet and to catch every pop-up with two hands at eye level, with the fingers pointing up (see figure 10.16b).

• Fielding bunts—As figures 10.17a-c show, the catcher should spring out quickly and throw the mask in the opposite direction from where the ball is. She should field the ball with her chest right over the ball, picking it up with a scooping motion if it is moving and bare-handed if it is stationary. The catcher should bend her knees to get to the ball and step in the direction of the throw after fielding the bunted ball.

• Pitchouts—The catcher should call for the pitch at chest height about a foot off the plate and assume a target toward the outside corner of the plate. While staying in a low position with bent knees, she brings her left foot to the right

foot spot and steps out with the right foot (if the batter is right-handed). For a left-handed batter, the catcher reverses the feet.

• Intentional walks—In an intentional walk the catcher stands up and reaches straight out with the right hand. Upon release of the ball the catcher must quickly bend her knees and move the left foot to the right foot spot and then move the right foot directly out to receive the ball.

CATCHER'S DRILLS

Pop-Ups

Purpose: To allow the catcher to work on pop-ups behind her, in front of her, and to her sides.

Procedure: The catcher assumes her position at the plate in full gear and a helper stands behind her where the umpire would be. The helper yells "Up" and throws a pop-up to various positions in foul and fair territory. The catcher must locate the ball and then throw her mask in the opposite direction of the ball.

Coaching point: A more advanced technique would be to have the helper fungo hit the pop-ups to give the true spin on the ball.

a   b

Figure 10.16a-b   When catching a pop-up, the catcher first finds the ball and throws her mask in the opposite direction (a), then makes the catch with both hands (b).

Balls in the Dirt

Purpose: To teach the catcher how to move to block pitched balls in the dirt.

Procedure: A simulated batter is in the batter's box and a helper simulates a pitched ball to the catcher's left and right.

Coaching point: First, pitch all of the balls to one side, then pitch all of the balls to the opposite side, and then pitch all of the balls down the middle. Finally, mix the pitch location.

Close Plays at the Plate

Purpose: To allow the catcher to practice thrown balls to the plate with a runner scoring.

Procedure: One player simulates a runner trying to score while another helper throws one-

and two-hoppers toward the plate. The catcher makes the catch and the tag.

Coaching point: Be sure that the timing is exactly like the game, where the ball and runner arrive at nearly the same time.

Stolen Bases

Purpose: To allow the catcher to throw to second and third base, simulating stolen base attempts.

Procedure: There is a simulated batter in the batter's box and a helper throws underhand to the catcher and a helper is at second or third base. The catcher is in full gear and receives the pitched ball and throws to second or third base.

Coaching point: Be sure the catcher executes proper footwork and arm action.

Figure 10.17 a-c   Catcher fielding the bunt: scooping up the bunt (a), beginning the throw (b), and following through after the throw (c).

Fielding Bunts

Purpose: To simulate game conditions while fielding bunts down the first and third baselines.

Procedure: The catcher assumes her position behind the plate with full gear. A helper is at first base and a helper is behind the catcher with softballs (where the umpire would stand). The helper rolls a ball out for the catcher to field and throw to first or third (see figure 10.18).

Coaching point: Be sure the balls are rolled out the normal distance a bunted ball would be hit. The catcher needs to practice removing and throwing the mask, along with proper footwork.

Figure 10.18   Fielding bunts drill.

Infielders

The four infielders must be united and work as a unit throughout the game. They hustle in and out together, keep track of each other's gloves in the dugout, and constantly communicate at the pitcher's circle and at their positions. They are the only ones who throw the ball around after an out and actually go into the pitcher's circle to talk with her during the game. They communicate with each other about outs, speed of the runners on base, the situation, and the plays. A team is as strong as the infield unit and there is no place for a weak player. Even if the players do not like each other, they must respect the talent on the field and be united. I look for infielders who all have solid skills. Please see chapter 11 for specific defensive drills.

The First Baseman

Some attributes of the first baseman are

- flexibility and athleticism;
- being tall and left-handed;
- the ability to make accurate throws to second and third base, even if she doesn't have the best arm on the infield;
- quick feet;
- soft, quick hands; and
- agility.

The first baseman's stance should be a low fielding position with the glove close to the ground facing the batter. Her weight is on the balls of her feet with her knees flexed, and her arms are extended out in front of her body. The basic footwork in covering the bag has her finding the ball and then moving to her right (toward her right shoulder) to find the bag, executing a drop step. She would then turn to face the throw and present the biggest target possible by having both shoulders squared toward the thrower. Her foot on the bag is opposite her glove hand and she touches the corner of the base with her full instep. She should not stretch until after the ball is thrown and she can judge its path.

The first baseman must prepare to field all balls hit without deflecting any ground balls. On balls to her right her range involves one step and a crossover step. Anything out farther is fielded by the second baseman. She can call for any ground ball; communication with the second baseman is important.

On a double play ball, the easiest play is to shift the feet and throw to second base. Shifting the feet gives power to the throw. The left-handed first baseman fields the ground ball, puts her weight on her left foot, and steps toward the target with her right foot. The right-handed first baseman places her weight on her right foot and steps with her left foot to the target. A tougher play would involve stepping on first base first and then throwing to second base. Of course, this play necessitates a tag by the shortstop.

The Second Baseman

It is very important that the player assigned to play second base be a very consistent infielder with quick feet, good hands, and a quick release. She must have an accurate throwing arm with good range, and she must have the skill to knock down every ball hit hard at her or to her left. The

second baseman should possess

- good range,
- quick hands and feet,
- a keen understanding of bunt coverage, and
- leadership skills.

The second baseman will possess the same physical qualities as the shortstop, with the only difference in the strength of her arm. The stronger arm would be at shortstop because of the long throw across the infield. But even if the second baseman does not have a strong arm, a quick release is critical. The second baseman will be involved in a lot of the defensive plays. She covers both first and second base.

The second baseman does not cover for stolen bases, but positions herself to back up the throw down to second, and she is utilized to pick off runners at first and second base.

I teach two footwork patterns to turn the double play at second. If the second baseman can get to second with a little time to spare, she will step over the bag with her right foot (with her heel about two inches away from the base). The right foot should land on the ground just as the ball touches her glove. As she transfers the ball to the throwing hand, she drags her left foot over the base and then plants it in a direct line toward first base.

If the second baseman arrives at second at the same time as the ball, she steps on the base with her right foot as she catches the ball. Her left foot then lands in a direct line with first base as the ball is released (see figures 10.19a-b).

The Third Baseman

The third baseman should have

- aggressiveness and athleticism,
- good anticipation for the ball,
- very quick reactions with soft hands,
- the ability to charge forward,
- a strong arm, and
- fearlessness.

a

b

Figure 10.19 a-b   The second baseman turning the double play: second baseman first steps on the base with her right foot as she catches the ball (a), then brings her left foot in line with first base as she throws (b).

The third baseman is keeper of the infield's "hot corner." She must handle everything from sharply hit line drives and short hops to slow-rolling bunts. The third baseman plays far enough in toward the batter to retrieve bunts, but not so far in that she cannot get back to cover the bag when necessary. The location, toward and away from home plate, is a compromise between two conflicting factors. First, the farther the third baseman is from home plate, the longer it will take for a batted ball to reach her, but the more time she will have to react to it and catch it. On the other hand, the farther back she is, the greater her vulnerability to a bunt or a slow roller, and the greater need of a strong arm. The distance she plays from the foul line is fixed to some extent by the baseman's speed, lateral movement, and ability to make a backhand catch.

The third baseman must be quick and have the ability to position her body in front of hard hit balls. She must be able to respond quickly and throw with speed and accuracy from a wide variety of set and off-balanced positions.

Protecting against stolen bases is a shared responsibility with the shortstop. I have the third baseman cover third on batter swings. If the batter swings and misses, the third baseman must get back. If the batter fakes a slap bunt, the third baseman must get back.

The Shortstop

The ideal shortstop should have

- great athletic ability,
- quick reactions,
- a strong arm,
- leadership skills, and
- a consistent glove.

This position should be assigned to your best right-handed athlete. She should have the strongest arm in the infield as well as possess great range and quick reactions. She must be a take-charge player with solid leadership skills. She must be the most consistent glove player, for the ball will touch her glove more than any other defensive player's besides the catcher, the pitcher, and the first baseman. I am willing to sacrifice some offense at this position if I have the player who can play this position well.

I have the shortstop cover second base on all stolen base attempts and on a first and third double steal. The shortstop will cover third on a stolen base there if the batter shows bunt.

The shortstop will cover second on all force plays that are thrown from the right side of the infield, the catcher, and the pitcher. If a pitcher is attempting to field a batted ball off of her right side, the shortstop will be in the backup position and will not cover second.

The shortstop's pivot at second base for a double play will include one of two patterns depending on the location of the other infielder making the play. If the throw is coming from the inside of the base path, the shortstop will hit the base with her left foot. She will then step onto the right foot a little off the line toward first base and then complete the play by stepping and throwing off of her left foot.

If the throw is coming from the outside of the base path—for example, a throw from the second baseman playing deep—the shortstop would receive the throw on the outside of the base. In this play, she would step behind the base with the left foot as she makes the catch, slide her right foot across the base, plant the right foot, and complete the throw (see figures 10.20a-b). She can eliminate steps by throwing right off the bag: She steps on the base with the right foot and then throws off the left foot step. I recommend that the shortstop try to get on the inside on all plays, if at all possible.

Basic Infield Plays

Some defensive plays are the same for all infielders. These include the ready position, ground balls, emergency plays, fake throws, going back on fly balls, intentional walks, and tag plays at the bases.

Ready Position

We teach an explosive ready position with the weight on the balls of the feet and the back straight. The corners have their gloves nearly on the ground while the middle infielders have their gloves slightly higher. The feet are squared and more than shoulder-width apart (see figure 10.21).

Fielding a Ground Ball

Infielders should get in front on every ground ball and only use backhands and forehands as

a

b

Figure 10.20 a-b The shortstop turning the double play: shortstop steps behind second base with her left foot as she makes the catch (a), then slides her right foot across the base, plants it, and completes the throw to first (b).

Figure 10.21 Infielder in ready position.

Figure 10.22 Infielder fielding grounder with arms in the "shovel out" position.

emergency plays. Their arms are in an L position, ready to run, and their heads stay at the same level as they move to field the ground ball. I want them to field the ball with their feet aligned and to have their hands scoop or shovel out in front (see figure 10.22). Both arms look identical with a slight flex at the elbows. When catching the ball the throwing hand goes on top and the ball is brought to the cradle position below the chest with the back of the glove up. Give your athletes these tips to keep in mind:

- Move down to the ball.
- Widen your starting position, staying on the balls of your feet.
- Position your feet wide apart when the ball is hugging the ground. If the ball hops, move your feet closer together.
- Point your knees out.
- Move your bottom down with the knee bend.
- Position your glove past an imaginary line from your forehead to the ground.
- Use a shovel movement.
- Position your forehead over the ball.

Emergency Plays: Forehand and Backhand

Emergency plays are ones that necessitate the fielder using only one hand to field the ball as she is moving to her left or right. I teach our players how to use these plays, but they are not to use them unless absolutely necessary.

- Forehand—The emergency forehand is used to field a ground ball to the fielder's glove side (see figures 10.23a-b). This is a play where she is unable to get both hands on the ball. The mark of a good infielder is one where she can range to her glove side, make the pickup and regain balance to make an on-target throw.

To field the ball on her forehand side, the right-handed infielder crosses over with her right foot in the direction of the ball. She must stay low and run on the balls of her feet. Keeping the head down and staying in low running form will allow the infielder to make a play without the ball going under the glove. The angle she takes to the ball is important so as to allow her the best possible hop. However, the deeper the angle, the longer the throw.

The glove should be carried in a running position to get the most drive from her arms.

a   b

Figure 10.23 a-b The emergency forehand. When fielding on the forehand side the infielder will stay low and drive for the ball (a), then field the ball with the glove leg in front, with her weight on the ball of her foot (b).

She should pump her arms as she runs to the ball just as she would in a sprint. The infielder must still try to field the ball with two hands and then bring the ball and glove up to the cradle position quickly. The infielder should always attempt to straighten her body, step in the direction of her throw, and raise her elbow up as she releases the ball. She should make the throw off her right foot to enable a more accurate and strong throw to first base.

• Backhand—The emergency backhand is used to field a ground ball to the throwing hand side (see figures 10.24 a-d). This play can prove very difficult unless proper mechanics are used. For the backhand, the fielder runs in the direction of the ball while pumping both arms. The infielder must become adept at cutting the ball off at the sharpest angle so that she can shorten the distance of her throw to the target. The infielder needs to cross over with her left foot while carrying the glove low. Once she sees that her best play on the grounder will be a backhand play, she must get her body under control. She needs to bend at both the knees and the waist as she extends her glove so that the upper part of her body goes to full extension. She must be sure to keep her head steady and her eyes on the ball.

The ball should be fielded about 8 to 12 inches in front of the glove-hand-side foot with the elbow of the glove arm slightly bent. The glove must be opened fully exposing the entire pocket of the glove to the ball. As soon as the ball is in the glove, the infielder brings the glove up quickly to her throwing side shoulder where her bare hand grips the ball for the throw. When fielding the ball with the left foot forward, the infielder must take another step with the right foot. As she catches the ball, she must take a short extra step with the right foot in the direction that her momentum is taking her. This will allow her time to bring the ball up to the throwing position. Once she plants her right foot, the fielder brings the ball and glove up for the throw.

• Dives—Infielders may also occasionally have to dive to stop a hard hit grounder or line drive. The infielder will leave her feet for a ball in an emergency situation, like when she cannot backhand or forehand the hit ball. A dive by the corner infielders is reactionary, while a dive by the middle infielders permits them more time to set an angle. For all infielders, diving to their right necessitates a pivot and push off their right foot, driving their bodies horizontally with full extension of their gloves (see figure 10.25). The nonglove hand helps cushion the landing. When diving to the left the pivot push-off occurs with the left foot. In either direction the object is to stay low and parallel to the ground with full glove extension.

Fake Throws

An infielder should fake a throw anytime she has no play on the batter base runner and there are other runners aboard. This is much better than just holding on to the softball and not taking advantage of an overaggressive runner rounding another base. The infielder should use a full overhand motion and grip the ball tightly.

Going Back on Fly Balls

We do not want the infielder drifting back on the fly ball; rather, we want her to go back full speed on any fly ball that she has to turn on so that she can get herself under control before the ball reaches the glove. As the ball hits the bat, the infielder executes a drop step going back. The angle of the step depends on the direction the ball has been hit. She must pump her arms and run on her toes in order to increase her quickness.

Intentional Walks

When the batter is being intentionally walked, the infielders should assume their regular positions in the infield in case the pitcher throws a pitch near the strike zone. The first baseman will move in 30 feet from the plate in case the pitched ball gets away from the catcher. The first baseman would then cover the plate. In this situation the pitcher does not cover the plate on the passed ball because the first baseman is positioned closer to the plate, so the first baseman is able to get there faster.

Tag Plays at the Bases

On tag plays at bases the infielder must concentrate on getting to the base as soon as possible. As she nears the base she must get her body under control by shortening her steps and lowering her center of gravity. Once the infielder is under control and set at the base, she must focus all of her attention on catching the ball

a

b

c

d

Figure 10.24a-d The emergency backhand. When fielding on the backhand side the infielder will cross-step (a) and stay bent at the waist as she moves to the ball with the glove opened fully (b). When the ball is in the glove the fielder takes another short step (c) and plants the foot for the throw (d).

and making the tag. As the ball is caught, both knees quickly flex. On close plays I recommend a sweep tag. This means that the infielder catches the ball and moves the glove and ball down to the tag area, and then pulls the glove away as the runner slides into the glove. On a hook slide or a headfirst slide, the infielder must stay with the runner and keep the tag on her because there is always the chance she will overslide the base.

The footwork for the shortstop or second

Figure 10.25 To make the diving catch the third baseman drives off the foot on the side of the ball and stays low and horizontal as she reaches for the ball.

baseman covering second base for a steal consists of an explosive crossover step in the direction of second base. As the infielder nears the base, she must start getting her body under control by shortening her steps and lowering her center of gravity. I like her to hook her left foot on the ground on the back corner of second base, and to have her right foot in front of the base as she fields the throw from the catcher. The infielder should allow the ball to come to her, rather than reaching for it. By having control of the back corner of the base, the infielder can easily reach out right or left for the ball thrown near the base and still maintain control of the base.

The footwork for the third baseman covering third for a steal involves a drop-back step with her left foot and a crossover step with her right foot as the catcher sets up to throw. She would then execute the same footwork as the middle infielders use in covering second base.

On tag plays involving a throw coming from the outfielder to second base, the footwork would be the following: On a ball thrown from right-center field to the right-field line, the middle infielder should control the home-plate side of the base with her right foot, with her left foot in a direct line with the throw on the outfield side of the base. On a ball thrown from the left-field foul line to left center, the infielder would con-

trol the right-field side of the base with her left foot and her right foot would be on the outfield side of the base in a line with the throw.

FLY BALL PRIORITY SYSTEM

Plays that make or break a team are fly balls that drop between fielders when the play should have been made. The communication for this play must be taught and practiced throughout the season. Here is a list of principles that work.

- Break full speed to the ball—do not drift.
- Call for the ball on its downward flight.
- Yell "Mine" when you are absolutely sure you can make the play.
- Once a fielder yells "Mine" all other players in the area call the fielder's name.
- Once a fielder yells "Mine" all other players must clear the area.
- When going for a fly ball, do not look for other fielders.
- Never command another fielder to take a fly ball.
- Just because one fielder calls for the ball does not mean that she should be allowed to catch it. For example, an outfielder coming in on a fly ball would have the right

Figure 10.26 Fly Ball Priority System

Position	Has priority over	Has no priority over
Pitcher	No one	Catcher and infielders
Catcher	Pitcher	First and third basemen
First baseman	Pitcher and catcher	Second baseman and right fielder
Second baseman	Pitcher and first baseman	Shortstop and all outfielders
Third baseman	Pitcher, catcher, and first baseman	Shortstop and left fielder
Shortstop	Pitcher and all infielders	All outfielders
Left fielder	All infielders	Center fielder
Center fielder	All infielders and all other outfielders	No one
Right fielder	All infielders	Center fielder

of way, even if an infielder called for it first.

- When no communication is heard, it means no one thinks she can catch the ball. There is still the chance of a diving catch and the fielder should yell "Mine" before the dive.

When two or more players have a play on a fly ball, one player must have priority in fielding it. Figure 10.26 is a chart we use to show the responsibilities of each player on the team, listing who does and does not have priority over a fly ball. This system takes a little practice, but when taught correctly the danger of a collision is greatly reduced and more balls will be caught.

SUMMARY

When the defense takes the field, it is their territory to defend. Proper execution and teamwork can prevent runs from scoring. In this chapter we learned:

- To strive for a success ratio of over 90 percent.
- To correct any technical errors in your athlete's throw immediately.
- To maximize your throwing warm-ups by pairing like positions together.
- An ideal outfielder has speed, agility, a strong throwing arm, and the ability to anticipate.
- The catcher has more jobs on the field than any other player—she must be sure to cover all of them.
- The four infielders must be united—they should be able to be vocal and respect each other's talents.
- Communication among the defense is crucial in all plays.

Chapter 11

TEACHING DEFENSIVE SKILLS

In this chapter you will find defensive drills that aid in developing defensive skills. This chapter will describe simple individual drills for two to nine players as well as other advanced individual drills. Let these drills be your formula for developing and implementing additional practice opportunities. They can be used in circuits or as stand-alone drills. Some of them involve throwing and some do not. This chapter also contains team drills that are both complex and advanced. Any of these drills can be done either inside or outside as weather permits.

I have also included discussions of the varying amounts of space needed to practice the drills and suggestions for the amount of time needed. The players run some drills themselves, thus freeing up the coaches to instruct and work one-on-one with athletes. Other drills are run by the coaches. For example, in many of the team drills in the last section of the chapter, there is a person labeled "CO" at several stations hitting balls and performing other duties. Each "CO" position could be filled by a coach, a manager, or an athlete who is unable to perform the drill, but can assist in the running of it.

Similar to chapter 8, this chapter starts off with a drill finder. This table will help you locate specific defensive drills quickly. The drill finder is organized by defensive skill—such as fielding flys, ground balls, or bunts—followed by the drills that include practice for that skill.

Fielding skill	Drill	Page
Fly balls in front of the fielder	Up and Back	140
	Outfield Loop	142
	Shoestring Catch	144
	Slant	144
	Outfield to Bases	146
	Team Drills #3, #4, #7, #9	149, 150, 151, 153
Fly balls to the fielder	Outfield Loop	142
	Sprint Relay	144
	Outfield to Bases	146
	Team Drills #3, #9	149, 153
Fly balls over the fielder	Up and Back	140
	Ball	141
	Grapevine	142
	Outfield Loop	142
	Outfield to Bases	146
	Team Drills #1, #2, #3, #8, #9	148, 149, 152, 153
Ground balls to the fielder	Partner Bucket	139
	Short Hop	139
	Soft Hands	139
	Three-Way Ground Balls	140
	Chimp and Champ	140
	Reaction Fielding	141
	Infield Loop	142
	Infield to Bases	145
	Infielders Work—Outfielders Run	145
	Team Drills #1, #4, #7	148, 150, 151
Ground balls to the side	Worker-Helper	140
	Triangular Ground Balls	140
	Range	143
	Infield to Bases	145
	Infielders Work—Outfielders Run	145
	Team Drills #2, #4, #5, #6, #11	148, 150, 151, 153
Fielding bunts	Team Drills #2, #3, #4, #5, #8	148, 149, 150, 152

(continued)

SIMPLE INDIVIDUAL DRILLS

These simple individual drills take up very little space and a lot of repetitions can occur in a small amount of time. I like to name the drills so that when it is time to do the drill the players understand what is expected. In this way, after the first teaching of the drill the coach can focus on teaching the skills and not the drills. Listed in each drill is the purpose, the number of players required, the procedure, the time allowed, and any variations.

DRILLS FOR TWO PLAYERS

Partner Bucket

Purpose: To field a lot of ground balls without a throw.

Procedure: One partner has a bat and a bucket of balls. The fielder has an empty bucket nearby. The fungo hitter hits all the balls to the fielder, who fields them and puts them in the bucket. They then switch positions. Partners stand at their normal fielding distance from the batter. For example, if one partner is a shortstop and one is a third baseman, the partners stand far-

ther apart when the shortstop is fielding and closer when the third baseman is fielding.

Time allowed: 10 minutes

Short Hop

Purpose: To field balls on the short hop.

Procedure: Partners stand 30 feet apart with one ball and throw one-hop ground balls to each other. The ball should be thrown in a sidearm style with the ball bouncing once close to the fielder.

Variation: Use a pitching machine set at 40 feet and pitch softies at fielders.

Time allowed: 5 minutes

Soft Hands

Purpose: To field short hops with soft hands.

Procedure: Partners wearing paddles on their hands stand 30 feet apart and they throw one-hoppers back and forth. They need to use "soft hands" to field the ball and bring it to the cradle or heart position. Use a softer ball to start.

Variation: Use a real softball.

Time allowed: 5 minutes

Up and Back

Purpose: To practice footwork and glove work for balls hit over the player's head or balls dropping in front of the player.

Procedure: Partners stand 30 feet apart with one ball. One player is the worker and the other is the helper. The helper starts by throwing a shoestring-catch ball for the worker. The worker charges in, fields the ball, and throws it back. The worker then breaks back and the helper throws a ball that the worker has to catch while running back. The worker makes the catch, throws it to the helper, and charges in. The helper continues the drill, throwing balls up and then back. Let the worker work until a certain amount of time has elapsed or until a certain number of plays have been completed, then rotate.

Time allowed: 5 minutes

Worker-Helper

Purpose: To field a lot of ground balls in a short amount of time.

Procedure: Partners stand 30 feet apart. The helper rolls balls to either side of the worker, who fields the ball and throws it back. Let the worker work until a certain amount of time has elapsed or a certain number of plays have been completed, then rotate.

Time allowed: 5 minutes

DRILLS FOR THREE PLAYERS

Three-Way Ground Balls

Purpose: To field ground balls off a bat.

Procedure: The fungo hitter stands next to a receiver and the fielder positions herself at her normal fielding distance from the hitter. A bat and balls are needed. The fungo hitter hits five ground balls to the fielder, who throws to the receiver. The players rotate so the receiver becomes the hitter, the hitter becomes the fielder, and the fielder becomes the receiver.

Variation: Fielder works until she makes five perfect plays.

Time allowed: 10 minutes

Triangular Ground Balls

Purpose: To practice fielding emergency forehands and backhands.

Procedure: Three players stand 30 feet apart forming a box with a missing corner (see figure 11.1). One player is the fielder and she stands next to the open corner. The other two players are throwers and stand next to each other with a ball each. The thrower opposite the open corner rolls the ball to that spot. The fielder moves over, fields the ball, and throws it back. When the fielder releases the ball, the second thrower rolls the ball to the open corner, and the fielder moves over to field it and throw it back. Continue moving the fielder from side to side until 10 plays are made. Players switch positions so that they are at each of the three stations.

Time allowed: 5 minutes

Figure 11.1   Triangular Ground Balls.

DRILLS FOR FOUR PLAYERS

Chimp and Champ

Purpose: To field batted balls in competition.

Procedure: There is one hitter with two or three fielders in a line standing about 20 feet from her, and a receiver is standing next to her. The hitter hits a ground ball to the first one in line who throws it back to the receiver. The hitter continues hitting ground balls to the first player until an error is made. The fielder who commits the error replaces the receiver who replaces the hitter, who goes to the end of the fielding line and everyone moves up. The object is to be at the front of the line when the drill ends.

Variation: Game can continue the next day at the same places where the players finished.

Time allowed: 5-15 minutes

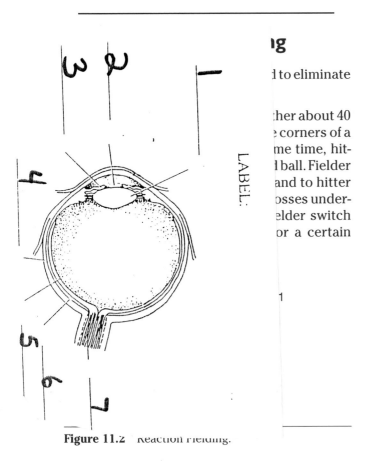

Figure 11.2   Reaction Fielding.

ADVANCED INDIVIDUAL DRILLS

The following eight drills focus on one player at a time as you have seen in the previous drills; however, now they become a little more challenging. There are more players involved in each of these drills and some take more time to learn than the simple drills. Again, once the drill is learned the coach can concentrate on teaching the skills involved.

Legend: In the diagrams in this section the following symbols are used:

Infielders	1B, 2B, 3B, SS
Outfielders	LF, CF, RF
Pitcher	P
Catcher	C
Coach	CO
Hitter	H
Receiver	R
Path of fielder	———
Path of throw	— — —
Path of batted ball	- - - - -

(To avoid confusion, the path of the batted ball has been omitted in many plays that also involve throws.)

Ball

Purpose: To improve players' confidence at turning, sprinting away from the ball, losing sight temporarily, and then finding the ball in flight while in a dead sprint and making the catch.

Number of players: 2-10

Procedure: The coach stands on the right side of a line of players and takes the ball from the first player in line and shouts "Go." The player sprints away from the coach without looking back or in the air. When she is about 15 to 30 feet away, the coach throws the ball at different angles and heights over the nearest shoulder of the player and out front. The coach then shouts "Ball." The player then looks up to find the ball in the air, making adjustments to make the catch with the glove in proper position. After making the catch, the player stays out and assists the next fielder by yelling "Hand" or "Glove" depending on the position of the ball. They both then take the balls they caught and sprint back to the end of the line. Next in line steps up and sprints away from the coach.

Variation: Throw higher flys initially, and gradually adjust and lower throws as players become adjusted to the drill.

Time allowed: 5 minutes

Grapevine

Purpose: To improve the footwork, concentration, and concentration, and catching ability of all fielders while they move in both directions.

Number of players: 2-10

Procedure: The coach stands about 10 feet in front of a line of players facing her and takes the ball from the first player in line. The coach points to the right. Player turns shoulder and hips to that side and runs perpendicular away from the coach. After about three or four steps, coach points in the other direction. Player, using the crossover step, turns the other direction, still running in a straight line away from the coach, never losing sight of the ball. After another three or four steps, coach points in original direction. Player then repeats previous crossover step and turns in original direction. Coach then throws a fly ball in the direction of the original point forcing the player to catch the ball by stretching over that side's shoulder. Player makes the catch and brings the ball back to the end of the line. It is important that the drill be executed full speed in a dead sprint, and that the player changes direction only when the coach makes the signal. Also, the player should never lose sight of the ball. The flys should be challenging and require a great deal of effort to make the catch. By the time the fielder has caught the ball, the next player in line has already set herself in the ready position.

Time allowed: 5 minutes

Infield Loop

Purpose: To field an assortment of ground balls and to field with different footwork positions. To throw to different bases and to condition.

Number of players: 4-8

Procedure: There are players at first and third, a ball in the pitching circle, and a player catching with a fungo hitter at the plate. One player works through all of the plays that follow (see figure 11.3).

1. A ground ball is hit to the third baseman who throws it to first base.

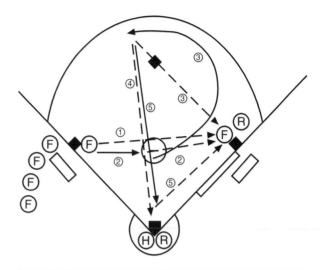

Figure 11.3   Infield Loop.

2. The player runs and picks up the ball in the circle and throws to first base.
3. The player then loops around second base toward the shortstop position and is hit a ground ball, which she throws to first base.
4. The player receives a ground ball at the shortstop position and throws it home.
5. The player charges the plate and the catcher rolls a bunt, which the fielder throws to first base.

After each player finishes she rotates to the next clockwise position. On-deck fielders wait their turn at third.

Variation: Begin at first base and throw the first three balls to third base. Reverse the loop so the batted ball is a backhand. The bunted ball is thrown to third base.

Time allowed: Each player gets five opportunities to go through the loop.

Outfield Loop

Purpose: To field an assortment of batted balls and to field with different footwork positions. To throw to different bases and to condition.

Number of players: 5-9

Procedure: Players are in left field and at second (with a ball) and third base, with a player catching and a fungo hitter at the plate. One player works through all the defensive plays that follow (see figure 11.4).

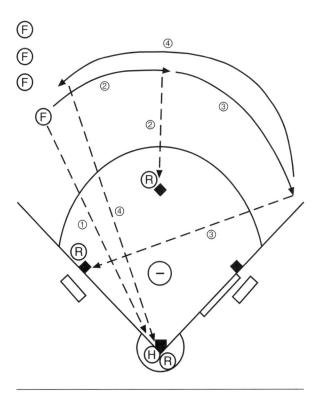

Figure 11.4   Outfield Loop.

1. A ground ball is hit to the left fielder who throws it home.
2. The left fielder runs into center field where the second baseman throws a fly ball. The player catches the fly and throws it to second base.
3. Then the player runs into right field where the second baseman throws a ground ball toward the foul line. The player fields the ball and throws to third base.
4. Lastly, the player runs to left field where the batter hits her a ground ball which is thrown home.

After the player completes the circuit, the outfielder becomes the catcher at home, the catcher rotates to third base, third base rotates to second base, and second base rotates to left field. Additional players are waiting their turns at the outfield position.

Variation: Begin in right field and reverse the loop.

Time allowed: Each player gets five opportunities to go through the loop.

Range

Purpose: To field forehands and backhands and to condition.

Number of players: 6-12

Procedure: Two fungo hitters stand diagonally opposite each other. One group of fielders stands single file facing one of the hitters, and another group of fielders forms a single-file line facing the other hitter (see figures 11.5a-b).

A and E go first

For A:

1. H1 hits a ground ball diagonally to the left.
2. A moves to the ball, fields it, and sprints toward H2.
3. A tosses the ball underhand to H2.
4. A sprints to the end of the opposite line.

For E:

1. H2 hits a ground ball diagonally to the left.
2. E moves to the ball, fields it, and sprints toward H1.
3. E tosses the ball underhand to H1.
4. E sprints to the end of the opposite line.

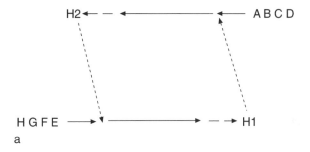

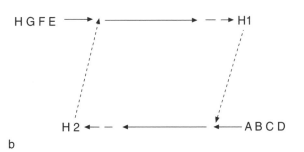

Figure 11.5 a-b   Range drill for the backhand (a) and forehand (b).

Variation: Have the hitters and fielders switch positions.

Time allowed: 10 minutes

Shoestring Catch

Purpose: To practice making diving and shoe-string catches.

Number of players: 2-10

Procedure: The players form three lines, standing about 60 feet from the coach. The lines are positioned about 20 feet apart. The coach has all the softballs. The first player in line A runs toward the coach. When she is about halfway to the coach, a soft underhand toss is made to the player's left, right, or straight ahead. If the player makes the diving catch, she should hold the ball up so the coach can see it. This will help the player remember to hold the ball up in games so the umpire can see that she caught the ball. The player attempts to make the catch, tosses the ball to the coach, and runs to the end of her line. The first player in line B then runs toward the coach and then the first player in line C.

Time allowed: 5 minutes

Slant

Purpose: To give outfielders practice at catching line drives and fly balls that tail away while in a dead sprint.

Number of players: 2-10

Procedure: Players line up in the center field gap and the coach stands with a bucket of balls on the foul line. Coach yells "Go" and a player sprints across the outfield toward second base, watching for the ball at all times. Coach then throws a variety of flys, grounders, and line drives just within the reach of the player. Upon catching the ball, the player tosses the ball back to the coach and starts a new line in front of second base. The next player in line takes off on command. Each player should get six to eight repetitions of the balls in each direction.

Variation: Coach throws varying types of flys and grounders.

Time allowed: 5 minutes

Sprint Relay

Purpose: To condition and to practice the relay pivot and long and short throws.

Number of players: 5-6

Procedure: Two players start on one end of the drill, two players start on the other end (about 80 feet apart), and one player starts in the center. The ball starts with F1 and each player makes a throw and follows her throw to the next position. The throw pattern is short, short, long. For example, F1 throws short to F2 and takes her place in the center of the drill. In the meantime, F4 steps up and takes F1's place. F2 throws short to F3 and takes F5's place. F3 throws long to F4 and takes her place, then F5 steps up to take F3's place. The drill starts again. Just remember to have your players follow their throws and sprint to the next spots (see figure 11.6).

Variation: Throw fly balls or ground balls to each other.

Time allowed: 5 minutes or 30 catches total

Figure 11.6   Sprint Relay.

COMPLEX TEAM DRILLS

A complex drill is elaborate and utilizes five or more players. The purpose of these drills is to give the players the opportunity to work together in game-like situations. It is important to thoroughly explain the drill and to tell the players the name you have given it so in subsequent practices the name will remind the players of what the drill entails. All of the drills in this section can be done outside or inside.

Bump Out

Purpose: To put game-like pressure on the infielder or the outfielder.

Number of players: Whatever the defensive drill chosen requires, plus one

Procedure: Set up for any of the defensive drills in this chapter. An additional player waits off to the side of the drill. When a fielder makes a throwing or fielding error, she leaves the drill and the player who is waiting replaces her. Every time an error is made the fielder steps out and the waiting player steps in.

Time allowed: Normal time for that defensive drill

Full Field in Between With Tennis Balls

Purpose: To practice communication among all outfielders handling in-between batted balls.

Number of players: 7

Procedure: All outfielders and infielders are at their positions. A fungo hitter is at the plate with a tennis racket and tennis balls. The fungo hitter hits balls into all sections of the field. Tennis balls are caught and thrown off to the sides of the field. All fielders need to stay focused on the hitter, as the hitter alternates hits to the left and right side of the field.

Variation: Use the pitching machine or hit real balls.

Time allowed: 10-15 minutes

Infield to Bases

In this drill the outfielders are used as fungo hitters and receivers. A hitter and a receiver are on either side of home plate. Directions must be specific on which pair of hitters is hitting to which pair of infielders (middle infielders or corners) so as to avoid any dangerous throws to receivers.

Purpose: To have all infielders field an assortment of batted balls and throw to all four bases.

Number of players: Minimum of 8

Procedure: Infielders are at their respective positions with two fungo hitters on opposite sides of the plate and two receivers next to them. The hitters hit four series (see figure 11.7). If there is more than one infielder per position, they alternate turns.

Series 1

1. The third baseman and first baseman work together for the play at first or third base.
2. The shortstop and second baseman work together for the play at second base.

Series 2

1. The third baseman and shortstop work together for the play at third base.
2. The second baseman and first baseman work together for the play at first base.

Series 3

1. The third baseman and second baseman work together for the play at second and third base.
2. The shortstop and first baseman work together for the play at second and first base.

Note. In series 3 use only one ball on the infield at a time as both groups are making throws to second base.

Series 4

1. The first baseman and second baseman throw home.
2. The third baseman and shortstop throw home.

Variation: Complete the double play to an additional player down the line of first base.

Time allowed: 5 minutes per series

Infielders Work—Outfielders Run

Purpose: To put the infielders in a game-like situation and to practice baserunning.

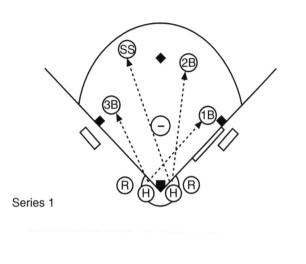

Series 1

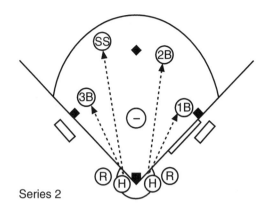

Series 2

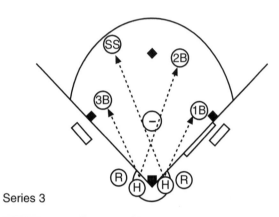

Series 3

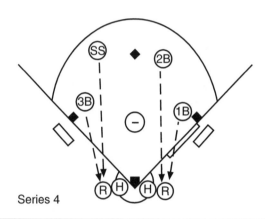

Series 4

Figure 11.7 Infield to Bases.

Number of players: All infielders plus the catcher, a fungo hitter at the plate, and base runners at home plate.

Procedure: The fungo hitter hits ground balls randomly around the infield and the infielders field the balls and make the appropriate plays. The base runners run to first until all runners are at first; then they run to second until all runners are at second; and so on.

Time allowed: 15 minutes

Outfield to Bases

Purpose: To field an assortment of batted balls and to throw to all four bases.

Number of players: Minimum of 9

Procedure: All outfielders are at their positions with two players at first, second, third, and/or home. These players are fungo hitters and receivers. The hitters hit four series of ground balls (see figure 11.8). Outfielders take turns in each field.

Series 1

1. The right fielder throws to first base.
2. The center fielder throws to second base.
3. The left fielder throws to third base.

Series 2

1. The right fielder throws to second base.
2. The center fielder throws to third base.
3. The left fielder throws home.

Series 3

1. The right fielder throws to third base.
2. The center fielder throws home.
3. The left fielder throws to first base.

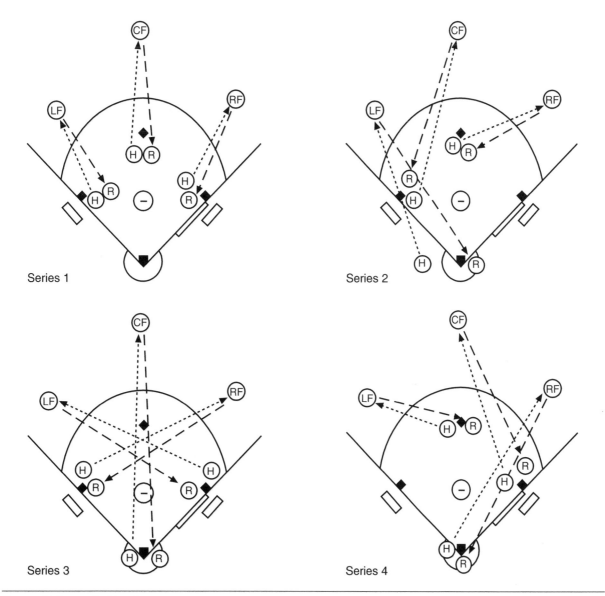

Figure 11.8   Outfield to Bases.

Series 4

1. The right fielder throws home.
2. The center fielder throws to first base.
3. The left fielder throws to second base.

Time allowed: Five throws to each base

Outfielders Work—Infielders Run

Purpose: To put the outfielders in a game-like situation and to practice baserunning.

Number of players: All outfielders, all catch-ers, necessary infielders, and additional players baserunning

Procedure: The outfielders are at their positions with a fungo hitter at the plate. There is a base runner at second base and one at home plate. The fungo hitter hits ground balls and fly balls randomly to the outfielders and they make the plays to throw home. A player or coach at third tells the runner "Go" or "Back," depending on if the runner can score.

Variation: Put a runner on third base and hit a fly ball.

Time allowed: 15 minutes

ADVANCED TEAM DRILLS

Advanced team drills are drills that have several groups of players working on various skills on different parts of the field. These drills also utilize all defensive players at the same time. For example, the catchers might be working on a play with the pitchers as the middle infielders are working on another play. The space required is a softball field. This series can be done indoors or outdoors and modified to meet your individual needs. A "CO" on the illustration shows where the coach should be in the drill.

Team Drill #1

Infielders and catchers

Purpose: To practice tag and force plays at the plate.

Procedure: The coach at home plate sets up situations and hits all types of ground balls to the infielders. Coach can set up every possible situation that can arise with a runner at third base. Catchers work on force plays and tag-play mechanics at the plate (see figure 11.9).

Pitchers

Purpose: To work on ground ball mechanics.

Procedure: Pitchers are in left field in pairs standing 40-43 feet apart facing their partner. One pitcher pitches to the other pitcher. She

catches the ball and throws a ground ball back. Pitcher fields the ball properly and fakes the throw to first base using the proper footwork. The pitcher now becomes the catcher and the catcher now is the pitcher. The ground ball should move the pitcher laterally as well.

Outfielders

Purpose: To work on fence communication and going back on a fly ball.

Procedure: Outfielders in right field alternate with one in right center yelling "Fence" when the other fielder is five or six strides away. Other outfielders are lined up about 70 feet from the fence. Manager or coach will throw a high fly ball near the fence with the outfielders alternating going after the ball properly. The coach or manager throwing the ball is positioned about 90 feet in front of the outfielder, who is in ready position to go back to the fence.

Team Drill #2

Catchers and first basemen

Purpose: To let catchers work on mechanics of fielding all types of bunts and throwing to first base.

Procedure: Catchers alternate fielding bunted balls with masks on. Bunt is thrown from behind the catcher. The first baseman should simulate a bunt situation by charging toward home plate until she reads catcher's ball, and then going back to cover first base (see figure 11.10).

Shortstops and second basemen

Purpose: To let middle infielders practice communicating on ground balls hit around second base.

Procedure: The coach or manager hits balls to either the shortstop or second baseman from a position about 20 feet from home plate so as not to interfere with catchers fielding bunts. There are no throws to first; fake the throw. If the middle infielder wants to make an unassisted double play she should yell "I've got it."

Third basemen

Purpose: To work on mechanics of fielding pop-ups around the fence area.

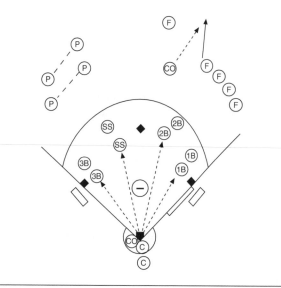

Figure 11.9 Team Drill #1.

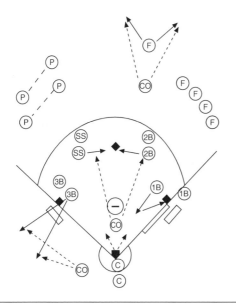

Figure 11.10 Team Drill #2.

Procedure: The coach stands near home plate and tosses flys to each fielder.

Outfielders

Purpose: To work on the mechanics of going back on fly balls.

Procedure: A coach or a manager throws balls over the outfielders' heads toward the outfield fence. The outfielder is about 70-90 feet from the coach and the same distance from the fence. The outfielder turns and goes back and finds the fence before making the catch.

Pitchers

Purpose: To work on ball spins.

Procedure: Pitchers pair up in left field and throw ball spins back and forth.

Team Drill #3

Pitchers and first basemen

Purpose: To work on communication when fielding bunts and ground balls.

Procedure: Coach hits ground balls or bunts to the first baseman or the pitcher from about five feet on the first-base side of home plate. The extra first baseman will cover first if the primary first baseman is fielding the ball or if the pitcher is fielding a bunt. This extra player is simulating

the second baseman's responsibilities (see figure 11.11).

Catchers and third basemen

Purpose: To work on bunt communication, along with the mechanics of fielding a bunted ball.

Procedure: The catchers alternate fielding bunted balls with their masks on. The bunt is thrown from behind the catcher and goes toward the third-base side of the diamond. The other third baseman covers third (would be the shortstop on a real play). Balls are fielded by both the catcher and the third baseman.

Outfielders, shortstops, and second basemen

Purpose: To let outfielders work on coming in on fly balls, while the middle infielders work on going back on the same fly balls.

Procedure: A coach or manager stands between second base and the pitcher's mound and attempts to throw fly balls in the area of the outfield where two or three players are attempting to make the play. The fielders go to the fly ball priority system and communicate with each other to make the catch. The coach is throwing the ball toward the "X" on the diagram. The fly ball priority system is discussed in detail in chapter 10.

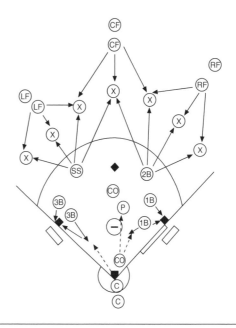

Figure 11.11 Team Drill #3.

Team Drill #4

Pitchers, first basemen, second basemen, and catchers

Purpose: To work on ground ball communication and backing up first base.

Procedure: The coach stands to the right side of home plate and hits ground balls from the mound to the right side of the infield. Catchers will alternate backing up the play at first base. The first baseman may occasionally intentionally miss the ball so the catcher can check herself on backup location. Balls can also be bunted for the catcher to field (see figure 11.12).

Shortstops and third basemen

Purpose: To work on communication during situational ground balls.

Procedure: The coach hits ground balls from the left side of home plate to the left side of the infield. Fungo hitter sets up the situation: possible force play at third or runner on second not forced to advance. Hitter tries to move the third baseman to her left and the shortstop to her right. Shortstop must let the third baseman know quickly when she can make the play by saying "I've got it." The third baseman must make all the plays to her left unless the shortstop can make the play much easier. With no force play at third base, the shortstop fields the ball and simulates the runner at second breaking for third base.

Outfielders

Purpose: To practice charging ground balls with a possible play at third base or home.

Procedure: All plays are do-or-die. The manager or coach will hit balls and the outfielders will fake the throw to either third or home plate.

Team Drill #5

Pitchers, third basemen, shortstops, and catchers

Purpose: To work on bunt communication on bunted balls to the third-base side of the infield.

Procedure: Simulate base runners at first and second with less than two outs. Coach throws bunted balls from behind the catchers at home plate. Catchers have masks on and call the play when the third baseman or pitcher fields the bunt. If instructed to throw to third, either the third baseman or shortstop will be at the base depending on the bunt play in effect. If the throw is to be made to first base, the fielder fakes the throw (see figure 11.13).

First basemen and second basemen

Purpose: To work on situational ground balls.

Figure 11.12   Team Drill #4.

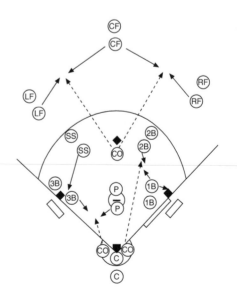

Figure 11.13   Team Drill #5.

Procedure: A coach hits ground balls to the right side of the infield from the right side of home plate. The hitter attempts to force the second baseman to her left and the first baseman to her right. The second baseman needs to let the first baseman know when she can field the ball by saying "I've got it." The first and second basemen practice throwing to first.

Outfielders

Purpose: To work on communication on balls in the gaps that can be caught.

Procedure: Coach or manager throws balls from the second-base area. Outfielders have to position themselves closer than normal to each other to take into consideration the ball is being thrown rather than batted from home plate. The outfielders should also work on their paths to the ball so that the center fielder catches the ball below the waist, and the side outfielders catch the ball above the waist, creating space between the two on the play.

Team Drill #6

Shortstops, second basemen, and pitchers

Purpose: To work on ground balls up the middle for the force play or tag play at second base.

Procedure: A coach stands in front of home plate and fungo hits ground balls to either side of the pitcher and at the pitcher. The pitcher fields the ball and throws to second for the force or tag. The middle infielders work on their backup responsibilities and covering the base (see figure 11.14).

Catchers, first basemen, and third basemen

Purpose: To work on pickoffs from the catcher to the third baseman or first baseman.

Procedure: One catcher is in front of the plate throwing to the catcher at home plate, who has her mask on. The catcher can alternate the pickoff attempt of a simulated runner at first or third base.

Outfielders

Purpose: To work on going to their right and left for ground balls.

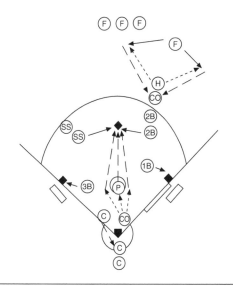

Figure 11.14   Team Drill #6.

Procedure: The manager stands next to the fungo hitter in deep second-base position, who hits balls to the outfielders. The outfielders are working on correct angles, fielding the ball properly, and throwing to the manager.

Team Drill #7

Pitchers and first basemen

Purpose: To work on pop-ups to the left of the pitcher and the right of the first baseman.

Procedure: A coach stands in front of home plate and throws pop-ups for the pitcher and first baseman (see figure 11.15).

Outfielders, second basemen, and shortstops

Purpose: To work on throwing behind the runner rounding second base on a well-hit ball.

Procedure: The coach stands between second base and the mound and hits hard line drives right at the outfielders. The second baseman and shortstop will alternate covering second base depending on where the ball is hit to the outfield. Anytime the ball is not hit well, the outfielder fields it properly and fakes the throw to third base. On a well-hit ball to left, the second baseman will approach the bag from behind the runner, preparing herself to receive a throw to second base. On a well-hit ball to right, the shortstop will break from the cutoff

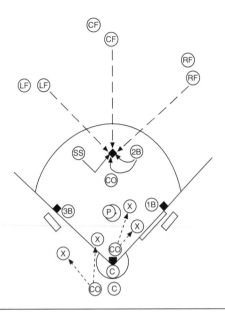

Figure 11.15   Team Drill #7.

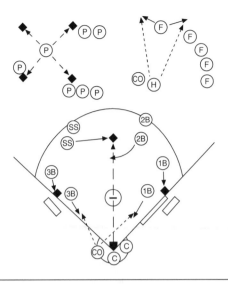

Figure 11.16   Team Drill #8.

position to second base when the ball leaves the right fielder's hand. On a well-hit ball to center, the second baseman will break to the mound side of second base and move into the base when the ball leaves the center fielder's hand. When the outfielders are in doubt about the status of the runner, they throw (fake) to third base.

Catchers and third basemen

Purpose: To work on pop-up communication.

Procedure: The coach or manager stands behind home plate and throws to the areas as designated by Xs on the diagram. Catchers must have masks on.

Team Drill #8

Catchers, shortstops, and second basemen

Purpose: To work on steals of second base and first and third double steals.

Procedure: An extra catcher delivers a ball to the catcher and the catcher throws down to second base. The shortstop covers second base and the second baseman is in the cutoff position between the mound and second base, so she can practice cutting off the throw to second in order to hold the runner at third or throw her out at home (see figure 11.16).

First basemen and third basemen

Purpose: To work on fielding bunted balls and throwing to either first base or third base.

Procedure: The coach throws out the bunts to either side from the left side of the batter's box. If the first baseman fields the ball and "One" is called, she throws the bunted ball to first base, where the other first baseman is simulating the second baseman covering the bag. If the coach yells "Three," then the first baseman fields the bunt and throws to third, where the other third baseman is simulating the shortstop covering the bag. The same drill applies if the third baseman fields the bunt.

Outfielders

Purpose: To work on going back to the fence to pick up a ball and throw to the relay player.

Procedure: The fungo hitter can either fungo or throw the ball to the right-field fence. A manager or coach serves as the relay player.

Pitchers

Purpose: To work on fielding ground balls and throwing to each base.

Procedure: The pitcher fields a ground ball and throws to first, second, or third base or home where additional pitchers are positioned. (The bases are set 60 feet apart.) The ball can be thrown or fungo hit by a pitcher with an additional player at first base.

Team Drill #9

First basemen, third basemen, and catchers

Purpose: To work on fly ball communication.

Procedure: The coach stands to the left side of home plate and tosses fly balls to the general problem areas as designated by Xs on the diagram. The catchers have their masks on (see figure 11.17).

Pitchers

Purpose: To work on getting to the proper backup position on balls hit to the outfield.

Procedure: Each pitcher will alternate on the mound faking the pitch and then reacting to the situation by the coach. After the pitch, the pitcher will break to the proper backup spot. For example, there is one out, a base runner at second, and a single is hit to left field. The pitcher should break to the backstop behind home plate. With a runner on first and a base hit to right field, the pitcher should break to back up third base.

Outfielders, second basemen, and shortstops

Purpose: To work on fly ball communication.

Procedure: The coach throws fly balls to the problem areas designated by Xs on the diagram.

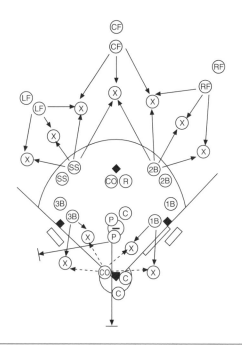

Figure 11.17   Team Drill #9.

All defensive players use proper communication as the coach throws balls with a receiver at her side catching the return throws.

Team Drill #10

Infielders, pitchers, and catchers

Purpose: To work on rundowns between all bases and home plate.

Procedure: Each player is at her position. The coach sets up behind the mound and throws to the first baseman at first base, the second baseman or shortstop at second base, the third baseman at third base, or the catcher at the plate. The outfielders will serve as base runners at each base, getting in a rundown as the play develops and attempting to get out of the rundown. Once the initial throw is made, the pitcher moves to back up or be involved in the rundown. The extra pitchers wait their turn in foul territory between third and home (see figure 11.18).

Outfielders

Purpose: To work on conditioning and baserunning.

Procedure: Outfielders serve as runners at first, second, and third base when infielders practice rundowns.

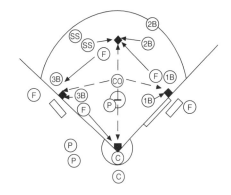

Figure 11.18   Team Drill #10.

Team Drill #11

Pitchers and catchers

Purpose: To work on the pitcher covering home plate on a passed ball or wild pitch with an imaginary base runner attempting to score.

Procedure: A coach sets up behind the catcher. The pitcher fakes a pitch to home plate, and as the faked pitch is made, the coach rolls the ball somewhere behind the catcher. The pitcher charges toward the plate and verbally directs the catcher to the ball location. The catcher will retrieve the ball, set up properly, and throw to the pitcher covering the plate (see figure 11.19).

First basemen

Purpose: To practice receiving bad throws.

Procedure: The first baseman sets up in the normal position and then breaks for the bag. The coach throws short hops, high hops, and throws from second base that will take the first baseman either left or right of the bag.

Outfielders, second basemen, shortstops, and third basemen

Purpose: To work on the tandem relay play on an extra-base hit.

Procedure: The coach fungo hits a ball from behind second base to all areas of the field, forcing the outfielders to go to all areas of the fence. Once the ball is hit, and a sure double is in effect, both the shortstop and second baseman

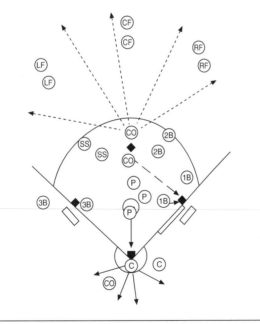

Figure 11.19   Team Drill #11.

go out for the tandem relay. The third baseman communicates where the play is to be made. The back player of the tandem will also communicate to the front player where to throw while listening to the third baseman.

DEFENSIVE PRACTICE

You should add defensive drills to your team's daily training by incorporating at least two drills per practice and setting aside 30 minutes to perform them. You will probably find that you will spend more time on your offense because you are less successful there than on your defense. I would say that we spend approximately 30 to 45 minutes on specific defensive situations and drills. We spend approximately 70 minutes on offensive situations and drills. You can divide simple individual drills into stations because these stations allow for specialty work for each position. This is something that is hard to get when doing team defensive drills.

Players need numerous repetitions. Team drills last about 30 to 45 minutes and we incorporate at least one each day. All team drills and individual drills should be experienced by all of the athletes. The player should always spend time polishing and refreshing her fundamentals.

SUMMARY

In chapter 11 we opened with a drill finder for defensive drills. This chapter introduced drills of increasing complexity, taking you from simple individual drills to combinations of plays involving many teammates, all of which can be used both indoors and outdoors.

- Defensive skills require a great deal of repetition.
- Teach the skills, not the drills.
- Offer a variety of drills, and add competitions whenever possible.
- Divide the simple drills into stations.
- Spend 30 to 45 minutes each day on team drills.

Chapter 12

DEFENSIVE STRATEGIES

Once the players have consistent individual fundamentals it is time to work on plays for the entire unit. In this chapter I present specific strategies to assist you in teaching how to defend against such plays as sacrifice bunts, squeeze bunts, and double steals, along with proper field coverage on ground balls, fly balls, and base hits. If the players know where to go to back up the hit or the throw, and who should cover the bases, an efficient defense will be produced.

We stress communication throughout the defensive alignments so that players are talking to each other about coverage before the pitch is thrown. For example, the middle infielders talk with each other with a fast runner on first and a possible bunt-and-steal play. The pitcher lets the defense know the order of batters up by yelling out, "Four, five and six up." Throughout the inning the infielders flash the outs and the outfielders flash the outs back. All pitches are given from the catcher to the pitcher and infielders, and the infielders flash the pitch to the outfielders. The middle infielders alert their side infielder when the corners cannot see the catcher's sign. The players will remind each other about the strength of the batter as well as where the batter hit the last time up. This information is shared throughout the game.

DEFENSIVE POSITIONING

Some of the factors that influence how players position themselves defensively include

- the inning,
- the score,
- the number of outs,
- the count on the batter,
- the field conditions,
- the batter's strength,
- the pitcher's strength,
- the fielder's ability,
- what pitch is coming,
- the position of the runners, and
- whether to expect a bunt.

Outfielders

Outfielders will move in toward the plate or out toward the fence, or toward the left-field foul line or the right-field foul line, depending on any one of the factors just listed.

Center fielders usually play closer to the plate than the side fielders, but all outfielders must communicate with each other and the infielders regarding their positions. For example, if the center fielder is playing deep, she will tell the middle infielders that they have more territory to cover on balls hit in between the infield and the outfield. The outfielders do not need to have the same amount of space between each other. For example, the center fielder should shade toward the outfielder with the slower foot speed. Also, outfielders need to check the wind direction and make a one-step adjustment. The idea is to be positioned where the hitter will hit the ball. We want a run-and-wait-for-the-ball mentality so that we do not have to dive or fall back when fielding.

The batter's ability will also determine an outfielder's location. Naturally, the outfielder will play the number three, four, and five hitters deeper than the rest of the lineup. On a left-handed slapper the left fielder is closest to the plate, followed by the center fielder, with the right fielder playing the deepest. The fielder should be able to judge the spin and the bat speed and already be gone by the time the ball is hit. The fielder must read the ball off the bat and take her first step to charge toward the area where she anticipates the ball to land or roll. This is considered getting a jump on the ball. Typically a left-handed batter will hit with more power to right field and a right-handed batter will hit with more power to left field. In these cases the opposite fielder can play a little shallower.

The outfielders adjust to the count on the batter by repositioning themselves according to the count. When the pitcher is behind in the count, the outfielders should take a step back and a step to the pull side. When the pitcher is ahead in the count, the outfielders should take a step in.

The outfielder must review the base runners on base before each pitch. This information will allow her to make the proper throw and to better anticipate steals, bunts, and pickoff plays.

The inning and the score dictate how deep the outfielder must play. For example, in a close ball game with a runner on third and less than two outs, the outfielder must play a little shallower so that she can throw out the runner at the plate on a fly ball. Similarly, late in the game with a two-run lead and a runner at second base, the outfielder positions herself to throw the base-hit single to second to keep the runner from reaching scoring position.

Infielders

The infielders also take similar considerations into account when positioning themselves. For example, the first baseman moves in toward the plate when the infield is wet and soft, when there is a weak but fast hitter at bat, or in a bunt situation. The first baseman moves back when a strong, left-handed pull hitter is at bat, when there is a slow runner at the plate, or when there are two strikes on the batter.

The second baseman adjusts her position depending on the defensive situation as well. The second baseman is responsible for all batted balls and slap-bunted balls between first and second base. She will also cover first base on bunted balls, unless the first baseman calls her off. She is responsible for backing up batted balls up the middle that are on the left side of the pitcher's body. The second baseman will cover second base on force plays from the third baseman and shortstop, and sometimes the pitcher. I like to have the second baseman cover second when the pitcher has fielded the ball on her right.

On all average or slow batters, I like the second baseman to play five or six steps from the baseline and to position herself closer to second than to first base. If the batter is a fast right-hander, I have my fielder take two steps in and two steps toward first base. If the batter is a fast left-hander, I have my fielder in the base path and an equal distance from first and second. With a slow left-handed batter, the second baseman plays four or five steps from the baseline and an equal distance between the bases. With less than two outs and a runner on third, the second baseman moves in front of the base path.

One of the most challenging plays for the second baseman is the play with a runner on first and third base. If the offense attempts to steal, the defense must prevent the run from scoring, and if possible, prevent the runner on first from getting into scoring position. We will bring the second baseman into the cutoff position for the throw from the catcher to second base. That position is halfway between the mound and second and slightly off the line so as to enable the shortstop, who is covering second, to see the catcher and the ball. I instruct the second baseman to catch the ball if (1) the runner on third breaks for the plate or takes a big lead and can be picked off or (2) the throw is wide of second on the line to the left of the second baseman. An experienced second baseman can make these decisions herself with practice. However, I sometimes will call the play in advance. I will have her catch any throw that is wide to her left because this ball will get by the shortstop as well.

Like the first baseman, the third baseman moves in toward the plate when the infield is wet and soft, when a weak but fast hitter is at bat, when a strong, left-handed pull hitter is at bat, or in a bunt situation. The third baseman moves back when a strong, right-handed pull hitter or a slow runner is at bat, when there will be a pitchout or pickoff attempt on a runner at third base, or when there are two strikes on the batter.

The shortstop's normal position is two or three steps from the baseline and an equal distance between bases. On very fast runners she will move toward the base path. This position decreases her range but allows her to reach the ball faster and shorten the throw to first base. The shortstop will play deeper on power hitters as well as slow runners, and she plays closer to second when her third baseman can move well to her left. With less than two outs and a runner on third, the shortstop should move in front of the base path. She will adjust toward third base on an inside pitch as well as on a change-up. It is her responsibility to alert the third baseman to a slow pitch coming. We usually do this with a secret word or number.

Figure 12.1 shows examples of good defensive positioning in certain defensive situations, pointing out the adjustments for the corners, middle infielders, and outfielders.

BASIC DEFENSIVE STRATEGIES

What follows are some key defensive strategies regarding bunt defense, backup position on throws and on batted balls, stolen bases and double steals, intentional walks, pickoffs, wild pitches and passed balls, rundown plays, and relay and cutoff plays.

Bunt Defense

To defend against the squeeze bunt look for signs by the offensive teams. They may tip off the fact that they are going to try to suicide or safety squeeze. Of course there will be a runner on third and the signal exchange for the base runner, the batter, and the coach may involve a longer amount of time or more glances toward each other. The batter might tip it off by looking at the corner infielders. If we even suspect it, we will pitch out and catch the runner well off third base. I believe it is the first baseman's role to take away the squeeze bunt on a right-handed batter. The baseman needs to carefully watch the hands of the batter and any sign she might give that she is going to squeeze. In like fashion the third baseman must take away the squeeze bunt on a left-handed batter.

My defense for a push bunt is to be sure the middle infielders commit toward the plate when the batter squares and hold their positions until

Figure 12.1 Defensive Positioning

Situation	Outfielders	Middle infielders	Corners
Sacrifice bunt	Move in five steps	Move in two steps	Move in two steps
Slapper	Move in three steps and two steps to the right	Move into the base path	Move in one step
Runner on third and less than two outs	Move in five steps	Move in front of base path	Move in one step
Power hitter	Take three steps back and two steps to the power foul line	Move behind base path	Move back one step
Ahead by three, 5th inning or later, runners in scoring position	Take three steps back	Move behind base path	Hold normal position
Change-up	Take five steps back and two steps to the right	Move behind the base path and one step to the right	Move one step back
Curve ball	Move three steps to the left	Move one step to the left	Hold normal position
Wind blowing in	Move in three steps	Move in one step	Hold normal position
Wind blowing out	Take three steps back	Take one step back	Hold normal position
Ahead in the count	Move one step in	Hold normal position	Hold normal position
Behind in the count	Take one step back and one step to right	Hold normal position	Hold normal position

the ball is down on the ground. We then follow bunt procedure in coverage. It is important to treat slap bunts as ground balls. The infielders move forward when the batter shows the bunt, but they must hold their ground while the ball is in the strike zone. By this I mean that they are completely balanced and can move laterally if necessary.

Backup Position on Throws and Batted Balls

When any player is responsible for backing up throws from teammates they should abide by two rules: First, allow 20 to 30 feet between players. This will allow for reaction time if the ball is thrown high, low, or wide. The distance is important because we do not want the backup person to have a difficult play. We want her close enough so that she does not have to field a tricky hop and deep enough so that the ball does not go over her head. Second, be stationary and in position before the ball arrives. For example, when the pitcher has to back up home plate she must be close to the backstop so as to increase the opportunity to field the ball if the catcher misses it. I like to have the pitcher actually touch the backstop. When she backs up third base she needs to be sure to have the fence or dugout within reach. The greater the space between the pitcher and the base or plate, the greater the chance of handling an overthrow cleanly.

When the fielder is backing up the batted ball she should abide by two rules: First, she should react to the batted ball as if she believes the fielder will miss the ball and the backup will have to make the play. The backup should not assume the fielder will make the play. Second, she must take the deepest possible angle to the ball so that the ball does not get by her.

Stolen Bases

When the base runner is stealing third, the third baseman will cover third if the batter takes the pitch, swings and misses, or fake slaps and misses. The shortstop will cover if the batter fake bunts.

If the base runner attempts to steal second base, the shortstop will cover while the second baseman backs up the throw to second. If the shortstop is pulled over to the left-field foul line with a runner on second, and the second baseman is pulled to the bag at second, the second baseman can cover second on the steal. It is more difficult for the second baseman to cover second than the shortstop because the second baseman must get to the bag and make a quarter turn to face first base. On the other hand, the shortstop can move directly to second base.

Double Steals

A very important aspect of defensive play in fastpitch is the ability to properly defend against the opponent's double-steal offense with run-

ners on first and third base. It is the coach's responsibility to determine which one of the defenses to utilize. The coach needs to take into account numerous circumstances before choosing the type of play she wants the defense to execute if the double steal is attempted. Those factors are as follows:

- Number of outs—The best time for an offense to run a double steal is with two outs, hoping to draw a throw toward second base so that they can score the runner from third. With less than two outs, most teams will allow the batter the opportunity to score the runner on third.

- Inning—Late in the game the offense will try a double steal more often with less than two outs because they can afford to lose the out to score a run.

- Score of the game—In almost all cases the offense will not attempt a double steal when they are down by a few runs early in the game or down by more than one run in the last two innings. Throwing the ball through to second is always preferred in situations where the runner at third base is not of importance at the time of the double steal. When ahead by two runs, the defense should always get an out, even at the expense of a possible run scoring. If the double-steal defense is done properly, a team should be able to keep the runner on third base from scoring and make a play on the runner from second.

- Strength of the shortstop's and second baseman's arms—Along with the ability of the catcher to throw through to second base, the strength of the arms of the middle infielders handling the throw to second base needs to be considered. If neither of the middle infielders can throw the ball well, then the defensive coach might be hesitant to throw through to second when an important run is at third late in the game.

- Hitter at the plate—Generally, with a good hitter at the plate, the offensive coach will be hesitant to take the bat out of her hands by running any type of double-steal play. A weaker hitter might prompt the offensive coach to attempt some type of double steal, especially with two strikes.

- Strength of the pitcher—If the pitcher is dominating the opposing team's hitters, there is more of a tendency on the opposing coach's part to try to score a run off the double steal or to advance the runner from first into scoring position.

• Count on the batter—The best time to run a double-steal play is when the batter has two strikes with two outs. This is really true with a weak hitter at the plate. With less than two outs, the offense may want to run with no strikes so that the batter might protect the runner by swinging and missing. The ideal time is a 3-2 count with one out, enabling the runner on first to execute a straight steal.

• Ability of the runner at first base—The better the base runner at first base, the more likely the chance the offensive coach will attempt the straight steal. It is advisable not to throw through to second base if there is little chance of getting that out.

• Ability of the runner at third base—The better the base runner is at third base, the greater the chance she will break for the plate on the throw through to second. In most cases with a poor runner at third base, the defense should throw to second.

• Opposing team's double-steal tendencies— A fastpitch coach usually has certain tendencies in regard to her offensive and defensive decisions, and this holds true for the double steal. When teams play each other or scout each other, each coach will know a little more about the opposing coach's philosophy. By knowing what these tendencies might be, the coach can make a better decision on the type of double-steal defense to utilize.

Each of the double-steal plays illustrated on pages 180 to 181 are shown with two outs. With less than two outs the same options exist, but now the middle infielders are in front of the base path. In fastpitch, it is vital to be sure middle infielders do not move laterally until the ball passes through the strike zone. If the middle infielders are moving to their cutoff positions and the batter slaps or hits the pitch, the first rule of defense is violated: Field the batted ball before covering bases.

As I discussed earlier, for all these double-steal plays the second baseman has three situations for catching the throw from the catcher. She should cut the ball if the throw is wide of second base, the runner on third breaks for

home, or the second baseman can pick the runner off of third.

Intentional Walks

When intentionally walking a batter, the pitcher and catcher must be sure the ball is not too close for the batter to reach out and hit, and that the pitch is catchable. In the intentional walk the pitcher is throwing to an invisible target because the catcher cannot set up outside of the catching box. The catcher should stand up and reach out to the side to give the target.

I will call for an intentional walk if the game is close, if first base is open, and if one of the opponent's best batters is up. I also want to be sure that the next batter we are facing is one my pitcher has gotten out, more often than not. If there are two outs and the above scenario is in place, it is an easier decision to intentionally walk that batter. Now with a ground ball the infielders can touch any base.

I Haven't Practiced It

I had a great pitcher from Canada who had complete mastery of her pitches. In one critical league game we were faced with the opportunity to intentionally walk a good batter in order to pitch to a weaker batter. I went out on the mound and told the pitcher what I felt. She told me she could not intentionally walk the batter because she hadn't practiced that. I looked at her and said, "Okay then, pitch to her, but get her out!" The pitcher did and no runs were scored in that inning. I am sure we had practiced pitchouts that spring, but this pitcher did not feel she could do it at that time.

Pickoffs

Occasionally the base runner will get a huge jump and you feel a properly executed pickoff will get her out. I like to use the play with a young runner or a pinch runner who has just entered the game. It is also effective if the ground is not firm. On the pickoff at first base I utilize two plays: the second baseman slipping behind the runner and the first baseman dropping back. The catcher calls a pitchout and the second baseman signals back. The second baseman then adjusts her position by taking two or three steps toward first base. This movement must be done so as not to be noticed by the runner or the first-base coach. As the pitcher begins her windup, the second baseman will sprint to first, straddle the bag, and wait for the throw. The first baseman comes in as if to field a bunt and the catcher fires the ball to the second-base side of first base. The second baseman will signal the right fielder that the play is on so that the outfielder can back up the throw and move with the second baseman. The catcher can also signal the first baseman and as the pitch approaches the catcher, the first baseman drops back with her left foot toward first base, crosses over with her right foot, and continues running to the bag. She receives the throw from the catcher and executes a sweep tag.

We do not attempt to pick off the runner at second very often, but if we do the catcher will throw to the second baseman covering. Again, I like to call the play and will call a pitchout if necessary. The second baseman must let the center fielder know the play is on so that the outfielder can back up the throw.

I think runners can be picked off third base as well, although the risk is greater. If the throw hits the runner or goes wide of the third baseman, the base runner will score. I will let the catcher know through a signal that it is okay to try. She will then signal the third baseman who will signal the left fielder. The catcher must throw on the second-base side of third base so as not to throw into the runner. We will not use a pitchout here, but the third baseman will stay back to prepare for the hit or the catcher's throw.

Wild Pitches and Passed Balls

If the pitcher throws a wild pitch or the catcher commits a passed ball, the pitcher must sprint to the plate and station herself off the plate on the infield side. She should give the catcher a chest-high target as she calls for the ball. The pitcher must hold her concentration on the ball coming toward her, make the catch, and use a sweep tag for the out. The catcher should throw her mask away from her route to the ball and

sprint to the ball. When picking up the ball, it is best if the catcher pushes it into the ground so a good grip is assured. A sidearm throw at medium speed to the target might get the runner, and the first baseman will sprint into a backup position for any overthrow from the catcher to the pitcher.

Rundown Plays

I want the rundown play to involve only one throw. Any more than that and the chance of error increases. Even better would be for the fielder to make a tag on the runner without a throw. It is the responsibility of the player with the ball to force the runner to go forward or backward at full speed. The fielder with the ball must start running full speed at the runner to force the runner to also run full speed toward the base or the plate. The fielder with the ball will establish the angle of her approach on the run so that the receiver of the throw can establish a position off the line. In this way the throw will not hit the runner and the receiver will have an unobstructed view of the ball. The fielder with the ball should have the ball up and should

not fake a throw; the throw should be a soft snap with the wrist. The ball should be thrown to the receiver's chest. After the throw, we want the fielder to veer out of the way and retreat back to the original base she was covering.

Here are some general rules to follow when the base runner is in a rundown:

- The runner is in trouble, not the defense.

- Always force the runner back to the base she came from.

- Throw the ball ahead of the runner to force her back.

- Throw the ball with moderate speed chest high.

- Ideally, six players are involved: two infielders at each of the bases and two players backing up. Those involved in the rundown will gradually move in and narrow the distance between themselves and the runner. The fielder about to receive the throw "closes the gap" between the two defensive players, so there is little room for the runner.

- As the ball is thrown, the fielder behind the runner will begin to move forward, trapping the runner between the two converging players.

- The infielder ahead of the runner will run toward the base runner to force her back before throwing.

Relay and Cutoff Plays

What is the difference between a relay and a cutoff play? I tell my players that the way to tell the difference is to think of a phone conversation. If I can tell a friend something directly on the phone and then something happens to our connection, we have been cut off. If I cannot reach my friend directly, I would have someone relay the message. Thus, a relay is needed when I cannot get the message or the throw to the desired person myself. I need someone to "relay" the message or "relay" the throw. When I can get the message there without the help of someone else, but then that message is interrupted, that is a "cutoff." I can get the throw to the base or plate, but it gets "cut off" to make another play or to hold a runner.

Relay Plays

I use the shortstop and the second baseman to relay all outfield plays. The shortstop will relay throws from the left fielder and the center fielder, while the second baseman will relay throws from the right fielder. If the shortstop is the relay she will go out to receive the throw, but only as far as needed. The outfielder should be able to throw 60 percent of the distance, leaving 40 percent for the infielder to finish. The second baseman positions herself in line with the shortstop and the ball and the plate, about 20 feet behind the shortstop. It is the second baseman's job to catch any overthrow in the air and to handle any other misplayed ball. As soon as the shortstop has the ball the second baseman must cover second base. The second baseman will also line up the shortstop and tell her where to make the play. The second baseman's relay and the shortstop's backup function exactly as the shortstop's relay and the second baseman's backup.

Some general rules for the relay are as follows:

- A relay play assumes the outfielder cannot get the ball to the desired base or plate because it is too long of a throw.

- Either the shortstop or the second baseman is the relay player. When one is receiving the throw from the outfielder, the other is in a backup position, 20 feet behind. They are a tandem. Wherever one goes, the other is right behind—just like a tandem bicycle. The back player backs up any bad throws from the outfield and tells the front player where to throw the ball.

- The relay or the tandem relay player has many things to consider before deciding where to throw the ball. Because of this, the third baseman or catcher can communicate her decision on where to throw the ball. Since both the catcher and third baseman will have the play in front of them, they can be of the best assistance to the fielder of the ball in making this decision. The command should be made prior to the ball reaching the glove of the relay. This will give the player plenty of time to see the runners, and to then decide what to do with the ball.

- The communication must be very loud so that every defensive player can hear. The third baseman is generally closer to the fielders and she needs to yell the following commands at least twice:

- "Four, four" for the throw to the plate.
- "Three, three" for the throw to third base.
- "Two, two" for the throw to second base.
- "Hold, hold" for the catch and to run the ball in.

- The back player of the tandem can also assist the front player in making the decision as to what the best play would be. As soon as the back player gets lined up behind the front player, and the outfielder is picking up the ball to throw to the front player of the relay, the back player should turn and check out where the runners are. While listening to the third baseman and the catcher, the back tandem player offers the commands as previously mentioned.

Cutoff plays

The first or third baseman will serve as a cutoff on certain balls thrown from the outfield or relayed to the plate (see figure 12.2). It is important that she be positioned slightly off a line from the ball to the plate about 35 to 40 feet from home plate. She must listen for the catcher's instructions and cut the ball if the catcher yells. We want her off the line so that she does not obstruct the view of the outfielder to the plate and the view of the catcher to the ball. When catching the ball she should step forward on her right foot and then use that foot to pivot toward the plate.

Some rules for the cutoff are as follows:

- A cutoff play assumes the fielder can throw the ball to the proper base or home plate. A player is in line with the ball and the base and this player is the cutoff player.

- A cutoff player can be assisted into the proper position by the defensive player at a base or the plate. The player can help line up the cutoff with the fielder throwing the ball by instructing her to move to her right or left by the commands "Right, right" or "Left, left." The cutoff player must move quickly until she hears "Okay." This alignment should happen before the fielder releases the ball.

- The cutoff player should have both arms up in the air so that she is an easy target for the

Figure 12.2 The first baseman in cutoff position from a relay throw.

outfielder or the tandem relay infielder making the throw. As the ball is coming toward her, she must anticipate what to do with it. Out of the corner of her eye she should be able to see where the runners are. By anticipating where the play will be made, she will be able to better position herself for the proper play.

- The defensive player at the plate or the base will inform the cutoff player if the ball should be cut or not. This should be done well in advance of the ball getting to the cutoff player. If the player at the base wants the ball to be cut off, she will yell "Cut" as loud as possible. Usually, if the ball coming in to the cutoff player is going to take the third baseman or catcher two steps off the line away from the tag area, she should have the ball cut off.

- Anytime an outfielder or a relay player is throwing to a cutoff player, she should aim for her knees. By aiming at the knees, there is less chance of an overthrow. The cutoff player needs to go after all bad throws, as if there was no one backing up the throw. The cutoff player can assume all bad throws will be cut, and therefore, should get into proper position to make the catch. The cutoff player should not get short-hopped on the throw from the outfielder or relay. There should be enough time to move forward or backward to keep this from happening.

• The cutoff player should always fake the catch if she is going to let the throw go through. This is why saying nothing if you want the throw to go through is more effective. This may keep the runner from taking an extra base. If a command like "let it go" is given, it will allow the runner to figure the play is going through, and give the base runner the chance to take an extra base.

• When the ball is coming toward the cutoff player and a play is going to be made on the runner, the cutoff needs to keep the ball lined up with the glove side. The player will be in a good position to catch the ball, if commanded, and then throw the ball, all in one motion. Anytime a cutoff player is throwing to a base or the plate, she should step and throw to the base.

Setting Up Situations in Practice

In each practice we spend at least 45 minutes on defense. In preseason we incorporate full field practice into our schedule with other offensive and defensive drills. This occurs after we have worked on individual skills or unit skills (such as infielders and outfielders). During the preseason we spend at least 15 minutes every day on situations. Once games have started, our full field defense is polished a few times a week. We also work on specific plays that have occurred during games where execution was lacking.

In practice, I suggest setting up the full defense, including the pitcher on the mound. The coach is at the plate to fungo hit. Runners can be placed at different bases, along with one at the plate, and must run full speed when the ball is hit by the coach. All types of balls need to be hit:

some between outfielders, some down the line, and some over the outfielders' heads. This type of defensive work allows the coach the opportunity to evaluate the defense's ability to cover their assignments.

GENERAL OBJECTIVES

In all sports, the object of the defense is to keep your opponent from scoring. Therefore, the number one objective of defensive fastpitch is to prevent the scoring of runs and the movement of runners into scoring positions. All strategy is keyed to these objectives, leading to the establishment of these basic rules for fielders:

1. Set the defense to field the batted ball.
2. Set the defense to back up the batted ball.
3. Cover all bases.
4. Back up throws to bases.

These four principles must be followed in this exact order. You cannot cover bases if you have not set the defense to field the ball and to back up the hit first. The defense must work to keep the ball in front of them and to throw ahead of the runner.

Within this basic framework, there are specific moves each defensive player should make in given situations. These defensive plays are diagrammed and explained on the following pages.

Legend: In the diagrams in this section the following symbols are used:

Infielders	1B, 2B, 3B, SS
Outfielders	LF, CF, RF
Pitcher	P
Catcher	C
Coach	CO
Hitter	H
Receiver	R
Path of fielder	————
Path of throw	— — —

GROUND BALLS

Situation: Ground ball to the third baseman with no one on base.

Objective: The play at first. The right fielder and the catcher back up the throw to first.

Catcher: Follows the runner toward first and backs up the base.
First baseman: Covers first and takes the throw.
Second baseman: Covers second.
Third baseman: Fields the ball and throws to first.
Shortstop: Backs up the batted ball.
Left fielder: Moves toward third to back up throw or hit.
Center fielder: Backs up a possible throw to second.
Right fielder: Moves toward the foul line to pick up any overthrow.

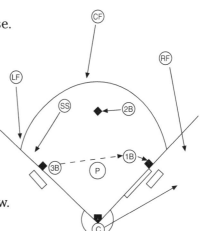

Situation: Ground ball to the second baseman with no one on base.

Objective: The play at first. The right fielder backs up the batted ball and then the right fielder and the catcher back up the throw to first.

Catcher: Follows the runner toward first and backs up the base.
First baseman: Covers first and takes the throw.
Second baseman: Fields the ball and throws to first.
Third baseman: Covers third.
Shortstop: Covers second.
Left fielder: Moves toward center field to back up a possible throw to second.
Center fielder: Backs up the second baseman for any deflection and backs up second for a possible throw.
Right fielder: (1) Backs up the batted ball and then (2) moves to the fence for any possible overthrow of first.

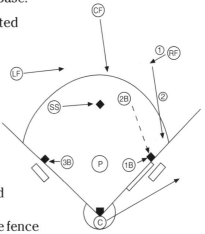

Situation: Ground ball to the pitcher with a runner on first and less than two outs.

Objective: The pitcher should know where the player covering second wants the ball. For example, if the shortstop is moving toward the bag the pitcher would throw a lead throw to her.

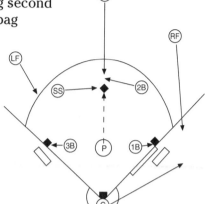

Pitcher: If the ball is fielded on the pitcher's right side, looks for the second baseman covering. If the ball is fielded on the pitcher's left side, looks for the shortstop covering.
Catcher: Follows the batter toward first and backs up the base.
First baseman: Covers first.
Shortstop and second baseman: The player who does not cover the throw backs up the play.
Third baseman: Covers third.
Left fielder: Moves toward third to back up the throw.
Center fielder: Moves toward second to back up possible throw.
Right fielder: Moves toward the foul line to cover any overthrow.

Situation: Ground ball to the first baseman with a runner on first and less than two outs.

Objective: The double play with the shortstop covering second. The first baseman should throw to second on either side of the baseline to avoid hitting the runner.

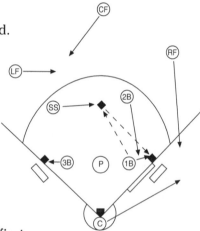

Catcher: Follows the runner toward first and backs up the base.
First baseman: Fields the ball and throws to second, then covers first for the throw from the shortstop.
Second baseman: Backs up the first baseman and is prepared to cover first if the first baseman cannot come back.
Third baseman: Covers third.
Shortstop: Covers second, takes the throw, and throws to first.
Left fielder: Backs up the throw to second.
Center fielder: Backs up the throw to second.
Right fielder: Moves toward the foul line to back up the throw to first.

Situation: Ground ball to the second baseman with a runner on first and less than two outs.

Objective: The double play with the shortstop covering second.

Catcher: Follows the runner toward first and backs up the base.
First baseman: Covers first.
Second baseman: Fields the ball and throws to second. The second baseman may also have the opportunity to tag the runner then throw to first.
Third baseman: Covers third.
Shortstop: Covers second, takes the throw, and throws to first.
Left fielder: (1) Backs up the throw to second and then (2) backs up the possible throw to third. Moves from position 1 to position 2 when the play is completed at second.
Center and left fielders: Back up the throw to second 30 feet apart and at different angles.
Right fielder: (1) Backs up the second baseman and then (2) backs up the throw to first.

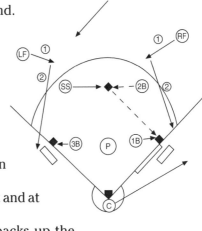

Situation: Ground ball to the shortstop with a runner on first and less than two outs.

Objective: The double play with the second baseman covering second.

Pitcher: Backs up third and moves to foul territory.
Catcher: Follows the batter toward first and backs up the base.
First baseman: Covers first and takes the second baseman's throw.
Second baseman: Covers second, takes the throw, and throws to first.
Third baseman: Covers third.
Shortstop: Fields the ball and throws to second.
Left fielder: Backs up the batted ball on an angle behind the center fielder.
Center fielder: (1) Moves to back up the hit and then (2) sprints to back up the throw from the shortstop to second base.

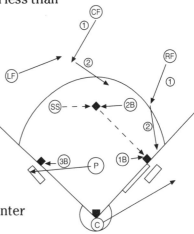

Right fielder: (1) Backs up the throw to second and then (2) backs up the throw to first. Moves to the secondary position as soon as the center fielder is in position to back up the throw from shortstop to second base.

Situation: Ground ball to the third baseman with a runner on first and less than two outs.

Objective: The double play with the second baseman covering second.

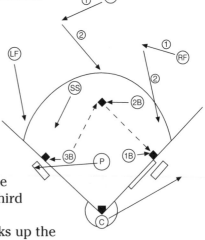

Pitcher: Backs up third.
Catcher: Follows the batter toward first and backs up the base.
First baseman: Covers first and takes the second baseman's throw.
Second baseman: Covers second, takes the throw, and throws to first.
Third baseman: Fields the ball and throws to second and then covers third.
Shortstop: Backs up the batted ball to third.
Left fielder: Backs up the batted ball.
Center fielder: (1) Moves to back up the hit at a deeper angle than the left fielder and then (2) sprints to back up the throw from the third baseman to second base.
Right fielder: (1) Backs up the throw to second and then (2) backs up the throw to first. Moves to the secondary position as soon as the center fielder is in position to back up the throw from shortstop to second base.

Situation: Ground ball to the shortstop with a runner on third and less than two outs.

Objective: To get the lead runner out at the plate if she goes; if not, the play at first.

Pitcher: (1) Attempts to field the ball and then (2) moves toward home plate in the event of a rundown.
Catcher: Covers home plate.
First baseman: When either the third baseman or the shortstop fields a ground ball with a runner on third (less than two outs), moves to the "short position." Sets up to receive the throw along the foul line, about 10 to 15 feet in front of the bag. From here, the throw to the plate on a delay by the runner at third will be a shorter throw. The baseman would get the batter out if there is no play at the plate.
Second baseman: Covers second.
Third baseman: First attempts to field the ball; if doesn't field the ball, covers third as the runner from third breaks for the plate.
Shortstop: Fields the grounder and throws home, then backs up third. If the third baseman fields the ball, the shortstop should cover third.
Outfielders: Move toward the infield and back up the base in front of them for a possible throw.

Note: With runners on first and third and less than two outs, the coach must decide whether to have the infielders try to hold the runner at third or go for the double play. Unless the runner on third is vital and there is no one out, instruct the pitcher, shortstop, and second baseman to go for the double play. This defense allows the middle infielders to play deeper and reach more ground balls. The first and third basemen, as their double play throws are longer, should check the runner at third and throw home if the runner breaks or throw to second if the runner at third holds.

HITS

In all of the following hit situations the play is the same regardless of the number of outs.

Situation: Long single, possible double, to left center with no one on base, with a runner on second, a runner on third, or with runners on second and third.

Objective: The play at second to prevent the batter base runner from reaching scoring position. A long throw from the outfield may require a relay.

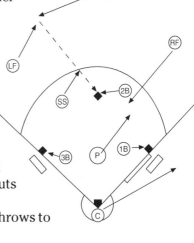

Pitcher: Backs up second. Does not stand in the base path where she may interfere with the runner.
Catcher: Follows the runner to first in case of a rundown.
First baseman: Covers first.
Second baseman: Covers second, is prepared to take the throw, and tells the shortstop whether or not to cut.
Third baseman: Covers third.
Shortstop: Moves to the outfield, in line with the outfielder and second base. Listens to the second baseman's instructions and cuts the throw or lets it go through.
Left fielder: Fields the ball, uses the shortstop as a possible relay, throws to second.
Center fielder: Backs up the batted ball.
Right fielder: Backs up the throw to second.

Note: This play is diagrammed for a ball hit to left center. The fielders' assignments are the same for a long hit down the left-field line.

Situation: Long single, possible double, down the right-field line with no one on base, with a runner on second, a runner on third, or with runners on second and third.

Objective: The play at second to prevent the batter base runner from reaching scoring position. A long throw from the outfield may require a relay.

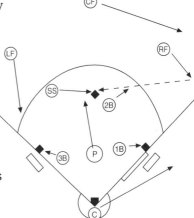

Pitcher: Backs up second. Does not stand in the base path where she may interfere with the runner.
Catcher: Follows the runner to first in case of a rundown.
First baseman: Covers first.
Second baseman: Moves toward the outfield, in line with the outfielder and second base. Listens to the shortstop's instructions and cuts the throw or lets it go through.
Third baseman: Covers third.
Shortstop: Covers second, is prepared to take the throw, and tells the second baseman whether or not to cut.
Left fielder: Backs up the throw to third.
Center fielder: Backs up the batted ball.
Right fielder: Fields the ball, uses the second baseman as a possible relay, throws to second.

Note: This play is diagrammed for a ball hit down the right-field line. The fielders' assignments are the same for a possible double to right center.

Situation: Double, possible triple, to left center with no one on base, with a runner on second, a runner on third, or with runners on second and third.

Objective: The play on the batter base runner trying to reach third. The shortstop is the relay and the second baseman concedes the double and backs up the relay.

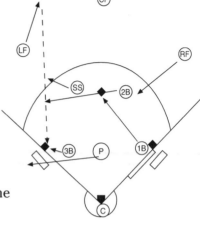

Pitcher: Backs up third.

Catcher: Covers home plate.

First baseman: Trails the runner to second for a possible pickoff throw from the relay player.

Second baseman: Backs up the shortstop about 30 feet behind in line with third base.

Third baseman: Covers third and prepares to take the throw. Tells the shortstop or second baseman whether or not to cut the ball.

Shortstop: Moves toward the outfielder so as to be able to catch the outfielder's throw in the air, in line with the ball and third base.

Left fielder: Fields the ball and throws to the relay.

Center fielder: Backs up the batted ball.

Right fielder: Moves toward second to back up a possible throw.

Note: The fielders' assignments are the same for a possible triple down the left-field line.

Situation: Double, possible triple, to right center with no one on base, with a runner on second, a runner on third, or with runners on second and third.

Objective: The play on the batter base runner trying to reach third. The second baseman goes to the relay position and the shortstop backs up the relay.

Pitcher: Backs up third.

Catcher: Covers home plate.

First baseman: Trails the runner to second for a possible pickoff throw from the relay player.

Second baseman: Moves toward the outfielder, in line with the ball and third base, so as to be able to catch the outfielder's throw in the air.

Third baseman: Covers third, tells shortstop whether or not to cut the ball, and prepares to take the throw.

Shortstop: Backs up the second baseman about 30 feet behind in line with third base and listens for third baseman's call about cutting the ball.

Left fielder: Moves toward third to back up possible throw.

Center fielder: Backs up the batted ball.

Right fielder: Fields the ball and, using the second baseman as a possible relay, throws to third.

Situation: Double, possible triple, down the right-field line with no one on base, with a runner on second, a runner on third, or with runners on second and third.

Objective: The play on the batter base runner trying to reach third. The first baseman serves as the backup when the second baseman goes out for the relay.

Pitcher: Backs up third.

Catcher: Covers home plate.

First baseman: Backs up the second baseman about 30 feet behind in line with third base. Instructs the second baseman on whether or not to relay the throw.

Second baseman: Moves toward the outfielder, in line with the ball and third base, so as to be able to catch the outfielder's throw in the air. Listens for the first baseman's instructions.

Third baseman: Covers third and prepares to take the relay. Third baseman tells either the first or second baseman whether or not to cut the throw.

Shortstop: Covers second for a possible pickoff from the second baseman.

Left fielder: Moves toward third in case of a rundown.

Center fielder: Backs up the right fielder.

Right fielder: Fields the ball and throws to the second baseman relay.

Situation: Triple, possible inside-the-park home run, to center.

Objective: Prevent the home run from scoring.

Pitcher: Backs up home plate.

Catcher: Covers home plate, prepares to take the throw, and instructs the first baseman whether to cut the ball.

First baseman: Moves directly in line with the second baseman and home plate about 40 feet from home plate. Follows the catcher's instructions, cuts off the relay or lets it go through.

Second baseman: Moves toward the center fielder in line with the ball and home plate so as to be able to catch the throw in the air. Listens for the shortstop's instructions on whether to cut the throw and throw to third or cut the throw and throw home.

Third baseman: Covers third.

Shortstop: Backs up the second baseman about 30 feet behind in line with home plate and instructs the second baseman on whether or not to relay the throw.

Left fielder: Backs up third in case of a pickoff overthrow from the first baseman or catcher.

Center fielder: Fields the ball and throws to the second baseman.

Right fielder: Backs up the hit.

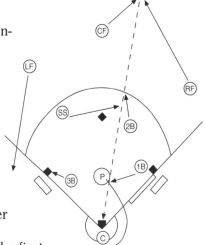

Note: On hits to the right-field side of the center fielder, the second baseman is the relay. On balls to the left-field side, the shortstop becomes the relay.

Situation: Single to right with a runner on first.

Objective: The play at third and holding the batter to a single.

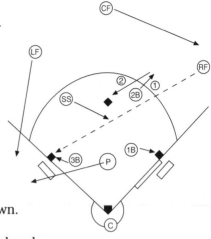

Pitcher: Backs up third.
Catcher: Covers home plate.
First baseman: Covers first.
Second baseman: (1) Moves out to field the hit and then (2) repositions to cover second.
Third baseman: Covers third, prepares to take the throw, and instructs the shortstop whether or not to cut the ball.
Shortstop: Moves in line with the right fielder and third base. Follows the third baseman's instructions, cuts off the throw or lets it go through.
Left fielder: Moves toward third in case of an overthrow or rundown.
Center fielder: Backs up the hit.
Right fielder: Fields the ball and, using the shortstop as a possible relay, throws to third.

Note: On hits to the right-field side of the center fielder, the second baseman is the relay. On balls to the left-field side, the shortstop becomes the relay. On a single to center or left, the play is the same coverage except there would be no relay needed and the second baseman would cover second. The center and left fielders would back up the batted ball.

Situation: Long single, possible double, down the left-field line with a runner on first, with runners on first and second, runners on first and third, or with the bases loaded.

Objective: The play at second to prevent the batter base runner from reaching scoring position.

Pitcher: Backs up third or home.
Catcher: Covers home plate.
First baseman: Covers first.
Second baseman: Covers second. Instructs the shortstop whether or not to cut the throw from the left fielder.
Third baseman: Covers third.
Shortstop: Moves into the outfield, directly in line with the left fielder and second base. Listens for the second baseman's instructions. Cuts off the throw or lets it go through.
Left fielder: Fields the ball and, using the shortstop as a possible relay, throws to second.
Center fielder: Backs up the left fielder.
Right fielder: Moves toward the infield in case of an overthrow at second.

Note: The diagram for this play shows a ball hit down the left-field line. The fielders' assignments are the same for a possible double to left center with a runner on first, runners on first and second, runners on first and third, or with the bases loaded. If the batter has a chance of reaching second, the runner on first will usually make third easily.

Situation: Long single, possible double, to right center with a runner on first, with runners on first and second, runners on first and third, or with the bases loaded.

Objective: The play at second to prevent the batter base runner from reaching scoring position.

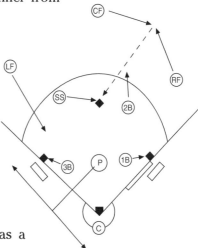

Pitcher: Backs up third or home.

Catcher: Covers home plate.

First baseman: Covers first.

Second baseman: Moves into the outfield, directly in line with the right fielder and second base. Listens for the shortstop's instructions. Cuts off the throw or lets it go through.

Third baseman: Covers third.

Shortstop: Covers second, prepares to take the throw, and instructs the second baseman whether or not to cut if off.

Left fielder: Moves toward the infield in case of an overthrow at second.

Center fielder: Backs up the right fielder.

Right fielder: Fields the ball and, using the second baseman as a possible relay, throws to second.

Note: The diagram for this play shows a ball hit to right center. The fielders' assignments are the same for a possible double down the right-field line with a runner on first, runners on first and second, runners on first and third, or with the bases loaded. If the batter has a chance of reaching second, the runner on first will usually make third easily.

Situation: Double, possible triple, to left center with a runner on first, with runners on first and second, runners on first and third, or with the bases loaded.

Objective: The play at the plate or the play at third.

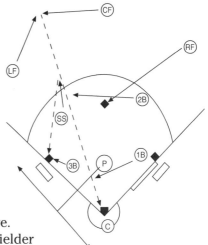

Pitcher: Moves outside the third baseline, close to home plate. Backs up third or home, depending on the play.

Catcher: Covers home plate. If the relay comes toward the plate, prepares to take it and instructs the first baseman whether or not to cut it off.

First baseman: Moves near the pitcher's mound, directly in line with the shortstop and home plate. Following the catcher's instructions, cuts off the relay or lets it go through.

Second baseman: Backs up the shortstop about 30 feet behind in line with home plate. Instructs the shortstop on where to relay the throw or to just cut it off.

Third baseman: Covers third and takes the relay if it comes there.

Shortstop: Moves into the outfield, directly in line with the left fielder and home plate. Listens for the second baseman's instructions. Relays the throw either to the plate, using the first baseman as a guide, or to third, or just cuts off the throw.

Left fielder: Fields the ball and throws to the shortstop.

Center fielder: Backs up the left fielder.

Right fielder: Covers second.

Note: In this play there is a relay player and a cutoff player.

Situation: Double, possible triple, down the left-field line with a runner on first, with runners on first and second, runners on first and third, or with the bases loaded.

Objective: The play at the plate or the play at third.

Pitcher: Backs up third and home.

Catcher: Covers home plate. If the relay comes toward the plate, prepares to take it, and instructs the first baseman whether or not to cut it off.

First baseman: Moves near the pitcher's mound, directly in line with the shortstop and home plate. Following the catcher's instructions, cuts off the relay or lets it go through.

Second baseman: Covers second.

Third baseman: Serves a dual role: backs up the relay, and covers third and takes the relay if it comes there. Both occur at the base.

Shortstop: Moves out into the outfield, directly in line with the left fielder and home plate. Listens for the third baseman's instructions. Relays the throw either to home plate, using the first baseman as a guide, or to third, or just cuts off the throw.

Left fielder: Fields the ball and throws to the shortstop.

Center fielder: Backs up the left fielder.

Right fielder: Backs up a possible throw to second.

Note: In this play there is a relay player and a cutoff player.

Situation: Double, possible triple, to right center with a runner on first, with runners on first and second, runners on first and third, or with the bases loaded.

Objective: The play at the plate or the play at third.

Pitcher: Backs up third and home.

Catcher: Covers home plate. If the relay comes toward the plate, prepares to take it, and instructs the first baseman whether or not to cut it off.

First baseman: Moves near the pitcher's mound, directly in line with the second baseman and home plate. Following the catcher's instructions, cuts off the relay or lets it go through.

Second baseman: Moves into the outfield, directly in line with the right fielder and home plate. Listens for the shortstop's instructions. Relays the throw either to the plate, using the first baseman as a guide, or to third, or just cuts off the throw.

Third baseman: Covers third and takes the relay if it comes there.

Shortstop: Backs up the second baseman about 30 feet behind in line with the throw to third. Instructs the second baseman on where to relay the throw or to just cut it off.

Left fielder: Backs up third in line with the first baseman in case the relay to the plate is cut off and the throw goes to third.

Center fielder: Backs up the right fielder.

Right fielder: Fields the ball and throws to the second baseman.

Note: In this play there is a relay player and a cutoff player.

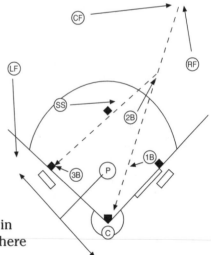

Situation: Double, possible triple, down the right-field line with a runner on first, with runners on first and second, runners on first and third, or with the bases loaded.

Objective: The play at the plate or the play at third.

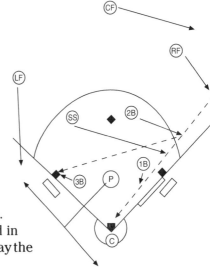

Pitcher: Backs up third and home.

Catcher: Covers home plate. If the relay comes toward the plate, prepares to take it, and instructs the first baseman whether or not to cut it off.

First baseman: Moves near the pitcher's mound, directly in line with the second baseman and home plate. Following the catcher's instructions, cuts off the relay or lets it go through.

Second baseman: Moves out into the outfield, directly in line with the right fielder and home plate. Listens for the shortstop's instructions. Relays the throw either to the plate, using the first baseman as a guide, or to third, or just cuts off the throw.

Third baseman: Covers third and takes the relay if it comes there.

Shortstop: Backs up the second baseman about 30 feet behind in line with the plate. Instructs the second baseman on where to relay the throw or to just cut it off.

Left fielder: Backs up third in line with the first baseman in case the relay to the plate is cut off and the throw goes to third.

Center fielder: Backs up the right fielder.

Right fielder: Fields the ball and throws to the second baseman.

Note: In this play there is a relay player and a cutoff player.

Situation: Single to left with a runner on second, or with runners on first and second, runners on second and third, or with the bases loaded.

Objective: The play at the plate and holding the batter to a single.

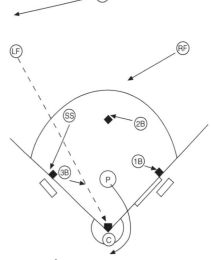

Pitcher: Backs up home plate.

Catcher: Covers home plate. If the throw comes toward the plate, prepares to take it, and instructs the third baseman whether or not to cut it.

First baseman: Covers first.

Second baseman: Covers second and takes the throw if it comes there. It may come from the left fielder, the third baseman, or the catcher.

Third baseman: Moves near the pitcher's mound, directly in line with the left fielder and home plate. Following the catcher's instructions, cuts off the throw or lets it go through.

Shortstop: Covers third.

Left fielder: Fields the ball and throws to the plate.

Center fielder: Backs up the batted ball.

Right fielder: Moves toward the infield in case of an overthrow at second.

Note: Do not let the tying run get into scoring position at second base by throwing to the plate when the runner is likely to score or has held up at third.

Situation: Single to center with a runner on second, or with runners on second and third.

Objective: The play at the plate and holding the batter to a single.

Pitcher: Backs up home plate.
Catcher: Covers home plate. If the throw comes toward the plate, prepares to take it, and instructs the first baseman whether or not to cut it off.
First baseman: Moves near the pitcher's mound, directly in line with the center fielder and home plate. Following the catcher's instructions, cuts off the throw or lets it go through.
Second baseman: Covers first.
Third baseman: Covers third.
Shortstop: Covers second and takes the throw if it comes there. It may come from the center fielder, the first baseman, or the catcher.
Left and right fielders: Back up the batted ball.
Center fielder: Fields the ball and throws to the plate.

Note: Do not let the tying run get into scoring position at second base by throwing to the plate when the runner is likely to score or has held up at third.

Situation: Single to right with a runner on second, or with runners on first and second, runners on second and third, or with the bases loaded.

Objective: The play at the plate and holding the batter to a single.

Pitcher: Backs up home plate.
Catcher: Covers home plate. If the throw comes toward the plate, prepares to take it, and instructs the first baseman whether or not to cut it.
First baseman: Moves near the pitcher's mound, directly in line with the right fielder and home plate. Following the catcher's instructions, cuts off the throw or lets it go through.
Second baseman: Covers first after the throw has been made to the plate.
Third baseman: Covers third.
Shortstop: Covers second and takes the throw if it comes there. It may come from the right fielder, the first baseman, or the catcher.
Left fielder: Moves toward the infield in case of an overthrow or rundown.
Center fielder: Backs up the batted ball.
Right fielder: Fields the ball and throws to the plate.

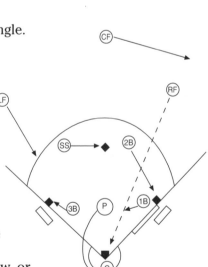

Note: Do not let the tying run get into scoring position at second base by throwing to the plate when the runner is likely to score or has held up at third base.

FLY BALLS

On all fly balls to the outfield with a runner on third, the first baseman is the cut off on all throws to the plate. The play will be the same for no outs and one out.

Situation: Possible sacrifice fly to left with a runner on third.

Objective: The play at the plate.

Pitcher: Backs up home plate.
Catcher: Covers home plate and prepares to take the throw. When the throw comes toward the plate, instructs the first baseman whether or not to cut it off.
First baseman: Moves near the pitcher's mound, directly in line with the left fielder and home plate. Following the catcher's instructions, cuts off the throw or lets it go through.
Second baseman: Covers first.
Third baseman: Covers third.
Shortstop: Covers second.
Left fielder: Catches the ball and throws home.
Center fielder: Backs up the batted ball.
Right fielder: Backs up second in case the left fielder drops the ball and throws to second.

Situation: Possible sacrifice fly to center with a runner on third.

Objective: The play at the plate.

Pitcher: Backs up home plate.
Catcher: Covers home plate and prepares to take the throw. When the throw comes toward the plate, instructs the first baseman whether or not to cut it off.
First baseman: Moves near the pitcher's mound, directly in line with the center fielder and home plate. Following the catcher's instructions, cuts off the throw or lets it go through.
Second baseman: Covers first.
Third baseman: Covers third.
Shortstop: Covers second.
Left and right fielders: Back up the batted ball.
Center fielder: Catches the ball and throws home.

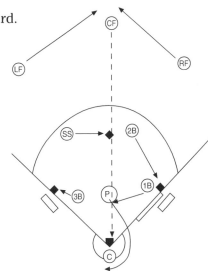

Situation: Possible sacrifice fly to right with a runner on third.

Objective: The play at the plate.

Pitcher: Backs up home plate.
Catcher: Covers home plate and prepares to take the throw. When the throw comes toward the plate, instructs the first baseman whether or not to cut it off.
First baseman: Moves near the pitcher's mound, directly in line with the right fielder and home plate. Following the catcher's instructions, cuts off the throw or lets it go through.
Second baseman: Covers first.
Third baseman: Covers third.
Shortstop: Covers second.
Left fielder: Moves toward the infield in case of a rundown or overthrow at third base.
Center fielder: Backs up the batted ball.
Right fielder: Catches the ball and throws home.

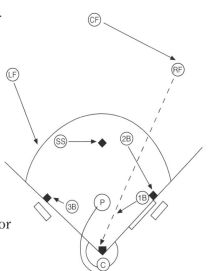

Situation: Possible sacrifice fly to left with runners on first and third.

Objective: The play at the plate and holding the other runner to first.

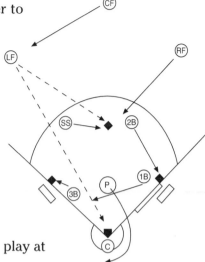

Pitcher: Backs up home plate.

Catcher: Covers home plate and prepares to take the throw. When the throw comes toward the plate, instructs the first baseman whether or not to cut it off.

First baseman: Moves near the pitcher's mound, directly in line with the left fielder and home plate. Following the catcher's instructions, cuts off the throw or lets it go through. If the first baseman cuts the throw because there is no play at home, she can hold the runner at first.

Second baseman: Covers first.

Third baseman: Covers third.

Shortstop: Covers second.

Left fielder: Catches the ball and throws home, or if there is no play at home, throws to second.

Center fielder: Backs up the batted ball.

Right fielder: Moves toward the infield in case of a rundown or an overthrow at second.

Note: An accurate throw and a properly positioned cutoff player will keep the runner on first from moving to second. With a sacrifice fly to right or center with runners on first and third, the defense is the same.

Situation: Possible sacrifice fly to center with runners on second and third, or with the bases loaded.

Objective: The play at the plate and holding the other runner to first.

Pitcher: Backs up home plate or possibly third base.

Catcher: Covers home plate and prepares to take the throw. Instructs the first baseman whether or not to cut it off.

First baseman: Moves near the pitcher's mound, directly in line with the center fielder and home plate. Following the catcher's instructions, cuts off the throw to hold the runner or lets it go through.

Second baseman: Covers first.

Third baseman: Covers third.

Shortstop: Covers second.

Left and right fielders: Back up the batted ball.

Center fielder: Catches the ball and throws home, or if there is no play at home, throws to third.

Note: An accurate throw and a properly positioned cutoff player will keep the runner on first from moving to second.

Situation: Possible sacrifice fly to right with runners on second and third, or with the bases loaded.

Objective: The play at the plate or the play at third.

Pitcher: Backs up home plate or possibly third base.

Catcher: Covers home plate and prepares to take the throw. Instructs the first baseman whether or not to cut it off.

First baseman: Moves near the pitcher's mound, directly in line with the right fielder and home plate. Following the catcher's instructions, cuts off the throw or lets it go through.

Second baseman: Covers first.

Third baseman: Covers third. If the throw comes toward third, prepares to take it, and instructs the shortstop whether or not to cut if off.

Shortstop: (1) Moves directly in line between the right fielder and third base. Following the third baseman's instructions, cuts off the throw or lets it go through. (2) Covers second.

Left fielder: Moves toward third in case of a rundown or overthrow.

Center fielder: Backs up the batted ball.

Right fielder: Catches the ball and throws home, or if there is no play at home, throws to third.

Note: An accurate throw and a properly positioned cutoff player will keep the runner on second from moving to third. On a possible sacrifice fly to left with runners on second and third, the defense would remain the same.

SACRIFICE BUNTS

On sacrifice bunts the catcher calls the play when she is not fielding the ball. When she is fielding the ball, the shortstop calls the play.

Situation: Sacrifice bunt with a runner on first.

Objective: A force play at second or the sure out at first. The infielders would play on the base runner going to first if they have the opportunity to get her out.

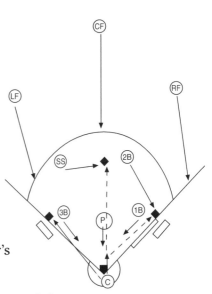

Pitcher: Breaks toward the plate after delivering the pitch. If she fields the bunt, follows the catcher's instructions and throws to second or to first.

Catcher: If possible, fields the bunt and makes the play—either to second or to first—or instructs the infielder who picks up the bunt where to throw. Covers third if the third baseman fields the ball.

First baseman: Breaks in and covers the area between the foul line and the mound. If she fields the bunt, follows the catcher's instructions and throws to second or first.

Second baseman: Covers first.

Third baseman: Breaks in and covers the area between the foul line and the mound. If she fields the bunt, follows the catcher's instructions and throws to second or first.

Shortstop: Covers second.

Left fielder: Moves toward the infield in case of a throw to third. Is in the backup position.

Center fielder: Backs up second.

Right fielder: Backs up the throw to first.

Situation: Sacrifice bunt with runners on first and second.

Objective: A force play at third or the sure out at first.

Pitcher: Breaks toward the plate after delivering the pitch. If she fields the bunt, follows the catcher's instructions and throws to third or to first.

Catcher: If possible, fields the bunt and makes the play—either to third or to first—or instructs the infielder who picks up the bunt where to throw.

First baseman: Breaks in and covers the area between the foul line and the mound. If she fields the bunt, follows the catcher's instructions and throws to third or to first.

Second baseman: Covers first.

Third baseman: Breaks in and covers the area between the foul line and the mound. If she fields the bunt, follows the catcher's instructions and throws to third or to first.

Shortstop: Covers third.

Left fielder: Moves toward the infield in case of a throw to third. Is in the backup position.

Center fielder: Covers second.

Right fielder: Backs up the throw to first.

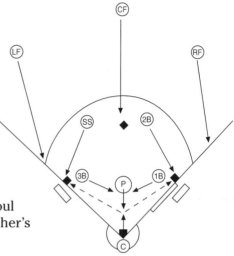

DOUBLE STEALS

Situation: Double steal with runners on first and third, and two outs.

Objective: To get an out and prevent the run from scoring. Second baseman moves into cutoff position and makes the play at second.

Pitcher: Delivers the pitch, moves off the line of the throw to second, and if there is a rundown with the runner at third, backs up the catcher.

Catcher: Receives the pitch, looks at the runner on third to freeze her, throws down to second and prepares to cover the plate and receive the throw from the infielder.

First baseman: (1) Moves to defend against the bunt and then (2) moves to cover first in case of a rundown.

Second baseman: Moves into the cutoff position an equal distance from the mound and second, just slightly off the catcher's throwing line to second base. Has two options: The first is to decoy the runner at third by making a fake attempt to catch the ball and letting the throw go through. The second is to catch the ball to freeze the runner at third and toss the ball underhand to the shortstop covering second.

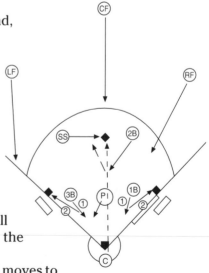

Third baseman: (1) Moves to defend against the bunt and then (2) moves to cover third in case the throw comes there from the catcher or the second baseman.

Shortstop: Covers second.

Left fielder: Backs up the throw to third from the catcher or the second baseman.

Center fielder: Backs up the throw to second and is ready for a possible rundown.

Right fielder: Breaks for first as soon as the catcher receives the pitch and the runner breaks for second to help on a rundown between first and second.

Situation: Double steal with runners on first and third, and two outs.

Objective: The out at the plate. The second baseman moves into the cutoff position and makes the play at the plate.

Pitcher: Delivers the pitch, moves off the line of the throw to second, and if there is a rundown with the runner at third, backs up the catcher.

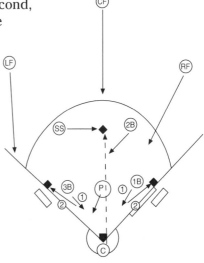

Catcher: Receives the pitch, looks at the runner on third, throws down to second and prepares to cover the plate on a return throw from the infielder.

First baseman: (1) Moves to defend against the bunt and then (2) moves to cover first in case of a rundown.

Second baseman: Moves into the cutoff position an equal distance from the mound and second, just slightly off the catcher's throwing line to second base. Catches the ball and throws to the plate.

Third baseman: (1) Moves to defend against the bunt and then (2) moves to cover third in case the throw comes there from the catcher or the second baseman.

Shortstop: Covers second.

Left fielder: Backs up the throw to third from the catcher or the second baseman.

Center fielder: Backs up the throw to second and is ready for a possible rundown.

Right fielder: Breaks for first as soon as the catcher receives the pitch and the runner breaks for second to help on a rundown between first and second.

Situation: Double steal with runners on first and third, and two outs.

Objective: Keeping the runner at third. To keep the runner at third, the second baseman must check both runners.

Pitcher: Delivers the pitch, moves off the line of the throw to second, and if there is a rundown with the runner at third, backs up the catcher.

Catcher: Receives the pitch, looks at the runner on third, and picks her off if she is off the base. The catcher can also fake the throw to second and possibly pick the runner off. The catcher can also check the runner at third and throw to the second baseman in the cutoff position.

First baseman: (1) Moves to defend against the bunt and then (2) moves to cover first and be involved in a rundown.

Second baseman: Moves into the cutoff position an equal distance from the mound and second, just slightly off the catcher's throwing line to second base. Catches the ball and throws to the plate or throws to third to pick off the runner.

Third baseman: (1) Moves to defend against the bunt and then (2) moves to cover third in case the throw comes there from the catcher or the second baseman.

Shortstop: Covers second.

Left fielder: Backs up the throw to third from the catcher or the second baseman.

Center fielder: Backs up the throw to second and is ready for a possible rundown.

Right fielder: Breaks for first as soon as the catcher receives the pitch and the runner breaks for second to help on a rundown between first and second.

SUMMARY

The defensive plays illustrated in this chapter should provide an objective for the defense as a whole and as individual players.

- These plays designate a specific job for each individual to practice. For example, outfielders do not need to practice being the relay or cutoff player.
- The defense should be set up to (1) field the batted ball, (2) back up the batted ball, (3) cover the bases, and (4) back up the throws to bases. If all these areas are covered and performed in this prescribed sequence, the defense will be a strong unit.
- There are numerous defensive situations in the game of fastpitch. These 35 plays cover many possible defensive alignments the team would need to execute through the course of the game.

Chapter 13

TEACHING PITCHING

Pitching is a big part of the game, up to 80 or 90 percent. Because of your pitching staff's impact on each competition you need to make sure you incorporate some aspect of pitching in your daily practices. This chapter will help give some insight into how you can do this. It should also help you to become more familiar with pitching mechanics and the different types of pitches your staff can utilize.

There is so much strategy in the game of fastpitch softball and a good majority comes from the mound. Learning how to throw to batters is a tool that every coach and pitcher-catcher combination need to become familiar with.

PITCHING: MORE THAN GOOD MECHANICS

I look for several different attributes in a pitcher. I like to see one who runs to the mound as if she cannot wait to get out there. I want her to behave in such a way that she gives me and the rest of the team a feeling of being led. The pitcher controls a great deal of the game and has a large responsibility: The ball is handed to her and she begins each inning with her motion. The team will feel confident in the pitcher if she shows she is in control. Her poise and choice of emotions on the mound will help set the pace of the game.

Pitchers need to have strong personalities and good recovery skills. I have always been impressed with the pitcher who, after throwing a ball that ends in a home run hit, gets a new ball and goes after the next batter. I have seen some pitchers have trouble recovering from a home run and, unfortunately, someone else goes in to pitch their game. I have lost 1-0 ball games where that one run was a home run. The pitcher threw a great ball game holding the team to one run and, most important, the home run did not take her out of the game. She fought back and held the opponent. I know that most pitchers hate the idea of the ball going over the fence; it is a very isolating moment. That's why two characteristics of the pitcher should be resilience and confidence to overcome the momentary failure and to push on to success.

PITCHING PLAN

Our pitching plan has changed throughout the last couple of years in response to the changes in fastpitch softball. Pitching once dominated the game. It was standard to have a ball game that lasted an hour and a half because of all the strikeouts and the lack of hard hit balls, but fastpitch has since become more of an offensive game. Today, pitchers control the game because they handle the ball for the majority of the game but they are not sitting down as many batters anymore. There have been more hits and higher earned run averages because of the development of the athlete, location of fences, high-tech bats, and a new core in the college ball. With these changes in the offense, we have had to make adjustments on the mound.

Today we emphasize keeping the ball low, using the corners, and mixing speeds. It is a must to have a change-up and to be able to aid the batter in hitting a ground ball.

We want our pitchers to have great control on their drop balls and a good change-up. After these pitches have been polished, we will work on something else to add to their mix. The pitch

Too Many Pitchers on the Mound

One time when I was coaching the Macomb Magic, we were playing in regionals. It was double elimination and we already had one loss to the opposing team, so if we were to lose the next game, we would be done. Our pitcher on the mound was Cathy Staskus and the game was in the 12th inning. Her pitches were losing a little bit of their edge, so I went out to the mound to talk with her. When I asked her if she wanted to finish the game she said, "Well, here comes Robin now." I turned and our other pitcher, Robin Lindley-McConnell, was walking toward the mound. I asked Robin, "What are you doing out here?" She replied, "Someone said you wanted me to come in." I answered, "We don't need you now. We will pitch you in the next game." She walked away into the dugout and Cathy continued pitching and we won the game in the 13th inning. Now we were tied with our opponent, each of us having one loss. Robin pitched the next game and we won. This allowed us to advance and to move on to nationals, where we placed fourth.

I love this story because it shows the true characteristics of pitchers. Both Robin and Cathy wanted to pitch the game and win it. I know I could have used Robin in relief, but Cathy sold me by wanting to stay in and finish the game. Her confidence helped us win regionals by making it possible for us to keep Robin fresh for the next game. You want the pitcher to want the ball and to want the challenge. Both of these young women did just that!

they usually go with is a rise ball, though lately I have seen more use of the curve ball in Division I softball. I have never been a big fan of the curve ball. The only time I like it is when it is way out of the zone. If we can get our pitchers to mix their speeds, throw low and outside, and combine these with a solid third pitch, we should have a strong pitching staff.

Three pitches will take your pitchers through a ball game if they know how to use them and what they are for. The pitcher's goal for each batter is to make her commit an out by either striking out, popping out, or grounding out. You need to help your pitchers create a mix that will help them get one of the above results. In high school they might have been able to survive with two pitches: a fastball and a change-up. But in college, pitchers definitely need three pitches: a drop ball, a change-up, and a high fastball or a rise ball. If the drop ball is your pitcher's best pitch, it is the one she wants the batter to swing at or hit. Her other two pitches should help set the stage for that to happen.

Here is an example of how I might throw to a batter. I might start off with my drop and throw it inside for a first strike. If the right-handed batter swings and hits the ball, I should have a ground ball situation to the left side of the field, and if the batter is left-handed I should have a ground ball situation to the right side of the field. If the batter misses, I have to make my next pitch selection for the 0-1 count. Because I am ahead and I have had a swing and miss, foul ball, or called strike, I might want to go with something out of the zone. I choose my high fastball. The batter takes the pitch and I am now at a 1-1 count. In this count I would throw my change-up for a low strike. If the batter hits the change-up, I hope for either a routine fly ball or ground ball. If the change-up becomes another strike, I will now be ahead 1-2. I know the batter has to protect the plate, so I will go to where I feel is the weakest area for hitters and pitch my drop ball low and outside. This drop ball will be a ball. I do not want the batter to be able to take this pitch to the right or left side of the field. I am hoping that she will swing and miss. If she does not, I end up in a 2-2 count and am still ahead of the batter.

With the count at 2-2, I will throw my best pitch. If she lets the one on the outside corner go by, I might put it right back there, only in the zone. If hit, hopefully I have made this my best pitch and I'll get a ground ball to the second baseman or to the right side of the field. If she takes the pitch, it will be strike three. If I were to miss the corner or not get the called strike, I am in a full count and I would then throw my change-up for a strike. This pitch, with its accuracy and low velocity, would help us earn an out. Either the batter will swing and miss, look at a called third strike, or hit off balance for an out.

This is an example of how three pitches can lead you through a count. You could very well have used the high fastball again after the change-up. I often go with a low and outside pitch when the batter needs to protect because she seems more likely to swing at this pitch than one above her waist.

As the head coach I often call the game or have my assistant call the game with the catcher. I do this because we have scouted and kept track of our opponents' batters. If you have a catcher with whom you feel comfortable calling the game alone, that works just as well. We work with our catchers and review situations so that we all feel we are on the same page as far as how we would pitch in a given situation.

PITCHING STRATEGY

Batters show five different characteristics when they are in the batter's box. Any one of these traits will enable the pitcher and catcher to find a weak area in the batter's strike zone.

1. How she stands and where she positions her feet
   - Closed stance
   - Open stance
   - Square stance
2. Where she holds her hands
   - Hands drop during the swing (a hitch)
   - Has a long, sweeping swing where the hands go out away from the body
3. Where she stands
   - Crowds the plate—The batter is looking for an outside pitch and is blinded to an inside pitch.
   - Standing away from the plate—The batter cannot reach the outside pitch and is indicating that her strongest pitch is the inside pitch.
   - Stands in front of the plate—The batter is trying to catch the ball before it breaks. This may indicate a defensive situation such as a bunt.
   - Stands back in the box behind the plate—The batter is trying to let the ball break before swinging so she has more time to see the ball. Lefties utilize this position for the run-and-slap.

4. How she transfers her weight
    - Weight shift in the batter's upper body is back—This takes the bat out of the point of power, usually resulting in a pop-up.
    - Weight shift in the batter's upper body is forward—This takes the bat out of the point of power and eliminates the lower body power.
    - Weight shift in the batter's stride is over the front foot—This eliminates lower body power.
    - Weight shift in the batter's stride remains back over the rear leg—This eliminates the batter's trigger.

5. How she strides
    - Short stride
    - Long stride
    - Strides across her body, toward the plate
    - Strides away from the plate, toward the third-base coaching box

Selecting the right pitch depends on any one or a combination of the batter's five characteristics. See figure 13.1 for a pitching chart containing suggestions about which pitches are best against batters with the above characteristics.

Mechanics

To create an efficient throwing pattern your pitcher should throw in a line of force. The best way to teach the line-of-force technique is to put down tape (or draw a line) and observe her as she goes through her pitching motion. The motion should begin with, open up on, and close on the tape. The tape or a drawn line will give great feedback as to whether she's accomplishing these things.

The pitcher's feet should be shoulder-width apart on the mound with her weight on her front foot. Her glove arm should rest on her body with her throwing hand inside it (see figure 13.2). She will signal the beginning of her motion with a slight rock backwards and then push her glove down with a curve at the end as if she were making the curve in the letter J. The head should follow the glove and lead the body. The back foot then steps out and her body pivots and opens up into a star position (see figure 13.3) with the toe of her left foot pointing at one o'clock and her right foot pointing at three o'clock. Make sure she has her weight on the balls of her feet. The pitching arm should be reaching out and high, slightly bent at the elbow.

Now that the pitcher is opened up, she must close. When the closing process occurs, the pitcher will pivot and push. The front foot (the left foot on a right-handed pitcher) will be the pivot foot and will pull the hips closed and the back foot will provide the push in closing the hips (see figure 13.4). If she loses the push or pivot because of mechanics, the pitcher will be less efficient. The pitcher needs to stay flexed so that she can continue to drive through the motion and end tall. Her pitching arm passes her hip before it closes and the release occurs.

The pitcher's arm should pass her chest after release for a high finish (see figure 13.5). The glove arm is often overlooked. It is important to keep this arm on the line of force and not let it drift out to the side of the body.

When the pitcher's body performs with all its parts working together as an engine, it will produce the most efficient pitching style for the desired pitch and speed. You want your pitchers to throw well, throw fast, and keep throwing for a considerable amount of time. For these things to occur, the pitcher must work on her motion daily to keep it efficient and to give her body the time to learn through muscle memory.

Fastball

The fastball grip is one in which the ball should feel sturdy and comfortable in the pitcher's fingers. The middle finger rests on the seam and the thumb should be directly across from the middle finger. This is a four-seam rotation grip (see figure 13.6); there is also a two-seam rotation. It is important that the ball rest in the fingers of the pitcher's hand. If the ball is deep in the hand it will not allow for a good wrist snap or a fast-spinning rotation. The body mechanics for this pitch are the same as described earlier in the section labeled "Mechanics."

We want to make sure the pitcher can throw the fastball at all four spots (high in, high out, low in, and low out), making minimal changes in her motion. To do this we have our pitchers make small changes in the direction of their front foot on the mound and their release point

Figure 13.1 Pitching Chart

Stance and Characteristics	Optimal Pitch(es)
Up in front of the box	Rise ball, fastest pitch, change-up
In back of the box	Drop ball, breaking ball
Crowds the plate	Rise ball or fastball high in or out, inside curve or screwball, drop inside, rise inside
Off the plate	Drop outside, curve ball or fastball outside
Closed stride	Inside rise, inside drop
Open stride	Outside drop, outside curve
Hands held close to the body	Rise ball or fastball high inside or out, drop inside
Hands above the strike zone	Drop ball or low fastball in or out
Long stride	Rise ball or fastball high in or out, change-up
Hitch	Rise ball or fastball high in or out, change-up or off-speed pitch
Lunges	Curve ball or fastball outside, change-up or off-speed pitch
Sweep swing	Inside curve or screwball, rise ball in or out
Big swing	Change-up

Game Situations	Pitch Selection
Runner on first, bunt situation	Rise ball or fastball high in or out, inside curve or screwball
Runner on second, right-handed batter	Drop inside or low fastball inside
Runner on second, left-handed batter	Drop outside or low fastball outside
Runner on third, right-handed batter, squeeze is on	Rise, pitchout, drop inside, or low fastball
Runner on third, left-handed batter	Drop ball or low fastball outside
Suspected squeeze or suicide bunt, hit-and-run, slap-and-steal, or bunt-and-steal	Pitchout
Slapper	Outside change, rise inside, drop ball or low fastball outside, inside curve or screwball
Aggressive batter	Off-speed, change-up
Pull hitter	Drop outside, curve ball or fastball outside, change-up or off-speed pitch inside

and finish. These changes are so small they are difficult for the batter to recognize. The perfect strike down the middle is a good pitch only for the batter. Since this chapter is on how to teach a pitcher to be successful, we will avoid having her throw the ball down the middle of the plate.

When throwing the ball high in or high out, the pitcher should adjust the front foot so that it turns approximately a half inch to the desired side of the plate, release further out, and finish tall and with a high arm. When throwing low in or out, the pitcher again adjusts her foot and then releases sooner, finishing with a lower arm and having a slight bend forward in the hips.

Figure 13.2 Start of pitching motion.

Figure 13.3 Star position in pitching motion.

Figure 13.4 Closing the hips before releasing the ball.

Figure 13.5 High finish of the pitching motion.

Figure 13.6 Fastball four-seam rotation grip.

Change-Up

The change-up grip is much different from the fastball grip because we want it to do the exact opposite. Where the fastball's desired motion is fast and with spin, the change-up is its counterpart—slow with little spin. There are a few ways to throw this pitch, including the backhand flip change and knuckle ball change. Our team has been most successful with the palm change so that is the one I will describe.

The palm change is one where the pitcher keeps the ball deep in the palm of her hand. You should not be able to see space between the ball and the palm (see figure 13.7). If you can see space, she is not holding it correctly and the ball

Figure 13.7 Change-up grip.

will not change in speed drastically enough for this pitch to be effective.

The mechanics of this pitch are similar to that of the fastball; however, the ending is slightly different. The pitching arm should pass the hip and then the hand should turn down at the release point. This motion is similar to reaching out and shaking someone's hand. The pitcher wants to keep the hand and pitching arm close to the body (see figure 13.8).

The objective of the change-up is to catch the batter off-balance. To assure this, the pitcher tries to throw the pitch with little change in her motion and always keeps the grip hidden in the glove until the motion begins.

Drop Ball

I think the drop ball is one of the easier pitches to learn. Our pitchers throw the roll-over drop. The basics of throwing this pitch are similar to the motion you use when dribbling a basketball. If you can get your pitchers to get on top of the ball and then push it into the ground, you have the beginning of a great drop ball. The spin used

Figure 13.8 Change-up release.

for this pitch can be either a two-seam or four-seam spin. Some people feel that the four-seam grip gives the ball a more gradual drop, whereas the two-seam causes it to drop more suddenly. I have seen both used and think that they both are good drop balls. It's more a matter of comfort for the pitcher. The grip is a split-finger grip with the first finger on the side of a seam and the middle finger on the side of the next seam. If your pitcher is throwing the two-seam, her index finger will be parallel to the large C-curve seam (see figure 13.9). The four-seam requires the index finger to rest parallel to the straight seam (see figure 13.10). The thumb is in a com-

fortable spot for the pitcher's hand, either directly under the middle of the two split fingers or resting on the side.

The pitcher needs to begin the roll-over when passing her hip after the star position. The hand then rolls over the top of the ball causing the ball to spin downward. After the release the hand ends facing down over the right leg. There will be a slight bend in the waist with the shoulder leaning over the body (see figure 13.11).

Rise Ball

The rise ball may be the most difficult pitch to learn. It demands that the body be efficient and that the timing be on. When teaching the rise ball, you must be patient.

The rise ball has various grips. The objective of these grips is to get the ball spinning in a backward rotation so that when the air hits the seams, they push off the air and the ball rises. It again comes down to what is comfortable and successful for your pitchers. The C grip is the one we have gone with for many years. Here is the grip for a four-seam rise ball (see figure 13.12).

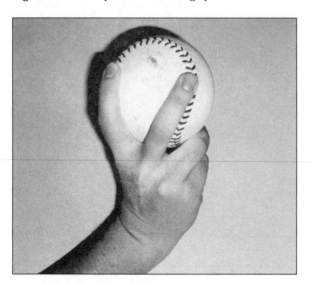

Figure 13.9   Drop ball two-seam grip.

Figure 13.10   Drop ball four-seam grip.

Figure 13.11   Drop ball finish.

Figure 13.12   Rise ball grip.

1. Take your right hand and make a backward C, with all your fingers close together. Now spread your fingers, not losing the curve in all your fingers or the backward C created with your thumb and first finger.
2. In your other hand, hold the ball so that the seams of the ball make a C. Place the ball in your pitching hand so that the C made by the seams of the ball are facing your backward C.
3. Place your first finger on the lower half of the top seam. Your thumb should rest comfortably on the ball close to the two lower seams. Let the other fingers cradle the ball in their tips.

Now that you have the grip, let's work on the wrist: It should be slightly cupped. In the star position, the wrist should be turned with the hand turned outward from the body (see figure 13.13). The wrist should remain cupped until the release point. The first finger will then pull off the ball, spinning it backward into the air. There should be a slight arch in the back with the chest pointing out and the follow-through high (see figure 13.14).

Curve Ball

The curve-ball grip is the same as for the rise ball only the first finger pulls around the ball instead of down. The ball must remain in the fingertips, which all pull around the ball. This pitch requires a straight back and that the arm pull across the body during and after the release

Figure 13.13   Rise ball star position.

Figure 13.14   Rise ball release.

Figure 13.15   Curve ball finish.

(see figure 13.15). The release point for the curve is a later release than for the others, occurring in front of the body. The curve ball is one of the easier pitches to learn, and as I mentioned earlier, it is the most effective if it ends completely out of the hitting range. I say this because some curve balls stay on the same plane as the bat. Pitches that do this are easier for the batter to track and hit.

PITCHERS' DAILY ROUTINE

I have my pitchers throw for an hour and a half five or six days a week, throwing around 400 pitches each day. This helps them create their daily routine for practice. For a younger pitcher in junior high, you might want to lower the amount of pitches to 100 pitches every other day. Once her stamina increases, so can the time spent and pitches thrown.

I like our pitchers to go for a run for 5 to 10 minutes, followed by a 10-minute full stretch. When they get their gloves and cleats on, they play overhand catch with their catcher and then move into a nice and easy, slow underhand toss. This warm-up usually takes about 10 minutes. Once the pitcher feels ready she begins a faster underhand pitch and works her way into throwing at about 70 percent of her actual speed. When warm we will move into drills that we have designated for that practice session. When the pitchers have been successful in their drills, they begin to throw off the mound starting at 50 percent and working their way into full speed. Once they reach full speed, they will work on the designated pitches for about half an hour and then cool down with some light throwing and stretching again.

Each pitching session is designed to give the pitcher ample time to warm up, throw hard, and cool down. To keep your pitchers healthy and strong I suggest allowing them this time. If you try to rush a pitcher, you could hurt her arm. It is very important to cool down and stretch after all physical exercise.

Pitching Drills

In this section I present several different pitching drills and variations to each drill. We put specific time aside for the pitchers to work on these drills during practice. We often do some team drills that do not call for a pitcher to throw, and in these cases we put the pitchers in the bull pen to do drills and spins.

It is important that pitchers get time to do their position-specific drills and also just as important that they are involved in team drills and hitting drills. It takes a little time to arrange a practice to include all these things, and you will find sometimes there must be a little give-and-take. I suggest that if your pitcher requests more time to throw, you give it to her. You want her to be ready to pitch.

Mirror Drill

Purpose: To teach the body muscle memory of the proper mechanics.

Procedure: Your pitcher will need her glove (for balance purposes) and a full-length mirror. Have her stand four to five feet from the mirror. The pitcher is to go through the proper pitching motion at a slow speed, while watching herself perform in the mirror. Each pitch should be performed 20 to 30 times to help the body learn the motion.

Variation: If you cannot get a mirror, have your pitcher face someone with proper mechanics, and after the pitcher goes through her motion she is to watch the coach or other pitcher go through the pitching motion. In this case the coach or other pitcher is taking the place of the mirror.

Coaching point: Make sure the pitchers go slowly and make each movement have a purpose.

Time allowed: 10 minutes

Wall Drill

Purpose: To teach the pitcher to keep her arm straight and to open up into the star position. The wall acts as a deterrent to improper mechanics. If the pitcher does not keep her arm straight, get her hips open, and close strong, she might hit the wall with her arm or body.

Procedure: You will need either a wall or fence that the pitcher can walk down. The wall should be around 30 feet long. If you use the fence of your softball field, make sure it is higher than the pitcher's reach. You do not want the pitcher to come down on the top of fence wire. The pitcher stands sideways about four inches from the wall with her pitching arm closest to the wall. She begins her motion keeping her arm straight so that it does not hit the wall. The pitcher will need to open her hips up when she approaches the star position. If she is in this position correctly, she should be facing the wall with both arms at shoulder height and legs opened shoulder-width apart. After the pitcher is in the star position, she should finish up her motion keeping her arm straight so that when she closes it again it does not rub or bump the wall. The pitching motion should be continuous while she walks down the 30-foot wall. Have each pitcher do 10 sets (one time down the wall counts as a set).

Coaching point: Walk through the motion with the pitchers, standing next to them so they can follow your tempo and not rush the drill.

Time allowed: 10 minutes

Walk Drill

Purpose: To strengthen the lower body and build endurance.

Procedure: One partner stands 60 feet away from the other partner with the ball in a grassy area, gym space, or ball diamond. She begins walking and takes approximately three steps before she steps into her pitching motion. Once in the motion she attempts to throw the ball to her partner. She wants the ball to reach her partner in the air. To make this possible she must use her legs and lower body so she gets a good lift on the ball. After she releases, she takes three steps back to the 60-foot distance. Once the partner receives the ball, she will then do the same technique back to the first thrower. This drill works the legs and teaches the athlete to use the lower body as the generator for the pitch. Have each player pitch 20 to 30 balls.

Time allowed: 10-15 minutes

Spin Drill

Purpose: To teach the fingers the proper grip and ball spin.

Procedure: The pitcher stands three feet from her partner, either a catcher or another pitcher, grips the ball for the pitch she chooses, and then spins it to her partner (see figure 13.16). She does 15 of each of her pitches. If the partner is a pitcher, she can do the spin back; otherwise the catcher can catch it and give feedback.

Coaching point: Make sure you are observing spins if you can. You do not want the pitchers to practice the wrong spin. If you can stand by and watch, you can reinforce the proper spin and help the athlete to continue that proper manipulation.

Time allowed: 15-20 minutes

Drop-Ball Drill

Purpose: To reinforce the correct drop-ball mechanics (getting on top of the ball and pushing it into the ground).

Figure 13.16   Spin Drill.

Procedure: Give your pitcher a bucket of 30 balls (they can be softies) and either a net, tarp, or fence. The pitcher stands approximately three feet away from her catch net. She goes through her pitching motion and exaggerates her release of the drop ball by pushing it directly into the bottom of the net. Let each pitcher throw three buckets of balls.

Variation: The pitcher can throw these to an experienced catcher if she moves back a few more feet.

Time allowed: 15 minutes

Rise-Ball Drill

Purpose: To reinforce the correct rise-ball mechanics (getting under the ball, ball spin, long arm, high follow-through).

Procedure: Partners stand six feet apart with one ball. The pitcher stands in the star position and finishes her motion while working on her rise-ball technique. She wants to be sure to keep her hand cupped and to get backward rotation on the ball. The player receiving the ball is standing. It is the partner's job to give feedback on the spin and the pitcher's mechanics. This is a good drill for muscle memory and breaking down the pitch; it's also a good warm-up drill. Have each pitcher throw 20 pitches.

Variation: Have the pitcher get down on her right knee with her left leg extending out, or in the case of a left-handed pitcher, her right leg. Her hips should be open and her pitching arm straight up (see figure 13.17). From here her arm should come down and pass her hips, and then her release occurs. Her arm should have a high follow-through. This variation to the Rise-Ball drill helps the pitcher finish high because her catcher is standing up and she feels the need to throw the ball higher. This is an excellent drill for those pitchers struggling with their follow-through or getting their hips open.

Time allowed: 10-15 minutes

Figure 13.17   One-knee variation of Rise-Ball drill.

Work in the Bullpen

Bullpen time is an important part of the pitcher's practice. We use our bullpen as a warm-up, conditioning, and polishing area.

When using the bullpen as a warm-up area, we send our pitchers to get warm for a drill or game play. During this time they are to go through the routine with their catchers that they would go through on game day. This helps them know what it takes to get warmed up, how much time they need for each pitch, and how each pitch is working.

Conditioning our pitchers in the bullpen means we have them throw a certain number of pitches. Sometimes it could mean that we have one of the pitchers throw a certain number of drop balls and that is how she spends her time in the bullpen. This is not warm-up; it is conditioning her body to throw the same pitch even under fatigue. After awhile it is hard to tell her 10th drop ball from her 50th.

Once the pitchers have their endurance built up and know their warm-up patterns, they need to do what every finished product needs—polishing. We polish by doing certain drills or by working on our ball spin, but mostly just by breaking down the pitch and making the pitching

motion very efficient. By purifying the motion and reinforcing the movements needed to deliver the desired pitch, the pitcher begins the polish.

Conditioning

The most important conditioning that our pitchers do at Western Illinois University is run. Our pitchers run at least 12 miles a week. We put aside time for them to run in practice and encourage them to run on their own also. Running strengthens their legs and builds their endurance. It is as much mental as it is physical. The athlete sets goals as to how far she will run in what amount of time. Then once she meets her goal she goes out the next time and tries to better it.

This type of conditioning teaches the pitchers not only about goal setting and intrinsic rewards but also how to train the body to work the physical and mental components together. Mind over matter is a game we all play with ourselves when it comes to exerting ourselves physically. If the pitcher can see the way her mind can control her performance, she will have more control over her game. We try to make everything the pitchers do a learning experience. The running offers much more than just physical benefits and has made our pitchers mentally tough.

MENTAL APPROACH

Applying a cookie cutter mental approach to your pitchers is not feasible because everyone is different and will respond differently when faced with a challenge.

I tell our pitchers in the very beginning that they are going to get hits, but not as many times as they are going to get outs. The pitchers have an advantage because a great batter is one who gets a hit four out of ten times, and the majority of the batters they face will not be that successful. This is to the pitcher's advantage because she will be successful at forcing the batter to commit an out over 60 percent of the time. Knowing these facts helps the pitcher feel a little more at ease and definitely more confident.

The second thing I talk to the pitchers about is being committed to the pitches they throw. If they throw a pitch that they do not believe is right for a certain batter or that they don't feel is working well, they are probably right, and because they are not committed to it the pitch will most likely fail. To be successful they must first believe they can be.

The advice I seem to give the most is that they do not have control of what goes on around them. If it is cold or rainy or the fans are heckling them or even if the shortstop dropped two balls, they cannot control these things. The best thing the pitchers can do is control how *they* respond to what is going on around them. My advice is to have them shrink their focus to just their catcher and the task at hand. They should try to focus on throwing one pitch at a time. If they can bring their focus into that tunnel, they will be in control of the one thing that they can control—their performance.

OTHER CONSIDERATIONS

Now that you have worked with your pitchers' mechanics you will want to refresh them on some of the situations they will encounter while preparing to compete and during the competition: for example, how to polish the day before a game, how to find a routine on game day, and how to handle being replaced on the mound.

Day Before a Start

Throughout the years my philosophy on the pitcher throwing the day before a game has changed. This change is mostly due to the pitchers themselves and their requests as far as what they can do and what we can do to help them feel prepared. I have had pitchers who felt they should not throw at all the day before, but this has been very rare. Most of the pitchers who have played on my teams have wanted to throw a little. They use this practice time to iron out some of the kinks they have discovered in previous practices. Most of them choose this time to be one-on-one with a catcher in the bullpen or with the pitching coach. They might also do some light throwing and ball spins and possibly a few drills. We make an effort to ensure all of our pitching staff have worked with all the members of the catching staff. This is important so that everyone is familiar with each other's style.

Pitchers who choose to throw harder the day before usually throw for a maximum of a half hour. I do not include any pitching to live batters or other such drills that would force our pitchers to throw hard at batters on the day before a start. The only time pitchers throw is if they feel comfortable, and we still try to tone it down.

The best suggestion I have is to communicate with your pitchers and ask them what they are comfortable with. If you have more than one pitcher on your staff, you may find that they have different needs. You need to accommodate those needs so that when game time comes your pitchers feel and are prepared.

Pitching Routines

In sport psychology they talk a great deal about establishing routines to help the athlete be in control. Every person goes about getting prepared differently. Pitchers always seem to have a routine of some kind. It is important for the coach to know what his pitcher's routine is on the day of the game. I have had some pitchers

who take a good hour to get warm and others who take 20 minutes. I need to know this about each pitcher so that I can plan our pregame activities accordingly.

We try to give them what they need to pitch *their* game. There are times when we have arrived late for games for whatever reason and I have changed who would start the game because the pitcher who we were going to start needed more time to warm up than one of the others. I have found through my years of coaching that routines are important to the athlete. It is crucial that you do not interfere with the routine. Let them have their way to get prepared as you do yours, as long as it does not disturb the team or interrupt someone else's routine.

Handing Over the Ball

I also have some routines that I perform on game day, although I see them more as rituals than routines. On game day I take the game ball and hand it to the starting pitcher before she begins her warm-up and I ask her if she wants to pitch this game. We then discuss goals for the game and anything else she wishes to talk about. It only lasts a few minutes, but I feel these moments are crucial. This ritual helps her have a routine before each game, and because I choose to go about handing over the game ball the same way every game she can count on that moment. I believe that in her mind she has a way she does things before each game. Her mental thoughts might be something like, "I will put on my cleats, fix my visor, and then Coach will hand me the ball." I am involved and together we have created a moment where we are in control and can make our plan for the upcoming competition.

Relief

Remember to make a small note to tell your pitchers that they are not expected to do it all. I live by the theory that there is not a pitcher that will be on her game every day. In this case your pitcher has to be reminded that when it is not her day you will give another pitcher a chance to make it her day on the mound. When you pull a pitcher from a game she should not take it personally. The change is made because somebody else might be able to get the opponent out at that time in the game.

What a Relief

In the inaugural National Invitational Championship in 1987, Brenda Heyl was our ace. The previous weekend she had pitched five straight games to win the conference title and a few days later was pitching all of the NIC games. We came to the final day of play; her arm was tired and we discussed the next game. We both decided that she would start, but if she got into trouble she would come out. It was agreed and we were comfortable with the decision.

During the game Brenda was holding them to one run, but we were on the short end 0-1. Our opponents had been hitting shots and our defense was making the plays to get us out of many jams. We were in the top of the seventh and they had runners on first and second and only one out when I took the trip to the mound and told her I was going to be making a pitching change. Brenda just stood there, looking away and clutching the ball. I reminded her of our discussion and she finally flipped the ball to me and walked off the field. When she got near the dugout she whipped her glove into the fence.

The relief pitcher delivered one pitch which resulted in a ground ball that was turned into a fine double play. We then came to bat in the bottom of the seventh, trailing by one run. We loaded the bases with one out. Our batter hit a ground ball to the second baseman, who fielded it cleanly and fired to the plate. The catcher had set up for the catch and the throw to first to end the inning and the game. However, she never made the catch! Our runner on third scored and our runner on second brought home the winning run to end the game.

The jubilation that followed was awesome and I have a picture that has Brenda running out of the dugout to join in the celebration. She has a stunned, excited, and tearful face. Of course, the entire team was celebrating and enjoying that special win. After the game I pointed out to Brenda that Laura Pierce had gotten the win and had only thrown one pitch. But that's what a team is for—all the credit to the pitching staff!

SUMMARY

Pitching is a major part of the game of softball. If you want to be successful and have a successful team there is no better place to start than the mound. This chapter should help you get started.

- When choosing a pitcher, look for good leadership qualities.
- Teach your pitchers to focus on keeping the ball low for playable hits.
- Make sure your pitchers have three good pitches.
- Work on solid mechanics through a number of drills.
- Keep your pitchers in good shape; they need stamina.
- Discuss the mental aspect of pitching and put time aside to strengthen it.
- Communicate with your pitchers about what is working for them and what is not.

Part V

COACHING GAMES

Chapter 14

PREPARING FOR THE GAME

I want my team to have the best chance to win every game we play. I prepare my players by teaching and honing individual and team skills, and when the time comes, we put that preparation to the test against our opponent. But in order to give our team an additional advantage, I want us to know as much as we can about that opponent when we walk on the field.

My staff and I prepare a scouting report to study the other team's offense, defense, and pitching. Prior to the game, we will seek out as much information as we can from other coaches who know about or have already played our opponent. In this chapter I will discuss the preparation of scouting charts as well as pregame practices and preparing for big games.

THE SCOUTING REPORT

I like to go into every game having some idea of how the other team stacks up. This information gives me some idea of how to prepare and what we need to focus on to win the game. The main questions I have about the opponent are as follows: How fast do their pitchers throw? What are their main pitches? Who is their number one pitcher? What type of hitting team are they? Who is their best hitter? Has anyone shut her down and how? Does their catcher have a good arm? What is the steal percentage against her? Who has the most steals on the team? When all these questions are answered, I can usually come up with a few more. I feel comfortable that I have this information to share with the team so that we can know our opponent a little better.

I believe in scouting and feel it serves its purpose with our team. However, there are appropriate times to share and not to share such information with the team. If I know we are facing a great pitcher who has yet to lose a game or has a huge strikeout record, I might save that knowledge for the end of the game. I save it because I want my players to focus on the fundamentals and their own goals. If they have too much information, their goals might become fogged. Winning the game should be about you and your team. Too much information about the other team distorts this and could make the game too much about the opponent.

Offense

One of our best-kept scouting reports is our pitching cards. The purpose of the pitching card is to assist the pitcher, catcher, and coach in calling the game. If, for example, we face a team whose number four batter cannot hit a drop ball, we will record this on the card. When she is up to bat again, we can look at her card and know her weakness. We save all our cards for future games against the opponent. These cards are the size of a 4×6 note card, and they help us keep track of who pitched against whom and how the batter performed against that pitcher. They also give good feedback on the batter's weaknesses and strengths (see figure 14.1).

In creating the card we tried to make it easy to read and easy to keep. The game is so fast paced you do not want it to be too complicated. In keeping the card we draw lines for where the ball goes, using a dashed line for a ground ball, a dotted line for a line drive, and an arched line for a pop fly. We also initial by the line the type of pitch that was thrown. So, if the hitter hit a pop fly off an inside drop ball, we initial the arched line with a DI for drop inside. We keep track of who threw what by using different colored pens for each pitcher, because one pitcher's drop ball might be different than another's. The more specific you can keep the card the better it will serve your purpose. Players who are not playing in that game can help assistant coaches update these cards.

When going into a game against a team that we have not yet faced, we will try to find a time to watch them play. During this time we will write what we see in each batter on the back of the card. This helps us in not getting confused with how the batter did against our pitchers but still makes the information accessible.

I would definitely recommend charting your pitches and the opponent's batters if you have the staff or the time. Pitching cards, if kept correctly, are one of our best scouting tools.

Defense

When we are watching our upcoming opponents play another team, we take advantage of this opportunity to keep a defensive scouting chart on them (see figure 14.2). This chart helps us keep track of who is strongest in her position and how we can offensively take advantage of a weak link.

Pitching

We also keep scouting records for our opposing teams' pitchers. We want to know what their best pitches are and what pitches they might throw in certain situations. We record how fast they are and who the best pitcher on the team is. See figure 14.3 for a sample of that card.

Getting the Information

I like to utilize several methods to obtain scouting information about future opponents. First we gather all necessary opponent schedules. We

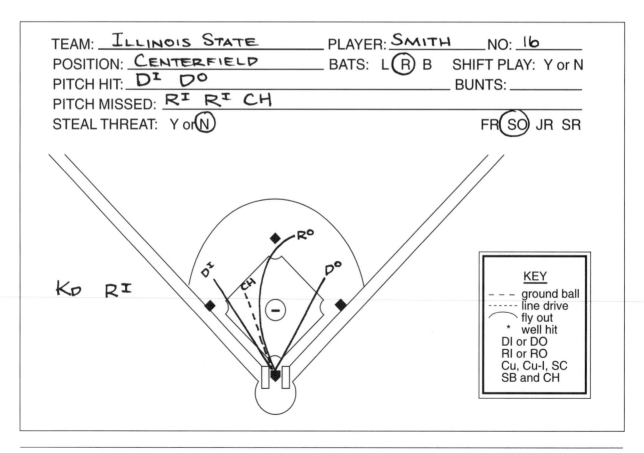

TEAM: _____ PLAYER: _____ NO: _____
POSITION: _____ BATS: L R B   SHIFT PLAY: Y or N
PITCH HIT: _____ BUNTS: _____
PITCH MISSED: _____
STEAL THREAT: Y or N   FR SO JR SR

KEY
– – – ground ball
------ line drive
⌒ fly out
* well hit
DI or DO
RI or RO
Cu, Cu-I, SC
SB and CH

TEAM: _ILLINOIS STATE_ PLAYER: _SMITH_ NO: _16_
POSITION: _CENTERFIELD_ BATS: L ⓡ B   SHIFT PLAY: Y or N
PITCH HIT: _Dᴵ Dᴼ_ BUNTS: _____
PITCH MISSED: _Rᴵ Rᴵ CH_
STEAL THREAT: Y or Ⓝ   FR ⓈⓄ JR SR

Kᴅ Rᴵ

KEY
– – – ground ball
------ line drive
⌒ fly out
* well hit
DI or DO
RI or RO
Cu, Cu-I, SC
SB and CH

Figure 14.1 A blank and a completed scouting card that charts the opposing batter.

202

Figure 14.2 Sample Defensive Chart

Date _____   Team _____

Opponent or Scouting (circle one)   Weather conditions_____

Field conditions_____

	Player & Number	Position	Arm strength	Range	Speed	*Comments
1.						
2.						
3.						
4.						
5.						
6.						
7.						
8.						
9.						
10.						
11.						
12.						

* Rookie, out of position, chokes, lacks lateral movement, cheats on steals, doesn't back up throw, etc.

Figure 14.3 Pitching and Special Defense Chart

Date _____   Opponent _____   Location _____   Weather _____

How do they defend first and third? _____

Weaknesses in their steal defense? _____

Weaknesses in their bunt coverage? _____

Who is their number one pitcher? _____

Who pitched against us? _____

Speed: Fast ___   Above average ___   Average ___   Below average ___

Types of pitches: Rise ___   Drop ___   Curve ___   Change-up ___   Screwball ___

"Go to" pitch: Rise ___   Drop ___   Curve ___   Change-up ___   Screwball ___

Primary location: Up ___   Down ___   Inside ___   Outside ___

What does pitcher throw when:

Ahead in the count _____

Behind in the count _____

First pitch _____

Full count _____

will then make arrangements to obtain or exchange videotapes with other opponents. Finally, we prepare a written scouting report for distribution to the coaching staff and team two or three days in advance of the game.

• Verbal input—We often talk with other coaches and knowledgable softball fans about our future opponents. We rely first on the observations of other coaches. This network is an excellent sharing cycle. Several times we have received phone calls from teams wanting to know how other teams looked when we played them previously that year, and several times we have called or asked other coaches at tournaments about some of our opponents.

• Written input—After discussing the opponent with other coaches, we will then go to our scouting forms, pitching cards, and defensive chart, and relay the information we have learned to our team. This helps create a relationship with coaches from different schools and we can

then ask them for some scouting information about teams we are preparing to face.

• Visual input—Before heading into a big game we usually like to be able to see our opponent play. If circumstances do not allow this, we will call one of the teams we share information with and ask if they have played the team we need information on and, if so, if they videotaped the game. Then we will ask if they would mind sharing a copy with us. This tape will give us the opportunity to fill out our scouting forms and prepare for the game. This is the ultimate sharing between teams.

Will They Still Give Us the Video?

We had invited a team from up north to come down and play us in a doubleheader. We had won our division for our conference and were going to be holding the conference tournament at our field. Two of the teams that we were going to play we had not faced or had an opportunity to watch. I called one of my former assistants who was coaching at another school and asked her for the video against one of them, Troy State. She sent it up to us. Now all we needed was a video of DePaul. While making arrangements for the northern team to come down I asked if they had played DePaul and if they would let us see a video of the game if they had one. Sure enough they had, and said they would bring it down for the doubleheader.

The day of the game, my assistant and I were out having lunch and talking strategy for our 3:00 P.M. game. After lunch we drove by the field and noticed that the northern team had arrived and was warming up two hours before the scheduled game time. We pulled into our office and called over to the field and had our equipment attendant make sure the northern team had checked their contract and knew the game time. Sure enough, they were confused and very upset. They had already checked out of their hotel, were all warmed up, and still had another hour to wait. Our athletes were in class so it was not going to be an easy thing to work out.

I checked the contract and 3:00 P.M. was the correct time, so I took a copy over to the head coach. She showed me her watch and we both knew instantly that the mix up was that she had forgotten the time zone change. She understood it was her mistake but wasn't happy to have made it. They hung out in the gym and warmed up again a half hour later.

The games were tense. They won the first game and then we came back to win the second. After the games, my assistant, Mindy, and I were getting ready to leave when I looked at her and asked, "Do you think they will still give us the video?" She told me she would go ask and reluctantly walked over to their dugout. The head coach was probably in partial disbelief but nodded to her assistant, who pulled the video out of a bag and handed it over to Mindy. As Mindy walked back to me she had a smile on her face and the videotape in hand.

TRAVELING TO GAMES

A few days before the travel date, I provide the team with a trip itinerary outlining all dates, times (including estimated times of arrival), and departure and housing information. This enables the players to record the information in their handbook and to share the travel plans with their parents and fans. I prefer that the parents make their own travel reservations but encourage them to stay at the same hotel as the team.

The players are assigned an equipment responsibility for all away games. They are responsible for picking up the equipment, packing it, and making sure it arrives where it is needed. For example, one player is assigned balls, another the extension cord, two others the catching equipment, and so on. This way no one can assume someone else took care of it. This plan makes for easy travel.

I think traveling together as a team is one of the most rewarding times for the players and the coaches. Seeing new cities and playing in different stadiums or fields allows everyone the opportunity to experience the adventure of competition. We normally travel by bus and encourage the players to arrive 15 minutes before scheduled departure. This allows them time to get their seats and all of their gear aboard without feeling rushed. It is important for athletes to hustle but never to "rush" on game day. Rushing causes the athlete to panic and worry, which is not conducive to top level play.

Before we board the bus, the entire travel party meets outside and forms a send-off circle. We join hands and a spokesperson for the group reminds everyone of the importance of leaving our worries outside the circle and to gain strength from the circle. The spokesperson can add anything else, including a prayer for safety and good health for all participants. I do the send-off circle for the first and last trips and the captains, team members, and assistant coaches have the opportunity to do the rest.

Before the send-off circle starts, we ask the players to mentally review their travel checklists to be sure they brought everything necessary. The most important items are spikes, gloves, socks, stirrups, all uniform parts, undershirts, sliders, and underwear. Anything else we feel we can do without.

When traveling we eat three hours before game time and strive for proper nutrition throughout the trip. We also have fruit and peanut butter and jelly sandwiches (made from low-fat peanut butter and whole wheat bread) in the dugout for all doubleheaders. On the bus we provide water bottles and fruit juices.

When we return from our trip, we empty the bus, check it over, put away equipment and luggage, and then meet back at the bus. We join hands again and make any quick announcements and reminders needed and wish each other a good night. The circle dissolves and everyone heads home.

THE PREGAME PRACTICE

After we have scouted the team and put all our information together, we begin preparing and polishing for the pending competition. The scouting helps us to know what we might work on in practice to take advantage of a possible weakness or create a strategy for the game. For example, we once prepared for a game against a team whose pitcher threw an outside curve. Since we had struggled a little with hitting outside pitching, we decided to focus at practice on hitting outside pitches. We started on the outside T and then worked our way to a toss and then live pitching. Not only did this help instill confidence in our batters but it made the opponent look familiar. Needless to say, we sent their pitcher's curve balls soaring into right field.

I use the practice before the game to tie everything together. It should be a time to rehearse and make last-minute adjustments. Sometimes we will bring in a new idea like the one mentioned above, but for the most part it is a simple polishing job. It is important on this day to ask your athletes what they feel they might need brushing up on before the competition and then create a practice that suits these needs. I sometimes leave open a slot of time to work on those things the athletes feel they need more of. For example, one day I had the infielders working on ground balls and double plays, the catchers working on pickoffs, and the outfielders going back on fly balls. When we were all done, they said they felt more comfortable because they had had the opportunity to fix what they felt were their problem areas.

It is difficult to always know what needs to be covered, so I suggest talking with the athletes to gather their input and make sure that they feel comfortable. After all is said and done, you all will feel more at ease come game day.

PREGAME MOTIVATION

Motivation before a game is as important as the pregame practice. Let me make a few general observations on the topic before I share the way I go about it. First, not everyone is motivated by the same techniques or talks; second, the delivery is crucial; and finally, honesty always works best.

Realizing that not everyone is motivated in the same way helps you not to be let down if many of your athletes do not respond or feel motivated after your talk or demonstration. The delivery is always important. If you are not feeling motivated how can you motivate others? If you do not believe in what you are saying, your athletes will not believe it either. Finally, do not

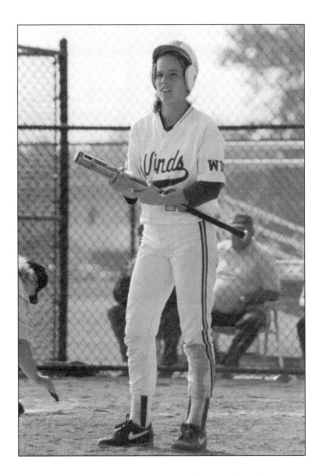

great quality would help make our weaknesses less apparent and strengthen our strong points. I purposely left out averages and percentages and talked more on effort and accomplishments. When we left the room I knew I was looking at a winning ball team. They all glowed with pride and esteem—two attributes that would help them be successful on the ball field. It was one of our more successful pregame motivational sessions, and we continue to do it a few times each year.

Who Is That?

One year we were preparing to play the biggest game of our season and all of the players were getting ready for practice the day before the big game. They were putting on their spikes and talking with one another when we noticed someone standing on top of the hill near our diamond. This person was about 100 feet away and at first, we could not make out who it was. One team member said, "That's Louise Cook!" Louise was the starting pitcher and star of the team we were about to play the next day. We were shocked that she was there in her uniform watching us practice. Well, after a few minutes we all began laughing because we recognized that it was our star pitcher, Robin Lindley-McConnell, dressed up in the opponent's uniform, hairstyle, and makeup. Robin's look-alike costume was so striking we all thought our opponent was spying on us. Our practice that day was great because everyone was relaxed. We went on to win that big game, and Robin was the winning pitcher.

tell your team they are something that they are not. It is very important in your motivational sessions that you are honest. The truth itself can be very uplifting. To admit your weaknesses and talk about overcoming them can be a very motivating experience. To strive to be the best is a better motivating tool than to be told you are the best when you might not be.

For example, after one pregame practice, I asked the team to sit in a circle. Then I went to each athlete in the circle and talked about her individual contributions to the team. This was a time for her teammates to recognize and hear how everybody gives and is a link to our mission. While I talked to individual athletes, I could see other athletes nodding and agreeing with me and smiling at their teammate. When I finished they often responded with "Good job" or "Way to be." This helped the individual feel like a contributor and know that her effort was noticed and respected. When I finished with all the teammates and coaches, I talked of the team as a whole. I focused on our strengths and how we had done one thing better than any other team in the past—hustled. I reiterated how this

UNDERDOG VERSUS FAVORITE

We try to make every opponent human and of equal ability to us. We do not try to think, "UCLA—they're great!" We instead work hard to be everybody else's UCLA. The athletes are aware of the talent pool and what teams are ranked and so on. I need not remind them very often. When we go into any game I want my team to feel it is a big game. Every opponent, every game, every time your team hits the dirt there is something to learn and to gain from the competition. I have seen my best teams lose to teams I thought we would beat the day after they played a ranked team and won. Fastpitch softball is a game of "any given day." That is, on any given day, any team can lose to or beat another. I believe the underdogs win because of their lack of expectation. If they don't expect to win or lose, they can focus more on playing the game. Thus, I do not want to make a giant or an elf of any of our opponents. I simply want my team to do the things they have practiced and do them right. If this happens, each game will be a success.

BIG GAMES

Every big game brings something to the ball field that we, as a team, work on overcoming all year—pressure. I feel that if you can create pressure-like situations in practice, your athletes will perform better under pressure in the game. This may seem very logical, but it is hard to produce the pressure of a conference championship at 6:30 on a winter morning in the gym. It is up to the coaching staff to get creative and produce competitions, awards, and losing consequences that will help put pressure into the practice and help the athlete develop a workable system to deal with it. The practice needs to be hard so that the game is easy.

A Gift to the Parents

In 1993 we were playing in a conference title game and it was televised on Sports Channel. It was the "if necessary" game in a double elimination tournament. Our pitcher, Mindy Dessert, was a fifth-year senior who had battled back through injury to earn the opportunity to pitch and subsequently win this very important game. Mindy's dad was very sick that year and did not make it to the game. My mom, also an avid fan, was unable to attend either.

We won the game against Northern Illinois University and Mindy and I celebrated with a hug on the mound. I said to her, "Now our parents get to see this great victory." We both had tears in our eyes as we realized the gift we were about to give. I called up my mom, told her we had won and told her it would be televised the next day and so she invited her brothers and sisters over to watch. She fixed lunch as they all watched the game. They kept asking her who won, and all she said was, "You'll have to wait and see."

Mindy's dad watched it that day as well and videotaped it. We heard that he had played it for every single visitor that came into his house that month.

SUMMARY

In this chapter we discussed the importance of preparing well for games.

- Find out all you can about your opponent at least a few days before the game so that you can share it with the team.
- Make scouting forms that are easy for you to use. Scout the offense, the defense, and the pitching, as well as any special defensive plays.
- Design the pregame practice to attack the opponents' weaknesses and nullify their strengths.
- In your pregame motivation try to be uplifting and honest.
- Let the team know that every opponent is human and equal to them in ability.
- To win the big game, the practice has to be hard so that the game can be easy.

Chapter 15

HANDLING GAME SITUATIONS

Game situations—everything from how you handle yourself on the field to how you pick your lineup—are extremely important to think about ahead of time. The game is the reason the players compete and put their talents to the test. As coaches and players, we want to be prepared for the challenge so that, win or lose, we know we performed at our very best. In this chapter I will present an idea for a pregame warm-up, as well as some statistics to help you determine the most effective batting order for your team. I will discuss your conduct as well as your players' conduct, and I have also included some information about game duties as well as game day responsibilities. The main focus of this chapter is on some of the normal and unique game situations that a coach will have to deal with that we haven't touched on before.

PREGAME WARM-UP

It is important to maintain team continuity before the game, and I've included an example of a consistent game day warm-up plan to help you create a pregame routine. This warm-up will take 65 minutes from the start of the warm-up to the beginning of the game. If you want to save seven minutes, stretch and do sit-ups and push-ups before getting to the field.

Pregame warm-up (65 minutes)

10 minutes	5-minute run, 5-minute partner stretch
2 minutes	Sit-ups and push-ups
10 minutes	Partner throw
20 minutes	Batting practice—pitchers and catchers go first (all players do 10 sprints during batting practice)
7 minutes	Defensive mini-drills (see chapter 11) • Ball drill • Grapevine drill • Shoestring Catch drill
10 minutes	Infield/outfield shuttle ground balls
2 minutes	Captains' meeting (all players meet for goal setting and a prayer)
2 minutes	Drink break
2 minutes	Final focus points

LINEUP

When my assistant coach, Mindy Dessert, asked me how I decide who starts, I thought about it and told her "the players with the most skill"—skill meaning the athlete who does the defensive job best at that position, coupled with the ability to hit. That seems easy enough if you have exactly nine players who fit the role. But what if you have matched talent at certain positions? In that case, there are other things I look at. Usually in practice the majority of the players give it their all. After practice, however, desire becomes more evident in the athlete who wants "one more" while the others are changing their spikes. I look to the player who creates opportunities to excel and takes advantage of them, rather than the player who waits for opportunities to happen.

You Be the Star

I had a pitching staff one year that consisted of a senior and a freshman pitcher. Neither one dominated, yet they both got the job done. This should have been the senior's year to shine. In her previous years, she had to follow one of Western's best pitchers, but now it was her opportunity to lead. Our defense was solid and our bats were hot, so even without a dominating pitcher, our spring was blooming into a great season. Our doubleheaders were being shared by the two pitchers: Usually the senior pitched the first game and the freshman the second. The majority of the time, if the senior won the freshman won as well, and if the senior lost the freshman lost, too.

One day we were playing the University of Iowa and the senior lost the first game 3-2. I knew we had another shot and I needed someone to go out and take charge. I knew right away that this could be our freshman pitcher's moment to shine. It is hard sometimes, as a freshman, to take charge, but I went to her anyway. I talked with her a little about her pitches and then I told her to go out there and be "the star." She looked at me and smiled and knew that this was a great opportunity for her to prove herself and replied, "Okay, Coach." The next thing I knew, we were in the bottom of the seventh and up 1-0. She pitched from within herself and played the game pitch by pitch. We defeated Iowa and she had proven to her team that she could be a leader.

The starting lineup is set during the practice sessions. I will pick a lineup before the season begins and stick with it if there are few problems. Once the lineup is set and the player has earned her position, it is hers to lose. The batting order is very flexible for me, and will change according to game performance. I do not change the defensive positions very often once they are set, but if two players are equal they will alternate until one clearly wins the spot. If a player does not produce in the game, then I meet with her in the office to let her know beforehand why I am making the change. Understanding the situation can help her to remain positive and enthusiastic. I also let her know that my decision may not be right, but sometimes decisions come down to coaching instinct.

When determining the batting order, I consider a number of factors. For example, the leadoff hitter must have the ability to get on base and enough speed, should she reach base, to avoid the double play or to go to third base on a single to right or right center. Therefore, good

pitch selection and discipline and a high on-base percentage are all important for the leadoff hitter, both for the first batter in the lineup and the hitter who has to lead off after the first inning. I conducted a 75-game study and found that the following positions in the batting order led off an inning:

Position	Led off an inning
First	68 (not including 75 leadoffs in first inning)
Second	31
Third	47
Fourth	65
Fifth	55
Sixth	62
Seventh	43
Eighth	56
Ninth	44

After the leadoff batter, the number four hitter also starts a lot of innings, with the sixth position a close third. What this research tells me is that the number one and four batters should be very much alike in terms of their attributes for leading off an inning.

The number two hitter in the lineup should be a good contact hitter who has the ability to hit the ball to the right side of the infield. The right-handed number two batter should have the ability to drive the ball to the right side and the left-handed hitter should have the ability to pull the ball. This hitter must have the discipline to look for a pitch in the hitting zone that she can drive to the area of the infield that will provide the best chance to stay out of a double play. We do not want a strikeout person here because a strikeout cannot advance a runner to scoring position for the big hitters following. Power is not essential here. The number two position will rarely lead off an inning according to our 75-game study.

What position is up most often with people on base? Here is a study of a 19-game fall season, showing the number of times each batting order position came up with runners on base:

Position	Runners on base
First	27
Second	35
Third	37
Fourth	41
Fifth	38
Sixth	36
Seventh	37
Eighth	26
Ninth	28

As coaches have suspected, the number four position comes to the plate with the most opportunities for advancing people on base. The number five spot is right behind, followed by the third and seventh positions.

The number three hitter should be the hitter who you feel is the best overall hitter on your team. In every game, this batter will be up in the first inning, sometimes with runners on base. To decide who this batter is, ask yourself this question: "Who demonstrates that she is the most consistent batter and scores the highest on offensive skill contests in practice?" This should be your most consistent hitter, someone who is the toughest to get out with few hitting weaknesses.

The number four, or cleanup, batter should be a clutch hitter with power, the team's top RBI hitter; her slugging percentage will be lower than that of the number three hitter, generally as a result of her lower batting average.

The fifth spot may be occupied by a power hitter with a lower batting average and on-base average than the two hitters ahead of her. Number six may be the same kind of hitter as number five, only not quite as proficient.

The seventh and eighth positions are usually filled by players who are starters by virtue of their defensive ability and who will be your two weakest hitters. The ninth batter shares the characteristics of the leadoff batter, while the seventh batter shares the characteristics of the second; but the seventh batter produces figures worse than the second batter. On an especially good hitting team, the seventh spot might be filled by a batter who hits a lot of long balls but has a low batting average and does not draw many walks.

The Home-Run Hug

In 1992 we were competing in the conference tournament against Indiana State University and the game was very tight. In the bottom of the seventh with the bases loaded, two outs, and a full count on their batter, I thought our pitcher had just thrown strike three. However, the umpire called "Ball four." That walked in a run, giving us a one-run lead with the bases still loaded. The next batter hit an RBI single to center field to tie the game, but the winning run was thrown out at the plate!

As I walked out of the dugout to go to the third-base coaching box I asked the umpire, "Where was that pitch?" He stared straight at me and I asked him again. He continued to stare at me, and so the third time I said, "Was it high, low, inside, or outside?" He finally answered and said that it was low. I said, "You're guessing—you don't know where it was." By now he was so puzzled he pointed to the sky. It was then that I realized I had just been thrown out. He also quietly said, "You're out of here." I thought if I just kept walking to the coaching box he would change his mind, but no, he turned and said he had thrown me out of the game. I couldn't believe it—all I had done was ask a question.

I walked back to the dugout and there was our starting pitcher and the first batter of the inning, standing in the door. I told them I had just been kicked out of the game. They both stared at the umpire and said, "Don't worry about it, Coach. We'll take care of it."

Having never been kicked out of a game before, I didn't know where I could be, and I sure did not want to miss the exciting conclusion of this one. The dugout was huge, so I stood down at the end of it, right across from first base.

The eighth inning started with our cleanup batter at the plate. On the first pitch she sent the ball flying over the left center field fence. Home run! She rounded the bases, met her teammates at home plate, walked into the dugout and gave me a huge hug and said, "That one's for you, Coach!" It was a wonderful feeling to be greeted in that manner and to feel important in the dugout. We went on to hold them in the bottom of the eighth inning for the victory but we did not stop there. We swept through the conference championship undefeated and earned a bid to the NCAA National Championship.

CONDUCT DURING THE GAME

Nothing is bigger than the game. Individual egos need to be managed in such a way that the attention of the audience is not on the individual but on the game as a whole. This can be accomplished when the coaches and players set a behavior standard that is beyond question. It is okay to get excited and show emotion, but not to disrespect the umpire, the opponent, or the game.

Your Conduct

Skills should have been taught in practice; the game is the time to coach the *game*, not the skill. For example, when the batter is on deck or in the batter's box, this is not the time to correct her swing. At this critical time the batter needs to be reminded to focus and make contact in order to hit the ball hard.

You should remain focused as well as your athletes. A good way to do this is not to get ahead of yourself. Play the game one out at a time. Try not to think of the what ifs. Let yourself see each play, out, or inning through. It is important for you to be focused on the situation at hand so that your athletes emulate your actions.

I feel it is always of utmost importance to never criticize or embarrass a player in public. Refrain from yelling at the athlete during the game or in front of others. Players do not want to disappoint with their performance, and I believe it is a serious flaw in a coach to belittle them by yelling at them.

There may be times when you need to raise your voice and these times are at practice. Practice is where the players learn to be disciplined. As a coach you have to teach discipline, hustle, and so on to make the practice efficient and an optimal learning environment. There are

usually no fans at practice so the yelling done there is only heard by the team. In the game, if an athlete makes a mistake or an error, she feels bad enough because she has let her teammates down.

I also have a rule never to use profanity during a game, not at the players, the umpire, or the fans. It looks awful, sounds awful, and is degrading to those you address, to your team, and to what you represent.

As a coach you must also show respect for the umpires. I have the greatest respect for umpires and for the difficult job they have, making split-second decisions on balls and athletes moving with great force and speed.

Your Underwear Is Showing

In a highly charged game against the University of Missouri in 1995, the plate umpire and I were in a heated discussion. I sensed I was going to get kicked out, so I walked around behind him on the way to the third-base coaching box and noticed his ball bag had pulled his pants down and about four inches of the top of his underwear was showing.

I stopped arguing, kept walking, changed and softened my tone and said over my shoulder, "Your underwear's showing." His right arm shot out and up ready to eject me as he yelled, "What? You're . . . ." At the same time he sensed something and reached back with his left hand and felt the back of his underwear. Meekly he said, "Oh." Down came the arm and I stayed in the game. Only rarely, in a season, can you win an argument with an umpire.

Your conduct during the game must be exemplary. Remember that you represent yourself, your school, and your family and that you are also the team's leader. You are the top of the pyramid, with assistant coaches below you, and the players forming the all-important base. Your players will look to you and follow your example during the contest. If you cannot keep your composure, it will be difficult for your team to keep theirs. If you lose your temper, your team may do the same. Stay focused on the game and the challenges at hand, and work to set the best

possible example for your players and your supporters.

Player Conduct

We expect our athletes to always behave proudly on and off the field. When on the field, they are representing the university and enjoying the privilege to play and showcase their talent in Division I fastpitch softball. But sometimes game situations will challenge their composure. For example, what happens if the umpire does not call certain parts of the strike zone? In that case the coach needs to tell both the pitcher and the catcher not to panic, and to keep throwing strikes. Instruct your catcher to talk to the umpire and to let the umpire know that the pitcher can throw that pitch for a strike and that she needs that pitch to get the batter out.

Differences of opinion about balls and strikes can be nerve-wracking for the umpire as well, and if it is early in the season it may take him time to return to form. The pitcher and catcher should not get emotional in their actions or their looks because no one wants to be embarrassed, including the umpire. If the pitcher has a question about a call the umpire made, have

her ask the catcher to ask him. The catcher and umpire must develop a relationship each game and it is quite permissible for the catcher to ask the umpire questions. It never works and you will never win the umpire's favor by being disrespectful, but you might win his favor by approaching him with respect.

We ask the same from our athletes on the bench, that when they disagree with a call, they do not question the umpire but respect his decision gracefully. We want all players to cheer for their own teammates and not to cheer against their opponents.

GAME PLAN ADJUSTMENTS

It is important for coaches to take full advantage of an opposing team's weaknesses on both offense and defense. In chapter 13 you found an in-depth discussion of pitching strategy. Coaches constantly need to evaluate their opponent's offensive and defensive weaknesses and must change the game strategy accordingly. Some topics included in changing the game plan are pitching changes, defensive changes, and pinch runners and hitters.

Pitching Changes

What happens if one or more of the pitcher's pitches is not working? During the course of the game usually one pitch will not work, but the pitcher cannot give up on it. The pitcher should try to establish all her pitches during the warm-ups, even if she finds that one pitch is not working. If the pitcher has no movement, then have her work on location. In like manner, if she is having problems hitting her location, have her work on ball movement. To make adjustments during the game, have the pitcher throw between innings with a catcher, working on location and spin. Do not let the pitcher give up on a certain pitch, because it may come around later in the game. If the pitcher is having trouble finding the strike zone, there are three ways the catcher can help—lowering her body or bringing her body up, thus moving the target, and exaggerating the target.

Changing the pitcher in the middle of a game is one of the toughest decisions a coach will have to make. There have been times when I hung with a pitcher who was struggling and we got the win, and there have been just as many times when I made the decision to take the pitcher out and we have sealed the victory. There is not a textbook answer, but the pitcher and catcher can help you make the call. The catcher can let you know how the pitcher's ball speed and movement are doing, while the pitcher herself can give some insight into her level of confidence. For example, does she feel her pitches are working and can she get herself out of the inning? Her challenge is to throw a good pitch and have it hit badly. Nothing more difficult than that.

Putting in a relief pitcher or staying with the one on the mound is a gut instinct call. However, do not put in a pitcher who is not completely ready to come in. The reliever must be mentally and physically ready to come onto the field. Finally, if you have any doubt about your pitcher on the mound—make the change!

Defensive Changes

If a player has made two errors in the game, when she leaves the field on defense I take her aside and talk with her one on one. I try to find out if she will be all right staying in the game or if she is having a hard time focusing on the task at hand. If I have to remove a defensive player, I want to make as few changes as possible within the entire team. You want to keep your players in their original defensive positions, because it is difficult for them to know all the aspects of each position. If I can keep players in the position they know the best they are more likely to excel.

A Substitution Nightmare

It is fun to think about the times when we found our opponent's weakness and snatched the win away by forcing the play. In one game in particular we did just that. We were down 3-0 going into the sixth inning. Our leadoff batter beat out a bunt and stole second. On the steal, she slid into their shortstop who twisted her ankle, and was forced to leave the game. Their next best shortstop was playing second base, so they moved her over. They moved their third baseman to second base and put in a new third baseman. Three people were out of their starting positions, the shortstop, the second baseman, and the third baseman. We saw this as a crucial opportunity for a comeback and we took advantage of it. We laid down bunt after bunt in the direction of their new third baseman. She had trouble getting to the ball and made some bad throwing decisions. Needless to say, they lost the game. We might have hit one ball out of the infield that troubled inning. The final score was 4-3. This is a great example of how you can capitalize on your opponent's weaknesses.

Pinch Hitters and Runners

There will be times when pinch hitters or runners can win a game for you. For example, a runner on third and one out with a batter due up who is a weak ground-ball hitter is a perfect opportunity for the pinch hitter, someone who has been hitting well at practice but maybe is not one of the starting nine. The hoped-for scenario is that your pinch hitter comes in and hits the long fly ball needed to score the runner at third. You can then reenter the fielder. It is important to know that pinch hitting is one of the hardest jobs for a player called from the bench. She has a one-time opportunity to put the ball in play. The pinch hitter needs to hit 1.000 every game. She doesn't get to try to go two for four or three for four. So, put your pinch hitters in the game when their hit or fly ball will make a difference on the scoreboard. Use them early in the game to get ahead or to add a run to cut into your opponent's lead.

Making the call on the pinch runner is fairly simple. Do you have someone on the bench who is faster than the base runner? If so, enter her early in the inning so that she has more than one out in which to score.

Time-Outs

The coach gets one trip to the mound each inning. Most of the time you will not need to use each time-out, but there are times when you should. The most obvious is when the pitcher is having problems and you either want to talk with her or make a pitching change. You might also go to the mound when your defense has made a series of bad plays. You want to take the time to get them to relax and break the negative rhythm. Just as you might go to the mound to break a negative rhythm, you might also go if the opponents are in a positive rhythm.

Your trip should give your team a moment to get themselves together. You want to make sure you are not breaking a good rhythm for your team, so don't make an unnecessary trip. If your pitcher says she is okay, give her the benefit of the doubt and let her try to pull herself out of any jam before you take her out. The pitcher and catcher can call a time-out and meet on the mound without you using your trip. Let them try that first if it is not a crucial situation.

Your conversations at the mound should help relax your players or refocus them. This is not a time for yelling; all eyes are on you. Find words of encouragement, or if they just need a breather, tell a joke. It is amazing how a smile can change the pace of the game.

If you use an offensive conference to talk to a batter, be sure you use few words and make eye contact. I have found that this is the most intense time for a player and when you look into her eyes you will see focus and concentration. Do not use this time to teach her how to bat or to explain a technique, but remind her of the exact needs of the team in this situation.

Game Duties

When the game begins, everyone on the team has a duty. Of course, there will be nine players on defense and nine or ten on offense. The remainder of the team has important responsibilities, too. The relief pitcher knows she is first relief at the start of the game. The relief pitcher and a catcher are to each have a ball in their gloves and to know where their gloves are. If we have a manager we teach her how to keep the score book and that will be her only assignment. She exchanges lineups in a timely manner with the opponent and the official scorekeeper and gives one to me to give to the umpire. Other nonstarters film one inning each game if we do not have a layperson doing the job.

Prior to the game one of the coaches works with the starting pitcher and catcher. The other will fungo hit to the infielders or the outfielders. I try to alternate so that on every other game I can work with all the players. A nonstarting catcher receives balls from the outfielders and a nonstarting first baseman can receive balls from the infielders. I then assign a fungo hitter to the station I am not working at.

During the game all nonstarters are expected to sprint to the foul-line fence and back each inning. Possible pinch hitters swing a bat every inning when we are on offense and additional defensive players play catch at least once in the first half of the game.

Coaches are in both coaching boxes when we are on offense, and when we are on defense the assistant coach is charting each batter as well as calling the game. Those pitching cards can be seen on page 204. I take notes during the game that I feel can help teach the game better. These may be on great defensive plays or mental errors that occurred. We will review these notes with the team after the game. With these notes I can evaluate our strengths and weaknesses as well as design future practices.

Postgame Procedures

I like to be consistent in my expectations of everyone after the game. We follow a prescribed course of action after each day's play.

1. First, of course, we all shake hands with each member of the opposition and compliment

the umpires on the good job they did as we walk through the line.

2. The players pack up their belongings in a reasonable amount of time while the coaches do the same.

3. The team works to gather all of the equipment. Each member attends to her specific equipment responsibility.

4. We meet in our regular location of the ballpark—for example, outside the fence down the first-base line—and players remove their shoes. At this time, the coaching staff can confer regarding announcements and the pluses and minuses in the game.

5. During our postgame meeting we have each player sit in the same place for the game discussion. For example, the pitchers and catchers that played in that game sit in the front, the infielders sit together, and the outfielders sit together. The players who did not play or who played as pinch runners or pinch hitters are together behind everyone else. In this way, I can make eye contact with each player during the discussion and I know where to look for each individual.

6. I then review the highlights of the pitching summary: hits, walks, how the pitcher did in tough or crucial situations, and the contribution of the catcher. I then cover our offensive performance—key hits, runs batted in, game-winning hits—and highlight situation hitting, such as crucial bunts, hit-and-runs, and so on. I end by reviewing sparkling defensive plays and any outstanding hustle performances.

7. Next, I review situations we can learn from in the game and mistakes we made as coaches, as a team, or as individual players. This is an important peak teaching opportunity; this is where necessary learning takes place. What did we do wrong and how can we learn from our mistakes? This discussion lasts 7 to 10 minutes.

8. We then make announcements regarding what happens next that day, who our next opponent is and what that game's itinerary will be.

9. After the postgame meeting with the team the coaches meet to select an offensive and defensive player of the game, and they announce their decisions at the next team meeting.

Winning With Class

After a win it is important to enjoy it. I remember losing one game 15-0 and hearing the winning coach berate her team for various mistakes they made in the game. I could not help but wonder what a team needs to do to be able to enjoy the completed contest. Surely in that 15-run romp there was something for our opponents to view as positive.

I think it is important to keep everything positive. Following a win, let the players enjoy the fruits of their labor. It is necessary to keep a win in perspective, but there is fun in playing and in being successful. Point out to the team all the things they did to be successful and remind them that it will take hard work to stay successful.

Following our games we always eat together and invite friends, parents, and families to join us. This is an important bonding time and it also gives the team a longer time together to enjoy the victory. After a win it is great to see everyone smiling!

Losing With Dignity

A peak teaching opportunity follows a loss—everyone can learn from a loss. A loss provides immediate feedback for the coach and player alike—the facts of the game play a part in the outcome. For example, if your catcher overthrows third base trying to pick off the runner and the runner scores, the catcher learns this is a risky play, especially late in the game. In my experience, the team is very receptive to what the coach has to say then. There are times in defeat when the players have given a winning effort and it is vital for the coach to acknowledge that effort. Praise them for it. After the loss, help the athletes to maintain a positive attitude that will carry them into the upcoming games and practices.

The coaches, too, learn from the loss. In the example of the catcher overthrowing third base, the coach who called the play learns the same lesson the catcher learned. Sometimes we are outplayed by our opponent, sometimes we are outcoached by them, and sometimes we don't execute well enough to earn the victory. Be sure to point out the differences. Handle the loss with dignity and fire up your players for the next contest. Every coach must set the tone for the

next game and practice in the most positive way possible. After each game I make it a point to walk through the dugout and acknowledge the effort each individual athlete gave.

After a loss, all the players are going to be disappointed; help them to lift their heads up and set the tone for a positive attitude, one that states, "We will be back, stronger than today." Athletes are very resilient, but it is often the coach who can lift the spirit of a discouraged player. Let them know you believe in them and that you care about the way they are feeling. Stay positive and your team will respond!

SUMMARY

Before the game, make the following preparations:

- Do your homework on your opponent.
- Be consistent with your starting lineup and place batters in the lineup where their attributes will work best.

- Know your players' skills, but do not forget their other strengths.
- Practice your pregame warm-up before game day.

Practice these strategies during the game:

- Stay focused.
- Take advantage of your opponents' weaknesses and take away their strengths.
- Have exemplary conduct at all times.
- Keep track of pluses and minuses.

Adhere to a routine after the game:

- Be consistent in your timetable of game review.
- Briefly discuss the team's pluses and minuses.
- Make important announcements.
- Allow the team to enjoy the victories.
- Lose with dignity and learn from the loss.
- Always focus on the positive.

Part VI

COACHING EVALUATION

Chapter 16

EVALUATING PLAYERS

This chapter emphasizes the importance of evaluating players fairly and explains how accurate preseason evaluations, as well as continuing evaluations during the season, can help the coach make better coaching decisions.

PRESEASON EVALUATION

We have returning athletes and recruited athletes in attendance at our first practice. That evening we will conduct tryouts for any additional athletes who are interested in walking on to the team. Procedures for tryouts are detailed in the following section. It is my goal to be sure that every player who either does not make it through tryouts or is cut from the program before the first game feels as though she was evaluated fairly, and that her lack of success on the field was due to her inability to perform the necessary skills that would enable her to be a contributing member of the team. With that in mind I have also included examples of the forms I use in my preseason evaluation process.

Tryouts

Figure 16.1 is an example of a tryout chart I use to select players. I rate them on a 1 to 5 scale for each of the skills and then add the scores together. To get additional opinions and increase your objectivity, you can also invite other coaches to watch the tryouts and to score the athletes.

After the tryout session we meet individually with each athlete and show her her evaluation form. We discuss what the form reveals and either tell her she has made the team or discuss why she did not. I feel it is best that we talk with the athletes face to face rather than having them find the results posted. This gives them the opportunity to ask about what they need to work on if they would like to try out again, and

---

Figure 16.1 Tryout Evaluation Form

- Take 2 laps, stretch, and do warm-up throws.

Ground balls   5   4   3   2   1
- Field 10 ground balls; 5 at SS and 5 at 2B—throw to 1B.

Fly balls   5   4   3   2   1
- Catch 10 fly balls; 5 in LF and 5 in RF—throw to 3B.

Throwing   5   4   3   2   1
- Evaluated during warm-up and when throwing to 1B and 3B during fielding and catching drills.

Hitting   5   4   3   2   1
- Swing at 10 pitches off of a machine.

Speed   1_____ 2_____ 3_____ AVG:_____
- Sprint from 1B to 2B 3 times—average the times.
- Group race; place 1st, 2nd, and 3rd overall.

Pitching   5   4   3   2   1
- Throw to catchers to demonstrate speed, accuracy, and movement of pitches.

Catching   5   4   3   2   1
- Catch pitches to demonstrate position and consistency.
- Throw to 2B 3 times, average the times   1_____ 2_____ 3_____ AVG:_____
  (from the time the pitch hits the catcher's mitt until the ball hits the SS's mitt at 2B).

they seem to feel more comfortable with this approach.

Evaluation During Practices

When we are three weeks away from our first game, we begin to chart various offensive situations and defensive tests. These results are posted for the next day's practice so that everyone can review her individual performance, along with seeing how she "measures up" to her teammates. For example, every other Monday, Wednesday, and Friday during the preseason we chart 10 swings off the pitching machine. We call this home-run derby. The athlete earns three points if she hits a line drive to the opposite field, two points for a line drive, one point for a ground ball, and zero points for a swing and miss, foul ball or pop-up. We do this in a batting cage and we incorporate this test within a circuit of other skills. We award a prize to the top point-getter.

Another method we use to evaluate during practice is to chart game plays off a pitching machine. We record well hits as we go through games in which we use a pitching machine. Every time the athlete hits the ball "well" she receives a point and we divide that by the total number of her at bats. For example, if she is up 10 times in three games and has four well hits, her average would be .400.

We chart defensive skills as well. For example, we will give a scorecard to a group of three infielders and they hit to each other 50 ground balls. A fungo hitter hits ground balls to a fielder, who scores a point when she fields the ball and throws it to the receiver. We do this objective test weekly and add the results for a total.

The players who are the most consistent at practice will start in games. During practices I look for the ones who can execute drills with pressure on, such as defensive players who can make the plays with live base runners. The more drills we can do that simulate game play and game situations, the stronger our individual players will be. The clutch player will stand out day in and day out, while others may do outstanding work on a more sporadic basis.

Videotape

We use the video camera as another coach. During the preseason we film each hitter every other Monday, Wednesday, and Friday and view the tape on the next Monday, Wednesday, or Friday. At the beginning of the season, we purchase one videotape for each player and use that tape at all recording sessions. Please see chapter 7 for the four-week hitting program.

We film our pitchers during practice at least once a week. As part of the practice we show the pitchers their films. After pitching and being filmed, they will go to a TV-VCR unit and review their practice with a coach. We film our defensive players once a week in circuit work or in game play. When we film a defensive player in circuit work, another station is set up for viewing.

It is also important that we film all of our games during the season so that we can be accurate with our statistics and so that the athletes can see themselves perform. We watch the recordings together as a team for general play and understanding of the game as well as individual performance. Players are also en-

couraged to meet with a coach to view their own performances during the game. Video technology is a vital tool and it is so true that "a picture is worth a thousand words."

Player Evaluation

Two weeks before the start of the season, we utilize a player evaluation system where all players and coaches are given the opportunity to evaluate each player on the team. I feel that at the high school and the college level the athlete is very much aware of the ability of her teammates, and because of this I want to involve everyone in the process. I want this procedure to be democratic, and I also want to know what my players' opinions are of each player at each position.

It is my obligation to each player to evaluate her performance as a potential team member and as a contributing factor to the team's success. Unfortunately there are subjective criteria involved in the selection of the personnel, but better evaluation will be in effect when we use as much objective criteria as possible. Subjective criteria involves opinion, like a coach's instinct about a performance, while objective criteria involves tangibles like a hitting chart kept at practices. Each player should be familiar with the methods used in the evaluation, since this evaluation will serve to determine the amount of playing time she can expect during the season. As the evaluations take place, the players will be able to see the results and we want them to feel that they can discuss the evaluation with any of the coaches involved.

At the evaluation session I explain to the entire team the reasons behind allowing them the opportunity to evaluate each other, along with what criteria they should use in making their decisions. I do not have them rank themselves until the final evaluation takes place before the opening of the regular season. They put their names on the forms so that the coaches know how each player ranked the team position by position. I tell the athletes not to use this evaluation as a personality contest, but rather, to base their evaluations on their estimation of each individual's worth to the team. They can use their observations over the past seasons and during the preseason as well to form their opinions.

I ask the players and the coaches to work independently of each other and to take a full day to contemplate the evaluation. A sample form is shown in figure 16.2.

When filling out the position part of the evaluation form, each player selects the best and the runner-up at the defensive positions. This allows each position player to see how she is evaluated against the other players at her position; then she can look at another part of the form to see how she stands with the other hitters.

When the evaluation forms are returned, the players are listed by their overall ranking. On this overall listing, the total points next to their ranking reflects the totals of the rankings—the fewer the points the higher the ranking. For instance, in the following sample, Martin was ranked the number one pitcher with a three-point total. One point is given for a first place ranking, two points for a second place ranking, three points for a third place ranking, and four points for a fourth. This pitchers' chart would then be given to each player or pitcher. The chart is returned to each pitcher so that she can see all other pitchers' points as well as her own.

Pitchers	Ranking	Coaches #1	#2	#3	Total points
Martin	1	1	1	1	3
Killion	2	2	2	3	7
Olachnovitch	3	3	4	2	9
Venes	4	4	3	4	11

The hitters' evaluations and the defensive positions' evaluations by the coaches are presented in the same way as the preceding chart. Each player receives the evaluation ranking done by her teammates. For the hitters' evaluations, each rank is also given its point value. For example, a hitter ranked second six times, third four times, and first one time would have a total of 25.

With the particular team in the following example, the pitchers are left off the hitting evaluations because of the DH. They could be evaluated too if we did not use a DH. An example of the hitters' evaluation by the players would look like this:

Figure 16.2 Sample Player and Coach Evaluation Form

Instructions: Place your name on the line below and rank each player in terms of worth to the team. Do not include yourself in this evaluation.

Name:_____

Pitchers	**Rank**
1. Killion	1. _____
2. Martin	2. _____
3. Olachnovitch	3. _____
4. Venes	4. _____

Hitters	**Rank**
1. Bonenberger	1. _____
2. Chambers	2. _____
3. Cousert	3. _____
4. DeRosa	4. _____
5. Dregely	5. _____
6. Hazelwood	6. _____
7. Johns	7. _____
8. Johnson	8. _____
9. Krick	9. _____
10. Krupa	10. _____
11. Maxwell	11. _____
12. Pearce	12. _____
13. Pierce	13. _____
14. Salerno	14. _____
15. Taylor	15. _____
16. Way	16. _____

Position	**Defensive player**	**Rank**
Catcher	_____	1. _____
	_____	2. _____
First base	_____	1. _____
	_____	2. _____
Second base	_____	1. _____
	_____	2. _____
Shortstop	_____	1. _____
	_____	2. _____
Third base	_____	1. _____
	_____	2. _____
Left field	_____	1. _____
	_____	2. _____
Center field	_____	1. _____
	_____	2. _____
Right field	_____	1. _____
	_____	2. _____
DH	_____	1. _____
	_____	2. _____

Hitter's Evaluations by Players

Hitters	Ranking	Points
Johnson	1	47
Salerno	2	63
Dregely	3	75
Maxwell	4	81
Taylor	5	123
Krupa	6	148
Chambers	7	187
Bonenberger	8	203
Johns	9	234
Cousert	10	251
DeRosa	11	275
Hazelwood	12	300
Pearce	13	313
Pierce	14	356
Krick	15	378
Way	16	400

I would then provide the players with the two sets of rankings, one from the coaches and one from the players. We have found that the coaches' and players' evaluations are very similar. The more times the evaluations are completed, the closer the results tend to be.

In the final player evaluations two weeks before the start of the season, each player is allowed to place herself where she thinks she belongs compared with other players at her position. This is an opportunity for the player to express how she estimates herself.

We also believe character and attitude should figure in this process, but it is very hard to set a standard of what you as a coach feel is the best type of attitude or character for your team members. You will know who brings a positive influence to your team everyday and who does not. This is where your coach's instinct comes into play—when looking beyond the athlete's physical capabilities and talents to make the judgment on her attitude and character.

Starting Lineup

On the final evaluations prior to the first game, I will give all of the coaches and players an actual lineup card to name their starting lineup. Everyone will pick the actual order of the lineup and positions. The following charts are examples of how this information can be provided to the players and the coaches. The players may put themselves in the lineup if they believe they should be there.

By the Coaches

In this example, there are three coaches voting. The number that follows the player's name means she received that many votes to be in the starting lineup. The number in parentheses is the most popular spot that was picked for her in the lineup. If there is only one number in parentheses, it means that two or more coaches indicated this spot in the lineup. For example, Johnson received all three coaches' votes and the 3 and 4 in the parentheses means she was selected to bat either third or fourth.

Player	Lineup
Bonenberger	3 (7)
Chambers	3 (2 & 8)
Cousert	0
DeRosa	0
Dregely	3 (4)
Hazelwood	1
Johns	2 (9)
Johnson	3 (3 & 4)
Krick	0
Krupa	3 (8)
Maxwell	3 (5 & 6)
Pearce	0
Pierce	0
Salerno	3 (4 & 5)
Taylor	3 (1)
Way	0

By the Players

In this example, 20 players voted. Again, the number in parentheses represents the most popular spot indicated for each player in the lineup. One number in parentheses means that over 75 percent of the players indicated this spot in the lineup. For example, 14 players put Krupa in the lineup and the most popular spot was batting eighth. Twenty players put Johnson in the lineup, batting third or fourth.

Player	Lineup
Bonenberger	18 (7)
Chambers	20 (2 & 8)
Cousert	0
DeRosa	0
Dregely	20 (4 & 5)
Hazelwood	5
Johns	15 (8 & 9)
Johnson	20 (3 & 4)
Krick	0
Krupa	14 (8)
Maxwell	20 (3 & 6)
Pearce	8 (8 & 9)
Pierce	2 (9)
Salerno	20 (4 & 5)
Taylor	20 (1)
Way	0

Using the Results

Of the preseason evaluation methods, we give more weight to practice evaluations done by the coaches than to the self-evaluations done by the players. It is the coach's job to observe, evaluate, and select the starting team. We receive valuable information from self- and practice evaluations, but ultimately, what happens on the field day in and day out plays into the final decision. After the coaching staff has decided who the nine or ten starters will be, we meet each athlete individually in the office and discuss what her role will be for the season.

I think it is very difficult for the high school star to come to college and find out that many of her new teammates are better than she is. To ease this situation, the coach should tell each athlete what her role on the team is prior to the start of the season. This gives the athlete a clear picture of what is expected of her, along with areas she needs to improve on to make the starting lineup.

The basic question is "Who plays and who doesn't?" When comparing two players at second base, who starts at second base and who doesn't? The answer is based on practice observations, defensive and offensive charts, video study evaluations, and game performance. The coach weighs all of these factors in deciding who gets onto the field and who sits on the bench. This procedure should be in constant flux until one player clearly beats out the other.

Choosing a starting lineup is a difficult task. I feel all my athletes bring something great to the game. When it comes time to announce who will start in what position I struggle with some of my decisions. I always want to play the nine or ten athletes who want it most, the ones with the greatest hearts. Yet I know there will always be some athletes who outshine others with pure, raw talent. It comes down to an athlete who plays ball like she would run a business. Her play is a career investment for her. She does everything perfectly well and makes the great plays. Do I bench her because she doesn't smile after she makes that tremendous diving catch? No. I have come to the conclusion that I try to put the best nine on the field. Every coach would like to think that all their athletes love the game like they do, but that is not always the case. Some athletes express their love of the game differently and as a coach you need to recognize that.

Regardless of whether a player is a starter or nonstarter, you should make it a point to treat all of your players equally. For example, I do not give my starters more time in the batting cage, and they are not the only ones given the opportunity to hit live pitching. In the preseason each athlete receives equal treatment. As we get closer to games there may be times when the starters are on the field longer in game-like situations, but I try to have each player receive the same total number of repetitions.

Let's Discuss . . .

One spring an athlete left a message on my office phone saying she was thinking about quitting the team and she wanted to know if we could get together and discuss it. This message caught me off guard because it was the first time an athlete wanted to discuss quitting. Usually the athletes just come into your office without warning, sit in the chair across from your desk or stand in front of your desk, look at you, take a breath, and announce they are quitting the team. Then we begin the discussion, if they do not run out of the office. I admired this athlete for wanting to discuss her quitting the team with me. She

was giving me a fair shake at keeping this from happening.

Later as we were having a team dinner, I invited her to sit next to me so we could discuss the message she left. She told me she wanted to quit and I asked her why. She said because she was not used to getting corrected at practice and that her last coach had worshipped her. I replied, "Give me something to worship." She smiled, nodded her head, took a breath, and stayed on the team.

The next day at practice the athlete who had wanted to quit, but did not, was wearing a shirt that I felt summed it up for the both of us. It read on the back, "The only losers are quitters."

EVALUATING GAMES

During the game we keep a defensive chart of assists, putouts, and errors (see figure 16.3) as well as a defensive chart of important plays and an offensive chart that documents execution of plays which nonstarters keep. We will use this information to evaluate the players after every game and we keep the data on a complete sheet for each player throughout the season. In the points column we keep a running total for the

---

Figure 16.3 Assists, Putouts, and Errors Chart

Date_____   Opponent_____   Final score_____

LF
assists/putouts/errors

CF
assists/putouts/errors

RF
assists/putouts/errors

SS
assists/putouts/errors

2B
assists/putouts/errors

P
assists/putouts/errors

3B
assists/putouts/errors

1B
assists/putouts/errors

C
assists/putouts/errors

year. We use this information throughout the year to help us evaluate where we have our athletes playing and where they are in the lineup.

During the game our manager keeps a score book that has the rest of the information we need for postgame evaluation. The manager records a "*" in the batter's box for a well hit (well-hit ball). The scorekeeper also records the usual information, such as how the batter was put out, where the batter hit, and so on. From the "*" we can figure a well-hit average that is an important indicator of that player's performance. The score book also gives us hits, RBIs, and fielding changes and errors.

After each game we give awards to an offensive player and a defensive player of the game (sometimes there are more than one of each). We determine the best offensive player by the most important hits in the game. We consider her number of well hits as well. The best defensive player is determined by the most important defensive plays as well as the most consistent defensive work. If the defensive player is the pitcher, we award an additional defensive player decal. All of these athletes receive decals that they can put on their softball awards board. We also give a most valuable player award for the athlete who made the most impact in each tournament we played in.

SUMMARY

In this chapter we discussed evaluating players and making the decision of who will play and who will not. These are difficult challenges for the coaching staff, but in this chapter we looked at ways to treat each individual as fairly as possible.

- Use a tryout evaluation sheet to keep the procedure objective.
- Always chart some part of practice so that you can give feedback.
- Use video—it is one of the best types of feedback because the athlete can review and see what was done correctly or what was done wrong.
- Utilize a player evaluation system so that both the athletes and the coaches can evaluate each player. Do this many times during the season.
- Remember to ask your team who they feel should be starters and compare this with the coaching staff's view.
- Evaluate the game to give feedback to the coaches on the decisions they make, player for player.

Chapter 17

EVALUATING YOUR PROGRAM

An evaluation helps the program by letting those who are part of it see what they do well and where they can make improvements. It is important to be aware of not only the changes you may need to make but also what aspects of your program are successful so that you can continue to utilize them.

PRESEASON PLANNING

Before the season begins consult with your players and create a mission statement. This is important because the mission statement lays out the road that you wish to travel. It provides a vision and a blueprint of the season's goals and gives the team direction for their first steps into a winning year.

Mission Statement

In the beginning of our season, we get together as a team and create a mission. Then before every game we will review and talk about our mission statement. At the end of the season we meet again as a team to review our mission and see if we accomplished it. If we did, we discuss how; if we did not, we examine why. The mission usually consists of 10 major goals that we write on large signs and post in our locker room, weight room, gymnasium, and dugout all season long. At the last team meeting of the year, when we go through each mission statement, we talk to each other about how we can better our mission and have greater success in achieving it. I've included the Westerwinds 1997 Softball Mission Statement below:

1. Be the conference champions.
2. Play it game by game—live from present moment to present moment.
3. Develop consistency—play at the end of the season as if it were the beginning.
4. Want to be in every game—live out the season to its fullest: NEVER SAY DIE!
5. Communicate.
6. Give meaningful compliments to each other.
7. Become a family—get to know your teammates.
8. Field better than .963 as a team.
9. Bat .300 as a team.
10. Keep the fun in things—smile, be confident, and show no fear or doubt. Bottle your own individual energy.

Meeting With Players

I hold one-on-one player meetings before the season begins to formulate goals and to get feedback from each player. In these meetings I will get many of the ideas that go into our mission statement for the year. This individual meeting gives the athlete the chance to speak freely about her goals and team goals, and at the same time allows me the opportunity to help the athlete set her individual mission and to formulate that into the team mission.

Senior Input

I make the seniors my priority. They are the ones who have weathered the good times and the bad times, along with committing their careers to our university and the softball program. The four-year athletes are the ones who have truly given a lot to me in many ways, and I want to be sure their final season is one of fond memories and no regrets. During preseason and prior to the start of their last season, the seniors and the coaches meet. At this meeting I acknowledge the work and dedication the seniors have given to me and the program. I let them know how valuable they have been and will continue to be during their final "hurrah." I want them to know that their input is vital and I want to hear from them about anything regarding the program and the success of the team. It is our goal, together, to make their last year their very best. Any and all suggestions will be honored, if at all possible. After all, the seniors are what we are all about: successful and memorable careers.

The Last Hurrah

I had a four-year starter named Kimiko Chambers who was a terrific athlete. But during her senior year her class schedule took her away from numerous practices. This caused me to wonder if her last year was as important to her as it was to me. Did she want the most out of it? At our one-on-one meeting, the player is asked to bring in her individual and team goals so that we can discuss them about a month before games begin. It was then that I asked Kimiko about her softball dream. Her eyes sparkled and she smiled and said, "I want to experience going to nationals and regionals and to earn that conference title. I want this to be my 'last hurrah'." I realized then the tremendous importance Kimiko placed on her last season and that she wanted to pile in the good memories to carry through her lifetime.

Shortly after that session I met with the seniors and told them their input was vital to our success and that I wanted this year to be their happiest. Was there anything that we had missed so far? Kimiko calmly stated that she wanted to play the last game on our home field. (We had scheduled it at the city park with lights to help draw a larger crowd.) I told her it would be no problem to change the game so that they could finish their WIU career on the field where they had spent so much of their lives.

Meeting With Assistant Coaches

I have been blessed with outstanding assistant coaches. Patty Cutright, Dianne Davidson, Kathy Welter, Jackie Crescio, Pat Stoffel, Brenda Heyl, Candi Letts, Jim Webb, Lu Harris, JoAnn Gordon, Barb Schaff, Cathy Packer, and Mindy Dessert all played the game at the collegiate level and all played women's major fastpitch softball (except for Jim). Because of their expertise as players, they brought to our team a clear vision

of the art of playing softball and how to train for something you love to do.

To each of my assistants I give certain responsibilities that they can carry out without too much intervention from me. Based on their personal strengths and interests, these range from serving as the recruiting coordinator to being the pitching coach, junior varsity team coach, and strength and conditioning coach, to name a few. The rest of the coaching responsibilities are shared. I want and need their input and make it clear when they are hired that we are a team within a team. I let them know that we will work together for the best of the team, each of us focusing on our strengths, and that I am interested in what they think and how they feel the program is going. Finally, after the season is over, I ask the assistants to fill out an evaluation of the program. I have shared my office with my assistant for the last ten years and that lends itself to a comfortable exchange of ideas.

Early in the year I meet with the assistant to discuss her role as an assistant coach on the team. I ask her what she would like to learn and to accomplish and what area or areas she feels are her strong points. We then lay out each of the areas of the program and how the responsibilities will be divided and shared. Each month thereafter we review how all jobs are coming along. These are very informal meetings and the purpose is to give feedback to the assistant and to assess the status of the program. At this time I will let the assistant know if she needs to communicate better, or if she should be more positive or more assertive. When evaluating my assistants I go by my own personal observations.

There is so much to coaching that new assistants, as well as veterans, look forward to and need feedback about. We probably do not tell them nearly enough how important they are to the overall health of the team. In this case, more is always better.

EVALUATION DURING THE SEASON

I want to hear from our players because I believe they will give insight into what is and is not working in the program. This feedback comes about not only through their words, but also through their actions. Are they conditioned well enough? Did we overtrain? Are they excited about the team? I ask all the players from time to time if they like certain things we are doing or if they have any suggestions. Our coaches meet with our captains once each week for a breakfast or a lunch, to share ideas and to let them hear me ask the question, "How is your team and how are your teammates doing?" I sincerely believe that healthy teams talk and that on a team, everyone loses or wins together. I want the players to realize this and to bring their concerns to the coaches or the captains so that we can all work out problems and find solutions.

It Has to Be a Give-and-Take

When coaching athletes you give a lot. You give your time, thoughts, ideas, experiences, conversations, counseling skills—essentially you give your all. When the athletes respond to the giving by only taking, you run dry. It is important that they give back and know that

they should and are welcome to give back. My assistant coach and I were in our weekly lunch with our captains and we were trying to talk to them about how we like to hear "thank you" and "good job" as well as they do. To make this point my assistant looked at one of the captains and said, "There is someone on the team who brings something new to practice everyday. She always says 'Hello' and gives all she has that day. Who do you think it is?" Both captains shook their heads and named different teammates. My assistant went on a bit and then said, "She is sitting with you now," and nodded her head in my direction. Both the captains claimed it to be a trick question as they looked down. My assistant spoke clearly and replied, "My point is that Coach is on the team also, and gives every day. Just like you didn't think of her when I asked the question, her contributions are often overlooked." The captains shook their heads in agreement and smiled as if a light had gone on. I thanked my assistant for the nice words. Coaching is fun and a great job to have. It becomes satisfying when you see that you make a difference or an athlete stops for a moment to thank you for something you

have done for her. The athletes need to know that they are in a relationship that involves give-and-take. It is your job as a coach to make them aware of this relationship.

I believe the best way to evaluate is to write down or log what your strengths and weaknesses are *during* the season. Don't wait until it is over. I make it a habit to carry note cards to every practice and game. On these cards I write down things that stand out, whether it is a good play or a mental error. I review the card with the players after the practice or game, then I incorporate drills into practice to help us strengthen what we are weak at. When this is done I drop the card into a file folder. At the end of the year I will pull out the cards and read through them. The information gives me great feedback on what we struggled with and what our stronger areas were. The cards help me remember and feel more confident that I am not overlooking anything; plus they serve as a journal and are easy to keep.

Hit the Ball Hard

At Western we have always had good hitting teams. For several years I wondered what it was that made us such good hitters besides good recruiting and one-on-one coaching. After I looked back at our best years, I realized we did a great deal of circuit work and hitting off live pitching. It is not coincidental that the years our team excelled at hitting we excelled at pitching also. It makes a great deal of difference if you are facing a good pitcher every day at practice or a great one. When I put all these things together in my head, I realized that I have continued to do circuits, one-on-one teaching, videotaping, solid recruiting, and so forth. I do not want to leave out any of these components because I think they all add to the mix of what we do well at Western and that is hit the ball hard.

POSTSEASON EVALUATION

Just as we do a postseason evaluation of our players, we also evaluate ourselves as coaches and the overall health of the program. Success-ful coaching is an ongoing process of looking for areas that need strengthening, and acknowledging the things that have gone well. I try to study the successful programs and coaches in the country and to follow some of their examples. Whenever a top ten coach is speaking at a clinic or at our coaches' convention I try to attend.

The postseason evaluation involves taking an honest look at myself, my staff, my team, and our opponents. If I feel I need to replace staff because of failure to meet my team's goals and objectives, then it must be done. Evaluation is sometimes painful and the decisions you make for the program's best interests may be even more painful, but if you expect to succeed, change may be in order.

At the end of the season I meet with each player individually; I also hand out player program evaluation forms for the athletes to return. They can sign their names or leave it confidential; the choice is up to them (see figure 17.1). The coaches also meet individually with the athletes to acknowledge their strengths and weaknesses and to assess their future with the team. We will let them know the role we see them playing along with the amount of their scholarship. We go over their single season highlights and their career accomplishments. Finally, we suggest a plan of action for them to follow throughout the summer.

SUMMARY

When evaluating your program, be sure to seek input from your players, assistant coaches, and colleagues.

- Get player input when creating a mission statement through individual meetings. It is important to have a team mission to follow from day one.
- Give your assistants responsibilities and work with them to improve the direction of the team through its leaders.
- Do not wait until the end of the season to write down your coaching strengths and weaknesses—do it daily.
- At the end of the season ask for insight from those who know best how the season went: your team.

Figure 17.1 Program Evaluation Form

Name (optional) _____

Please be honest and constructive as you complete this evaluation. Your input into our program is vital for the future. On the scales below, 1 is the lowest rating and 5 is the highest.

1. Regarding softball strategies and skills I learned:

    1   2   3   4   5

2. My individual performance of softball skills and strategies improved:

    1   2   3   4   5

3. I enjoyed playing softball this season:

    1   2   3   4   5

4. The coaching staff helped me develop as a player:

    1   2   3   4   5

5. The coaching staff helped me develop as a person:

    1   2   3   4   5

6. Players are treated fairly on the team:

    1   2   3   4   5

7. Players on the team respected team rules:

    1   2   3   4   5

8. Practices were well organized, challenging, and fun:

    1   2   3   4   5

9. The role I played in games was the best for the program:

    1   2   3   4   5

10. I feel more positive about the program now than I did at the beginning
    of the season:

    1   2   3   4   5

What can the coaching staff do to make the softball program better than it was this past season?_____

_____

The best thing about being a Westerwinds softball player is: _____

_____

The worst thing about being a Westerwinds softball player is: _____

_____

What changes would you make to eliminate the worst things about the program?

_____

_____

INDEX

MEET THE COACHES

Coaches Veroni and Dessert.

Kathy Veroni has served as head softball coach at Western Illinois University (WIU) in Macomb, IL, for more than 25 years. A past president of the National Fastpitch Coaches Association and United States Fastpitch Association, Veroni has won over 1,000 women's premier and Division I college games, as well as founding a women's premier fastpitch team that she coached to two U.S. Olympic Sports Festivals.

Veroni is a member of both the Illinois State University Hall of Fame and the Illinois Amateur Softball Association Hall of Fame. She has also recruited, coached, and taught two Olympians: Dot Richardson for the United States and Kara McGaw for Canada.

When away from softball, Veroni enjoys golfing, gardening, and camping.

Veroni was assisted in the writing of this book by **Mindy Dessert**, an assistant softball coach at WIU who played Division I softball for Veroni for four years. While pitching at WIU, Dessert chalked up a 50-23 career record. Also a member of the National Fastpitch Coaches Association, Dessert serves as the recruiting coordinator for the Westerwinds, in addition to working closely with pitchers and catchers and teaching hitting fundamentals.

When away from the field, Dessert enjoys reading and running.

LEARN HOW TO BE A COMPLETE COACH

with these books from the American Sport Education Program

1997 • Paper • 200 pp • Item PFLE0556
ISBN 0-88011-556-4 • $18.95 ($27.95 Canadian)

Contains the latest guidelines and procedures that coaches need to become competent first responders to nearly 100 athletic injuries.

1996 • Paper • 208 pp • Item PRIN0715
ISBN 0-87322-715-8 • $18.95 ($27.95 Canadian)

Explains to coaches how to set a positive example, establish and enforce an effective athlete code of conduct, use position to involve others in drug prevention efforts, and respond effectively when an athlete needs help.

1997 • Paper • 232 pp • Item PMAR0666
ISBN 0-88011-666-8 • $18.95 ($27.95 Canadian)

Contains information on developing a positive coaching philosophy, applying the principles of sport psychology and sport physiology to coaching, teaching sport skills properly, and using management skills effectively.

1997 • Paper • 128 pp • Item PCLI0512
ISBN 0-88011-512-2 • $12.95 ($18.95 Canadian)

Provides coaches with a valuable tool to help them understand the basic principles of sportsmanship, the justification of these principles, and how to teach their players to understand and apply them.

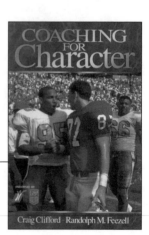

To request more information or to place your order,
U.S. customers call TOLL-FREE 1-800-747-4457.
Customers outside the U.S. place your order using the appropriate
telephone number/address shown in the front of this book.

American Sport Education Program

American Sport Education Program
A Division of Human Kinetics
http://www.asep.com/

Prices subject to change.